IMAGE BEYOND IMAGE :
NEW MEDIA ART OF CONTEMPORARY INDIA

Dr. ANIRBAN DHAR

NewDelhi • London

BLUEROSE PUBLISHERS
India | U.K.

Copyright © Dr. Anirban Dhar 2025

All rights reserved by author. No part of this publication may be reproduced, stored in a retrieval system or transmitted in any form or by any means, electronic, mechanical, photocopying, recording or otherwise, without the prior permission of the author. Although every precaution has been taken to verify the accuracy of the information contained herein, the publisher assumes no responsibility for any errors or omissions. No liability is assumed for damages that may result from the use of information contained within.

BlueRose Publishers takes no responsibility for any damages, losses, or liabilities that may arise from the use or misuse of the information, products, or services provided in this publication.

For permissions requests or inquiries regarding this publication, please contact:

BLUEROSE PUBLISHERS
www.BlueRoseONE.com
info@bluerosepublishers.com
+91 8882 898 898
+4407342408967

ISBN: 978-93-6452-727-9

Cover design: Yash Singhal
Typesetting: Namrata Saini

First Edition: January 2025

My parents, Akxina, Rajashree and all my readers

PREFACE

The involvement of images in human society has a very immense and significant history in cultural practices. From the prehistoric period to contemporary Visual Art, the methods of images have a very relevant meaning by their expression and also as conceptual aspects. In the development of contemporary Visual Art practices, New Media Art has enormous involvement to enhance the quality of postmodern art and art critique. New Media Art is a contemporary approach to postmodern art that encompasses artworks created with New Media technologies. The introductory chapter concentrates on how the evolution of New Media Art can be sketched to the moving photographic originations of the late nineteenth century. In global Visual Art practices, the 1960s witnessed a far-reaching re-evaluation of what Visual Art could be. Forerunners of New Media Art developed the new video technology, while an interest in the physical space in which art was engaged led to artists making installations, performances, videos for specific areas and circumstances. Contextually the new development of contemporary Indian art has been started from the sixties — this new trend which reflects a genre of non-conventional practices of Visual Art. The image became more conceptual from this era. With the relation of this new genre, the visual came to a point of zenith in the nineties when artists of India became involved with the broader area of art through the New Media works of art. The study limited to the evocation of New Media Art of late twentieth century to the till date highlighting the New Media Art of India since the nineties with studying and analyse the six artists' New Media Artworks as a referral to support the textual context of the video installation in the New Media Art practices of contemporary Visual Art of India. The artists are - Nalini Malani, Jitish Kallat, Ranbir Kaleka, Surekha, Bose Krishnamachari, Shilpa Gupta. The chapter also includes the operational meaning of the term used, statement of the problem, objectives of the study, scope of the study, limitation of the study, data and methodology, review of literature and organisation of research and chapterisation.

The chapter concentrates on the image beyond the image: New Media Art practices in 1990s India. The contemporary Visual Art of India has gone through a transitional phase of the early 1990s. The study focuses on the sub-topics like inception of interdisciplinary art practices in India, interdisciplinary collective-run groups in India, the role of art organisation in the exploration of

New Media Art of India in the nineties, role of art directorial in New Media Art of India through 2000 onwards: a connection to the discourses of New Media Art practices of India since the nineties, role of art institutes and Visual Arts pedagogy in India concerning New Media Art are described.

The video installations of Nalini Malani and Jitish Kallat have the interpretation of the legitimised narratives and the web of traffic. This chapter concentrates on the analytical study of New Media Art practices of Nalini Malani and Jitish Kallat. The study focuses on the sub-topics like art practices of Nalini Malani: transition from traditional painting to New Media Art, the role of the bodily and the local in Malani's art practice, the diverse techniques in Malani's New Media Art, myth as interclass vocabulary into Malani's art practice, the myth of Medea, the overhaul process in the works of Malani, the cathartic effect of Nalini Malani's artwork, a case study of the artworks of Nalini Malani, transformation from painting to New Media Art in Jitish Kallat's artistic journey , a case study of New Media Artworks of Jitish Kallat are described.

The New Media works of Ranbir Kaleka and Surekha have the visual and conceptual interactions of the third object / urban signs and the vulnerable body. The chapter concentrates on the analytical study of New Media Artworks of Ranbir Kaleka and Surekha. The study focuses on the sub-topics like artistic journey of Ranbir Kaleka: transforming from painting to video installation, Ranbir Kaleka's video art practice: exploration through co-founded film society, Kaleka as activist in theatre and the artist's days during teaching in College of Art, execution of monochrome into Kaleka's video installation: an analysis, narratives into Kaleka's video installation, sound is essential and visual borders on fantasy in Kaleka's video installations: an analysis, inspirations and philosophy in Kaleka's artworks, a case study of the video installations of Kaleka, New Media Artworks of Surekha, Surekha's art practice: the body represented to recurrently re-emerge as a polyvalent site, personifying beauty and pain into Surekha's art practice, a case study of New Media Art of Surekha are described.

Through the ways of memory and the techno-images are the re-interpretation of New Media works of Shilpa Gupta and Bose Krishnamachari. The chapter highlighted the analytical study of artworks of Gupta and Krishnamachari. The study focuses on the sub-topics like Gupta's art and the narrativity of the body in space and time, Gupta and Irit Rogoff's inhabitation, Gupta and Henri Lefebvre: rhythmanalysis, Shilpa Gupta and Michel de Certeau's anthropological space, a case study of the New Media Artworks of

Shilpa Gupta, artistic journey of Bose Krishnamachari: transformation from abstract painting to multimedia interactive installation, reading and travel, the significant fragment of Bose Krishnamachari's art practice, the artist and the Mumbai: Krishnamachari's art exploration, Bose Krishnamachari's works and the interactive audience participation: Beyond the artist's taste, questioning the idea of the formation of the canon in art: Krishnamachari as a curator, Bose's 3C theory: cricket, cinema and curry, Bose Krishnamachari as an art directorial: the visionary approaches, a case study of New Media Art practices of Krishnamachari are described.

The chapter concludes and summarises the study. It also highlights the research findings and suggests further research.

ACKNOWLEDGEMENT

There are a number of people without whom this research work might not have been written and to whom I am greatly indebted. I express my heartiest sense of gratitude to my supervisor Dr. Abhibrata Chakrabarty, Associate Professor, Department of Visual Arts, Assam University, Silchar, under whose guidance and motivation, I have been able to shape my this research.

I would also take the opportunity of thanking my teacher Prof. (Dr.) Nirmal Kanti Roy, HOD, Department of Visual Arts and Dean of Abanindranath Tagore School of Creative Arts and Communication Studies, Assam University, Silchar for his valuable suggestion.

I also express my gratitude to all the faculty members of the Department of Visual Arts, Assam University, Silchar for encouraging me in my research work. I also take this as an opportunity to thank all the staff members of the Department of Visual Arts, Assam University, Silchar, my friends, well-wishers, and many others who have directly or indirectly supported me all through.

I would also like to express my sincere thanks to Dr. Meghali Goswami, Associate Professor, Department of History of Art, Kala Bhavana, Visva-Bharati, Santiniketan for her valuable suggestion. She has been an immense help in motivating me to take up the research work and her initial motivation has helped me a great deal.

I also express my gratitude to all my fellow colleagues of past and present institution including faculty and staff members of Graphic Era Hill University, Uttarakhand, India for encouraging me in my research work.

I would express my sincere thanks to contemporaray artists for helping me in the field work by giving their valuable interviews for the research work along with discussions, thought of exchange regarding the New Media Art practices of India.

I would like to give special thanks to the different organisations and libraries of India as they provided space for my research study.

I would express my thanks to various art galleries and Museums of India as they shared their valuable documentations regarding New Media Art in India which helping me in the field work.

I most gratefully acknowledge my brother Agnik Dhar, my wife Rajashree Dutta Choudhury and my daughter Akxina Dhar for all their support throughout the period of research.

I must have forgotten many who helped me during these years, but I must thank all of them who have been of even the minimum help.

Last, but not the least, I would express my sincerest thanks to my mother Ms. Shibani Rani Dhar, who in her lifetime has been blessing me. I would also express my sincere thanks to my father Lt. Ashit Ranjan Dhar, who in his lifetime and also after his death has been encouraging me with his optimistic approach of thought process. I dedicate this work of mine to my parents, my wife Rajashree and daughter Akxina. I hope that they will always be with me during all the phases of my life.

(Dr. Anirban Dhar)

Contents

PREFACE V

ACKNOWLEDGEMENT IX

LIST OF PLATES XVII

Chapter-I: Introduction 1

1.1 Background of the Study *1*

    1.1.1 The Evocation of New Media Art in Late Twentieth Century 2

    1.1.2 Nam June Paik and Bill Viola: Significant Contributors in the Early Development of New Media Art 3

    1.1.3 The Emerging Practices of New Media Art in India 4

1.2 Some Indian Artists Who Are Working in New Media Art: A Comparative Analysis *5*

    1.2.1 Study of Some Artists and Their New Media Art in India 5

    1.2.2 'Desire Machine Collective' in New Media Art Through the Exploration of Mriganka Madhukaillya and Sonal Jain's Multimedia Artworks 11

    1.2.3 The Journey of New Media Art Through the Works of Desire Machine Collective 12

    1.2.4 New Media Artworks of Temsuyanger Longkumer: The Exploration of Socio-Cultural Traditions in Ethnic Societies and the Correlation Between Communities in the Microbial World and Our Own 15

    1.2.5 A Legitimised Analysis of Six Artists Who Make a New Genre in New Media Art of India 17

1.3 Operational Definition of the Term Used *20*

1.4 Statement of the Problem *20*

1.5 Objectives of the Study *21*

1.6 Scope of the Study *21*

1.7 Limitation of the Study *22*

1.8 Data and Methodology *22*

1.9 Review of Literature *22*

    1.9.1 New Media Art Practices in 1990s India 22

    1.9.2 New Media Art of Contemporary Era 24

    1.9.3 Miscellaneous / Related Referential Studies 25

1.10 Organisation of the Research and Chapterisations *27*

References *40*

Chapter-II: Image Beyond Image: New Media Art Practices in 1990s India 43

2.1 Introduction *43*

2.2 The Visual Art Practices of the Nineties of India *44*

    2.2.1 Inception of Interdisciplinary Art Practices in India 45

    2.2.2 Interdisciplinary Collective Artist-Run Groups in India 49

2.3 The Discourses of New Media Art of India in the Nineties *49*

    2.3.1 The Role of Art Organisational in the Exploration of New Media Art of India in the Nineties 52

    2.3.2 Role of Art Directorial in New Media Art of India Through 2000 Onwards: A Connection to the Discourses of New Media Art Practices of India Since the Nineties 53

    2.3.3 Role of Art Institutes and Visual Arts Pedagogy in India in Relation to New Media Art 54

2.4 Conclusion *56*

References *63*

Chapter-III: The Legitimised Narratives and The Web of Traffic: The Artworks of Nalini Malani and Jitish Kallat 65

3.1 Introduction *65*

3.2 The Video Installation of Nalini Malani *65*

    3.2.1 Art Practice of Nalini Malani: Transition from Traditional Painting to New Media Art 66

    3.2.2 Nalini Malani's Art Practice: The Role of the Bodily and the Local 67

    3.2.3 The Role of Nalini Malani's Technique into the Artist's Art Practice: Transformation to New Media Art 69

3.2.4 Myth as Interclass Vocabulary into Nalini Malani's Art Practice ... 70
3.2.5 The Myth of Medea into Nalini Malani's Art Practice 71
3.2.6 The Overhaul Process in the Work of Nalini Malani: An Overview 72
3.2.7 The Cathartic Effect of Nalini Malani's Artworks 73
3.2.8 A Case Study of the Artworks of Nalini Malani 75

3.3 New Media Artworks of Jitish Kallat 84
3.3.1 The Artistic Journey of Jitish Kallat: Transforming from Painting to New Media Art 85
3.3.2 A Case Study of New Media Artworks of Jitish Kallat 97

3.4 Conclusion 103

References 119

Chapter-IV: The 'Third Object'/ Urban Signs and The Vulnerable Body: New Media Artworks Of Ranbir Kaleka And Surekha 122

4.1 Introduction 122
4.2 Video Installation of Ranbir Kaleka 123
4.2.1 The Artistic Journey of Ranbir Kaleka: Transforming from Painting to Video Installation 124
4.2.2 Ranbir Kaleka's Video Art Practice: Exploration Through Co-founded Film Society 127
4.2.3 Ranbir Kaleka as Activist in Theatre and the Artist's Days During Teaching in College of Art, New Delhi 127
4.2.4 Execution of Monochrome into Kaleka's Video Installation: An Analysis 128
4.2.5 Narratives into Ranbir Kaleka's Video Installation 128
4.2.6 Sound is Fairly Important and Visuals Border on 'fantasy' in Kaleka's Video Installations: An Analysis 129
4.2.7 Inspirations and Philosophy of Ranbir Kaleka's Artwork 130
4.2.8 Video Installation of Ranbir Kaleka: An Overview 132
4.2.9 A Case Study of the Video Installation of Ranbir Kaleka 133

4.3 New Media Artworks of Surekha 153
4.3.1 Surekha's Art Practice: The Body Represented to Recurrently Re-emerge as a Polyvalent Site 154

  4.3.2 Surekha's Art Practice: Personifying Beauty and Pain 157

  4.3.3 Nature into Surekha's New Media Artworks:
    Forms/Contents/Processes 165

  4.3.4 A Case Study of New Media Art of Surekha 172

 4.4 Conclusion 177

 References 198

Chapter-V: Through The Ways of Memory and The Techno-Images: Re-Interpretation of New Media Works of Shilpa Gupta and Bose Krishnamachari 200

 5.1 Introduction 200

 5.2 New Media Art Practice of Shilpa Gupta 201

  5.2.1 Shilpa Gupta's New Media Art and the Narrativity of the Body
    in Space and Time 206

  5.2.2 Shilpa Gupta and Irit Rogoff's "inhabitation" 211

  5.2.3 Shilpa Gupta and Henri Lefebvre: Rhythmanalysis 212

  5.2.4 Shilpa Gupta and Michel de Certeau's "anthropological space" .. 215

  5.2.5 In conclusion: Shilpa Gupta, Michel de Certeau and Henri
    Lefebvre 220

  5.2.6 A Case Study of the New Media Artworks of Shilpa Gupta 221

 5.3 New Media Artworks of Bose Krishnamachari 226

  5.3.1 The Artistic Journey of Bose Krishnamachari : Transformation
    from Abstract Painting to Multimedia Interactive Installation 227

  5.3.2 Reading and Travel: The Significant Fragment of Bose
    Krishnamachari's Art Practice 228

  5.3.3 The Artist and the Mumbai: Bose Krishnamachari's
    Art Exploration 229

  5.3.4 Bose Krishnamachari's Artworks and the Interactive Audience
    Participation: Beyond the Artist's Taste 231

  5.3.5 Questioning 'the Idea of the Formation of the Canon in Art':
    Krishnamachari as a Curator 232

  5.3.6 Bose's 3C Theory: Cricket, Cinema, and Curry 232

  5.3.7 Bose Krishnamachari as an Art Directorial: The Visionary
    Approaches 233

    5.3.8 A Case Study of New Media Art Practices of Bose Krishnamachari 235

  5.4 Conclusion *240*

  References *252*

Chapter-VI: Conclusion 255

  6.1 Summary *255*

    6.1.1 Summary of Chapter-I 255

    6.1.2 Summary of Chapter-II 256

    6.1.3 Summary of Chapter-III 257

    6.1.4 Summary of Chapter-IV 258

    6.1.5 Summary of Chapter-V 258

    6.1.6 Summary of Chapter-VI 259

  6.2 Conclusion *259*

  6.3 Research Findings *260*

  6.4 Scope for Further Research *264*

    6.4.1 New Media Art Practices of Contemporary India in the 2000s of Twenty- First Century 264

GLOSSARY 267

BIBLIOGRAPHY 269

  Journal *288*

  Online Resources and Magazines *289*

LIST OF PLATES

CHAPTER-I

Plates	Descriptions
Plate 1.1:	V S Gaitonde. *Untitled*. 1963. Catalogue Cover
Plate 1.2:	Nam June Paik. *TV Cello* (detail).1971.
Plate 1.3:	Bill Viola. *Quintet of the Silent* (detail). 2001. Video Installation.
Plate 1.4:	Navjot Altaf. *Touch IV* (detail). 2010. 22 Channel Video Installation.
Plate 1.5:	Navjot Altaf. *Minus into minus equals ?* (detail). 2008. Single Channel Projection.
Plate 1.6:	Navjot Altaf. *Mumbai Meri Jaan* (detail). 2004. Four Channel Projection.
Plate 1.7:	Navjot Altaf. *Brief Case* (detail). 2004. Single Channel Video Installation.
Plate 1.8:	Navjot Altaf. *A dog a dog* (detail). 2001. An Animation Shot: Single Channel Video Installation.
Plate 1.9:	Navjot Altaf. *Water Weaving* (detail). 2005. Single Channel Projection.
Plate 1.10:	Navjot Altaf. *Relational Sensibility* (detail). 2003. Double Projection Video Installation.
Plate 1.11:	Navjot Altaf. *Catch* (detail). 2007. Three Channel Projection.
Plate 1.12:	Navjot Altaf. *Images of Images and Images in Images* (detail). 2001. Three Channel Projection.
Plate 1.13:	Desire Machine Collective. *Noise Life* (detail). 2015. Sound, Images, Elements of Plot.
Plate 1.14:	Desire Machine Collective. *Being Singular Plural* (detail). 2012. Video Installation.
Plate 1.15:	Temsuyanger Longkumer. *Gods Summit* (detail). 2018. Multimedia Installation.
Plate 1.16:	Temsuyanger Longkumer. *Portrait of a dance I* (detail). Multimedia Installation.

Plate 1.17: Temsuyanger Longkumer. *Portrait of a dance II* (detail). Video Installation.

CHAPTER-II

Plates	Descriptions
Plate 2.1:	M F Husain. *Theatre of the Absurd*. 1989. Water Colour on Paper.
Plate 2.2:	Nalini Malani. *City of Desires* (detail). 1992. Single Channel Site Specific Installation.
Plate 2.3:	Vivan Sundaram. *House from House / Boat* (detail). 1994. Video Screen into Sculpture and Installation.
Plate 2.4:	Ranbir Kaleka. *Man with Cockerel* (detail). 2002. Video Installation.
Plate 2.5:	Subba Ghosh. *Remains of a Breath* (detail). 2001. Installation.
Plate 2.6:	Sonia Khurana. *Bird* (detail). 1999. Video Art.
Plate 2.7:	Tejal Shah. *I Love My India* (detail). 2003. Video Installation.
Plate 2.8:	Tejal Shah. *What Are You ?* (detail). 2006. Video Installation.
Plate 2.9:	Umesh Maddanahalli. *Between Myth and History* (detail). 2001. Single Channel Video Installation with sound.
Plate 2.10:	Gigi Scaria. *Lost City* (detail). Video Art.

CHAPTER-III

Plates	Descriptions
Plate 3.1:	Jitish Kallat. *Dawn Chorus -7* (+ 2 others, bronze sculptures; 3 works) 2007. Acrylic on Canvas with Bronze Sculptures.
Plate 3.2:	Nalini Malani. *In Search of Vanished Blood* (detail). 2012. Video Installation.
Plate 3.3:	Nalini Malani. *Remembering Mad Meg* (detail). 2007. Video Shadow Play, Two Single Channel Animations.
Plate 3.4:	Nalini Malani. *Mother India: Transactions in construction of Pain* (detail). 2005. Video Installation.
Plate 3.5:	Nalini Malani. *Mutant* (detail). 1994-1996. Black and White Dye Painted On Milk Carbon Paper.
Plate 3.6:	Nalini Malani. *Stains* (detail). 2000. Animation Video Installation.

Plate 3.7: Nalini Malani. *Gamepieces* (detail). 2003. Video / Shadow Play.

Plate 3.8: Nalini Malani. *Unity in Diversity* (detail). 2003. Video Installation.

Plate 3.9: Nalini Malani. *Transgression* (detail). 2001. Video - Shadow Play.

Plate 3.10: Nalini Malani. *Hamletmachine* (detail). 1999-2000. Video Installation.

Plate 3.11: Nalini Malani. *Remembering Toba Tek Singh* (detail). 1998-99.

Plate 3.12: Nalini Malani. *Memory: Record / Erase* (detail). 1996. Animation Video.

Plate 3.13: Nalini Malani. *Medea video* (detail). 1991-1996. Video Installation.

Plate 3.14: Nalini Malani. *Now I See It Now I Don't* (detail). 2018 . Video Installation.

Plate 3.15: Nalini Malani. *Can You Hear Me ?* (detail). 2018-2019. 11 Projections With More Than 50 Video Animations.

Plate 3.16: Jitish Kallat. *P.T.O.* 1997. Catalogue Cover.

Plate 3.17: Jitish Kallat. *Random Access Memory* (detail). 2000.108 Works On Exposed Thermal Fax Paper, Applying Heat, Water and Pigments.

Plate 3.18: Jitish Kallat. *Rickshawpolis 3*. 2006. Acrylic on Canvas.

Plate 3.19: Jitish Kallat. *Artist Making Local Call* (detail). Digital Print.

Plate 3.20: Jitish Kallat. *Canis Familiaris / A Dog's Life*. 1999. Acrylic on Canvas.

Plate 3.21: Jitish Kallat. *Forensic Trail of the Grand Banquet* (detail) 2009. Video Projection.

Plate 3.22: Jitish Kallat. *Epilogue* (detail).

2010-11. Pigment Print on Archival Paper.

Plate 3.23: Jitish Kallat. *Untitled (Two Minutes to Midnight)* (detail). 2018. Sculptural Installation.

Plate 3.24: Jitish Kallat. *Public Notice* (detail). 2003. Burnt Adhesive on Acrylic Mirror, Wood, Stainless Steel.

Plate 3.25: Jitish Kallat. *Public Notice 2* (detail). 2007. Resin, 4479 Sculptural Units.

Plate 3.26: Jitish Kallat. *Public Notice 3* (detail). 2010. LED Bulbs, Wires, Rubber.

Plate 3.27: Jitish Kallat. *Covering Letter* (detail). 2012. Fogscreen Projection.

Plate 3.28: Jitish Kallat. *Covering Letter (terranum nuncius)* (detail). 2019. Installation.

CHAPTER-IV

Plates	**Descriptions**
Plate 4.1:	Ranbir Kaleka. *Sweet Unease* (detail). 2010-11. Oil and Acrylic on Canvas with Video Projection.
Plate 4.2:	Ranbir Kaleka. *Long sleep of the storyteller*. 2012. Oil on Canvas.
Plate 4.3:	Ranbir Kaleka. *Family Picture II*. 2009. Archival Inks and Oil on Canvas.
Plate 4.4:	Ranbir Kaleka. *Urban Utopia, Done Undone, Menaced by dragonflies*. 2014. Digital Print on Canvas.
Plate 4.5:	Ranbir Kaleka. *A- Panoramic-Spectrum Ground*.
Plate 4.6:	Ranbir Kaleka. *Kettle* (detail). 2010. Projection on painted canvas.
Plate 4.7:	Ranbir Kaleka. *Man Threading A Needle* (detail). 1998-99. Single Channel Video Projected on oil painting.
Plate 4.8:	Ranbir Kaleka. *Fables from the House of Ibaan* (detail). 2007. Oil and Acrylic on Canvas with Video Projection and sound.
Plate 4.9:	Ranbir Kaleka. *Crossing* (detail). 2005. Four Channel Video Projection on Painting.
Plate 4.10:	Ranbir Kaleka. *Cobbler*. 2003. Digital photograph on Metallic Paper.
Plate 4.11:	Ranbir Kaleka. *Reading Man*. 2009. Acrylic and Oil on canvas with aluminium sculptures and armature and wall clock.
Plate 4.12:	Ranbir Kaleka. *Cul-de-sac in Taxila* (detail). 2010. Single Channel HD Video Projection on Painted Canvas.
Plate 4.13:	Ranbir Kaleka. *Conference of Birds and Beasts* 2010. Digital Photograph and oil Painting on Canvas.
Plate 4.14:	Ranbir Kaleka. *The Great Topairist's Astonishing Dilemma*. Hand painted on Digital Paint on Canvas.
Plate 4.15:	Ranbir Kaleka. *Not from Here* (detail). 2009. Four Channel HD Video Projection on Painted Canvases.
Plate 4.16:	Ranbir Kaleka. *He Was A Good Man* (detail). 2008. Single Channel Video Projection on a Painting.
Plate 4.17:	Ranbir Kaleka. *Wall* (detail). 2009. Single Channel Video.

Plate 4.18: Ranbir Kaleka. *Forest* (detail). 2009. Video Projection on Painting.

Plate 4.19: Ranbir Kaleka. *Consider* (detail). 2007. Two Channel Video Projected on Two Canvases.

Plate 4.20: Ranbir Kaleka. *Man With Cockerel - 2* (detail). 2004. Single Channel Video.

Plate 4.21: Ranbir Kakela. *Man in Water* (detail). 2003. Two Channel Video Projection.

Plate 4.22: Ranbir Kaleka. *Windows* (detail). 2002. Single Channel Video-sculpture.

Plate 4.23: Ranbir Kaleka. *Music Room* (detail). 2002. Single Channel Video.

Plate 4.24: Ranbir Kaleka. *Video Lounge* (detail). 2002. Six Channel Video Loop with Sound.

Plate 4.25: Ranbir Kaleka. *Powder Room* (detail). 1999-2000. Single Channel Video-Sculpture Installation.

Plate 4.26: Ranbir Kaleka. *House of An Opaque Water* (detail). 2012. Three Channel Projection with Sound on Three Panel.

Plate 4.27: Ranbir Kaleka. *Fearsome Acquiescense of A Monotonous Life* (detail). 2019. Two Channel Video Installation with sculpture.

Plate 4.28: Ranbir Kaleka. *Not Anonymous_Walking to the Obscure Fear of A New Dawn* (detail). 2017-2018. Single Channel Projection on Multiple Screen.

Plate 4.29: Ranbir Kaleka. *Bound* (detail). 2018. Single Channel Projection on Burnt Wood.

Plate 4.30: Surekha. *Selving A Body* (detail). 1998-1999. Rice Paper, Pigments And Thread.

Plate 4.31: Surekha. *Communing with Urban Heroins* (detail). 2007. Culture Specific Video Installation.

Plate 4.32: Surekha. Between Fire and Sky (detail). 2008. Diptych Video.

Plate 4.33: Surekha. *eyes of a needle* (detail). 2003. Textile and Photographs.

Plate 4.34: Surekha. *cooking concepts* (detail). 2008. Video Installation.

Plate 4.35: Surekha. *f-lovers* (details). 2008. Video-Sculpture.

Plate 4.36: Surekha. *surveillance* (detail). 2008. Video-Sculpture.

Plate 4.37: Surekha. *they had their home here* (detail). 2009. Photo and Video Installation.

Plate 4.38: Surekha. *line of control* (detail). 2003. Video.

CHAPTER-V

Plates	Descriptions
Plate 5.1:	Shilpa Gupta. *Blame* (detail). 2004. Interactive Installation With Contains Stimulated Blood, Poster, Stickers, Video, Interactive Performance.
Plate 5.2:	Shilpa Gupta. *1278 unmarked, 28 hours by foot via National Highway No 1, East of the Line of Control* (detail). 2013. Interactive Installation.
Plate 5.3:	Joseph Kosuth. *One and Three Chairs* (detail). 1965. Wood Folding Chair, Mounted Photograph Of A Chair, And Mounted Photographic Enlargement Of The Dictionary Definition Of "Chair".
Plate 5.4:	Shilpa Gupta. *Speaking Wall* (detail). 2009-2010 Interactive Sensor Based Sound Installation, LCD screen, Bricks, Headphone.
Plate 5.5:	Shilpa Gupta. *Drawing in the D*ark (detail). 2017. Installation. Copper Pipe.
Plate 5.6:	Shilpa Gupta. *1: 998.9* (detail). 2015. Installation.
Plate 5.7:	Shilpa Gupta. *For, In Your Tongue, I Cannot Fit* (detail). 2017-2018. Site Specific Sound Installation With 100 Speakers, Microphones, Printed Text And Metal Stands.
Plate 5.8:	Shilpa Gupta. *Words Come From Ears* (detail). 2018. Motion flapboard.
Plate 5.9:	Shilpa Gupta. *We Change each other* (detail). 2017. Animated Light Installation.
Plate 5.10:	Shilpa Gupta. *24 : 00 : 01* (detail). 2010, 2012. Motion flapboard.
Plate 5.11:	Shilpa Gupta. *Untitled* (detail). 2012. Single Channel Video Projection.
Plate 5.12:	Shilpa Gupta. *Untitled* (detail). 2004-2005. Interactive Video Projection and Sound, Projector And Computer.
Plate 5.13:	Shilpa Gupta. *Untitled* (detail). 2005-2006. Interactive Installation With Touchscreens.
Plate 5.14:	Shilpa Gupta. *WheredoIendandyoubegin* (detail). 2012. Led Based Light Installation.
Plate 5.15:	Shilpa Gupta. *Singing Cloud* (detail). 2008-09. Objects Build With Thousands Of Microphones with 48 Multichannel Audio.

Plate 5.16: Shilpa Gupta. *Threat* (detail). 2008-2009. Interactive Installation, Bathing Soaps.

Plate 5.17: Bose Krishnamachari. *LaVA (labroratory of visual art)* (detail). 2006.

Plate 5.18: Bose Krishnamachari. *Ghost / Transmemoir*. 2008. 108 Used Tiffins With LCD Monitors, Amplifiers, DVD Players, Headphones, Cables, Jute Ropes, Scaffo

Plate 5.19: Bose Krishnamachari. *White Builders and the Red Carpets* (detail). 2008. One Table With Red Corean On Wood, Chairs, Red Carpet, 108 Conference Mikes With Cables And Stands.

Plate 5.20: Leonardo da Vinci. *The Last Supper*. 15th Century. Tempera, Gesso.

Plate 5.21: Bose Krishnamachari. *9 Rasas and One Soft Cut* (detail). 2020.

CHAPTER-I

INTRODUCTION

1.1 Background of the Study

"There is yet another man in me, not the physical, but the personal man; which has its likes and dislikes, and wants to find something to fulfil its needs of love. This personal man is found in the region where we are free from all necessity – above the needs, both of body and mind – above the expedient and useful. It is the highest in man, this personal man. And it has personal relations of its own with the great world, and comes to it for something to satisfy personality."

(Tagore, 2005, p. 10-11)

The traditional landscape genre was thoroughly transformed in the 1960s when many artists stopped merely representing the terrestrial and made their mark directly in the environment (Kastner, Wallis, 1998). Symptomatic of the countercultural impulses of that decade, artists rejected the gallery as a frame and economic system. They were drawn instead to entropic post-industrial wastelands or the vast, uncultivated spaces. Some artists moved the earth to create colossal primal symbols while others punctuated the horizon with a human-made signpost. This tendency also encompasses New Media Art and Conceptualism. For New Media artists, their physical and psychic experience of any space, the environment became works of art.

The title has been taken from a catalogue cover entitled "*Image-Beyond Image*" of a group exhibition of 1963 (Plate 1.1). Contextually the new development of contemporary Indian art has been started from the sixties —this new trend which reflects a genre of non-conventional practices of Visual Art. The image became more conceptual from this era. With the relation of this new genre, the visual came to a point of zenith in the nineties when artists of India became involved with the broader area of art through the New Media works of art.

New Media Art is a contemporary aspect of art, in an age of development of postmodern art of the nineties. The evolution of New Media Art can be traced in the moving photographic inventions of the late nineteenth century. During the nineteen sixties, the development of video art as a form of New Media with the combination of video-sound and installations, performance et al. was witnessed.

1.1.1 The Evocation of New Media Art in Late Twentieth Century

Visual Arts today is characterised by its vitality and diversity (Canfield, 2011). Contemporary artists utilise a whole range of media and methods to explore the world around them – everything from hybrid paintings using unfamiliar material, to digitally manipulated photographs and video works. In the development of contemporary and postmodern art; many art forms have their unique role, among these New Media Art, has massive involvement to enhance the quality of postmodern art and art critique. New Media Art is a contemporary approach to postmodern art. The evolution of New Media Art can be traced to the moving photographic inventions of the late nineteenth century. From the 1920s through the 1950s numerous forms of kinetic and light art can be seen as progenitors of New Media Art. This new kind of art form can be either temporary or permanent – depending upon the particular aspects of the artwork. The genre incorporates video art, sound and installation art to performance art et al.

New Media works can be constructed in any contextual place, and this is not such an important part of art gallery, museums for the display of New Media works. The works also are placed/produced at the public-spaces.

In New Media Art, traditional materials and techniques are far from having been abandoned. But today's artists no longer define themselves primarily in terms of disciplines. Artists have embraced new technologies as a means of expressing, reflecting upon, and competing with the unique cultural landscape of mass communication and entertainment (Canfield, 2011).

Earlier avant-garde movements made use of non-conventional materials and non-traditional media to attack the privileged status of art and the unique, precious character of the art object. With the institutional establishment of contemporary art, boundaries could be crossed without this being a negation of art as such.

In Western art from the 1960s, it has been witnessed a far-reaching reappraisal of what art could be. Pioneers utilised the new video technology, while an interest in the physical space in which art was placed led to artists making installations, performances, videos for specific areas and occasions. New Media artists have moved away from abstraction and towards an engagement with the world around them. Using photography, film and video-technologies that recorded impressions of actual, physical reality and the lives of ordinary people can be relayed in recorded images. Common concepts include people's interactions with their environment, relationships with one another, their hopes, fears, and self-image. People have also become not merely the subjects, but active participants in the creation of the works (Canfield, 2011).

Now some artists of the early development of New Media Art can be taken into account with few examples of their artworks.

1.1.2 Nam June Paik and Bill Viola: Significant Contributors in the Early Development of New Media Art

Nam June Paik is renowned as a pioneer of video art. Paik went on to explore its potential amid changing technology. The artist started as a musician and artist's interest is apparent in works such as '*TV Cello*'. In the 1960s; Paik moved to New York and became involved with Fluxus - a cross-disciplinary avant-garde art movement, influenced by the artist Marcel Duchamp and composer John Cage. Paik's video installations and performances question perception in a quirky and humorous way.

'*TV Cello*'

1971, Walker Art Center, Minneapolis, US

Nam June Paik's '*TV Cello*' consists of three TV sets stacked in the shape of a cello (Plate 1.2). The work was done for a performance with cellist and collaborator Charlotte Moorman. As Charlotte Moorman performed her bow along with the sculpture, Moorman produced video images on the screens.

The technology of video has been accused of spawning an external and disembodied virtual reality. In an extraordinary reversal of this Bill Viola has embraced video technology to create vivid visual experiences that explore the great mysteries of the human condition - love, pain, meaning, and morality.

'Quintet of the Silent' (Plate 1. 3)

With the dramatic lighting and composition of an Old Master Painting, five figures move in extreme slow motion and absolute silence.

2001, video installation, Indianapolis, Museum of Art, US

Viola's video installations often involve multiple projections, and act on the viewer visually, aurally, in space, and overtime. The experience is intensified by special effects, such as superimposition and extreme slow motion, opening up perceptions that transform our standard view and reality. Archetypal symbols, such as fire and water, recur in his work, while passageways and thresholds suggest the boundary separating life from death. Video operates in Viola's work not as an artificial disconnection from reality, but as a reconnection with the essential spiritual dimension of human life.

New Media Art draws attention to the artifice of its creation and to the structural cultural and historical context in which it is present (Canfield, 2011). Allusions to past works of art and movements are frequent, and techniques of framing, editing and digital manipulation are not hidden but revealed. It is this reminder of the artificiality of all images that allows contemporary art to engage with mass visual culture while maintaining a critical attitude towards it.

1.1.3 The Emerging Practices of New Media Art in India

The media, the visual dialogue and its language are evocative of the way we live. India and its art have gone through a sea change in the last decade. The situation is as exciting as it is intimidating (Matlin, 2019). The artists behind the lens compel us to see ourselves as we are. The discourse on New Media Art practices in India, such as it is, originates in the transitional period of the early 1990s, when western curators began to parachute into India, looking for idioms that they could recognize as "cutting-edge", such as the installation, the performance and video art. The narrative of the shift from art circumstances subjugated by painting, to an individual in which New Media practices set the tone, is acceptable as the Polaroid of a decade. Significantly, new-context media art is populated by artists whose education and interests are not restricted to a Visual Arts milieu, but enriched by diverse subcultures. While the nineties showed the beginning of an innovative gallery practice, it was larger cultural forces that brought photography, installation and video art into the conversation of the Indian art world, imparting to them both intellectual legitimacy and economic currency.

In most explorers of New Media Art, in postmodern art, the self and self-attachment are imaged through a class of signifiers. In India, more effective technological progress was achieved in video art when digital editing equipment became available after 1990. Once again, it was a TV and non-fiction film that prompted development. Nevertheless, it came as a boon to the New Media artists.

In India, artists are also exploring the creative matrix of tradition, spirituality, history, urbanisation and Western preferences to create a distinct India in the New Media arena where East is blended with the West.

1.2 Some Indian Artists Who Are Working in New Media Art: A Comparative Analysis

In the transitional phase of the early nineties in India, some artists emanated up with a practice of diversity of media like text, sound, video art, photography, internet, video projection on painting, installation, performance, digitally manipulated works, digital prints et al. (Kumar, 2014). Some of the projecting names are Nalini Malani, Navjot Altaf, Vivan Sundaram, Sheba Chhachhi, Shilpa Gupta, Shakuntala Kulkarni, Subba Ghosh, Subodh Gupta, Ayisha Abraham, Ranbir Kaleka, Sonia Khurana, Kiran Subbaiha, Aditya Basak, Abhijit Gupta, Sanjit Chaudhury, Gigi Scaria, Bharti Kher, Rummana Hussain, Anita Dube, Sudarshan Shetty, Pushpamala N., Veeneta Khanna, Shobha Thaparia, Bose Krishnamachari, Temsuyanger Longkumer, Shovin Bhattacharjee et al. Some of the collective artists- run groups in India, are Raqs Media Collective, Desire Machine Collective (DMC), Open Circle, Khoj - also devoted them in working to New Media Art.

1.2.1 Study of Some Artists and Their New Media Art in India

One of the most distinguished New Media artists; Navjot Altaf born in 1949 at Meerut. Navjot Altaf learned painting at the Sir J J School of Art. The artist grew up with the notion of artists as a universal political being. Outside the school in 1972, reading Marxist philosophy and writers like Ernst Fischer, Simone de Beauvior and later Edward Said, along with students from Bombay University and with Altaf in political and cultural studies circles exposed Navjot to another set of principles and a way of looking at the world rooted in a re-definition of power structures.

Mumbai-based artist Navjot Altaf is known for sculpture and video installations. For the previous three decades, the artist has produced sculpture and video installations addressing the theme of violence, memory, history and loss across India (Weaver, 2011) and the world, e.g. the communal disturbances in Bombay in 1993 following the Babri Masjid demolition in Ayodhya in 1992-3 and attacks connected with the rise of right-wing fundamentalism in India.

Altaf is credited with producing a series of interactive/collaborative works with composers, musicians, documentary filmmakers' technicians and craftspeople. These include community-based projects in Indian villages, revolving around the water situation, design and creation of water pump sites (Nalpar) and children's temples (*pilla gudis*) in collaboration with Adivasi artists from central India. As Altaf has written in a way that the *pilla gudis* appeared from the consciousness that village children were obliged to have no space of their own where they could verve to play or engage in other activities separate school hours. They are conscious as meeting areas in which young people could interact with each other and with community members with knowledge of oral and artistic traditions in their village as well as visiting and inviting artists from throughout India. Such interactions, Altaf continues in a way that can encourage the young minds to think about different ways of knowing and approaches of working, empowering them to utilise nourishment and sustenance from difference and similarities. The mainstream education system in India neutralises cultural difference in the hope of creating a sense of unity in diversity which touches students' perception of culture (Kester, 2005). The idea that Altaf notes is to encourage young minds to be able to question and take decisions, rather than merely receive. The artist's works have been extensively shown nationally and internationally.

'48°C PROJECT'
'Barakhamba in 2008'- 3 channel projection- 1 hour 20 minutes, colour, sound, loop projection: 20 Barakhamba Road.

Navjot Altaf's project will examine the complicated relationship between the urban environments, city development programmes, those who plan/build infrastructure and people who use them . The work is visualised through the cartographies of two major parallel roads in Delhi - Kasturba Gandhi Marg and Barakhamba Road. The former has old trees on both sides along with it, with personalities using the shady spaces below the trees to earn their livelihoods; the latter is without any greenery at all and fated to tall affluent business centres and high-rise corporate towers replacing its historic bungalows.

In Navjot's work, political authenticity is re-defined to locate the artist's subjectivity within the warp and woof of the human condition. In doing so Altaf makes many crossovers to the woman's terrain, the confined and often suppressed feminine situations. The technical virtuosity the artist brings to artist's work has of late been extended to installations and site-specific creations.

Contextual study on Navjot Altaf's video installation :

'*Touch IV*' (2010)

22 monitors video installation 2010

A projection in cooperation with Sangram: Sangli

'*Touch IV* ' (Plate 1. 4) emerged from a cohesive collaboration between the artist and the sex workers, where the entire footage of the documentation and stages of editing were shared in their environments in Sangli. They articulated their likes and dislikes as the project/video installation shaped itself through ongoing encounters and dialogues, which Altaf incorporated into the work.

'*Touch IV* ' is co-produced and co-authored by multiple voices and brings in Altaf's abiding engagement with the idea of participation, of not speaking 'for' / on behalf of the other but to relate to, to listen and understand as the artist says that the social context from which her interlocutors speak.

'*Touch IV* ' is a 22 channel video installation consisting of television monitors and headphones arranged in an adjacent form, depicting the voices of 22 professional sex workers, both women and of the third gender. The imagery used is layered and complex and like Navjot's earlier works, makes it difficult for the viewer to read and comprehend.

'*Touch IV* ' explores the politics of touch and representation, interrogating notions of gender, sexuality, security, class and identity. Navjot brings in an archive of images, words, atmospheric sounds, objects, symbols and play of light, conjoining both factual and fictional associations to the context.

The artist juxtaposes her own experiences of desire and intimacy (one that is accepted in society) with those of sex workers for whom such interactions are determined by commerce and class. There is an element of abstraction in both the visual and linguistic aspects of the work with each voice filling the screen, appearing and disappearing, articulating their choices to be in the profession willingly. The viewer encounters the ambiguities of their lives through a gamut of emotions, pain, trauma, confidence and resignation, through visual and aural experience.

Navjot introduces into the imagery several tools of her research and documentation – the recording machine, the typewriter, the computer and CDs while layering them with shadows and referential signs from the environment in Sangli – the shifts of a rotating fan, the tube-light in the narrow streets and the fire sparks from the torch of a welder or the wheel of the knife-grinder.

Images of nature - sunlight and water also appear with other ambivalent insertions such as that of a child who wants to swim but is wrenched back by a brutal force which is societal and circumstantial. Or is the water too murky to swim in, where the child chooses to step back to imagined freedom? What is the thin line between respectable and bad touch? When does a bit become desirable or repulsive? How does one negotiate with middle-class apprehensions and judgments of such contact, of erotic/ economic relations that occur beneath the surfaces of our lives? The artist probes at these anxieties , questioning the insider-outsider positions of both the artist and the viewer, layering realism and abstraction in such a way where they lived experiences of the protagonists can never be fully grasped.

The construct of the sex workers is not only of distress but as individuals with opinions of the right to one's body, issues of consent, who question the 'sacred' institution of marriage while dealing with battles of human rights, AIDS, sexual health, class, economics and power.

'Minus into minus equals ?' (2008)

Single Channel Video, 1.26 minutes, 1.8 minutes and 6 minutes, colour, sound, loop

'Minus into minus equals?' is a video art by Navjot Altaf (Plate 1.5). Regarding the work, Navjot Altaf reflected that with so many killed and so many more suffering all over the world, with human way of lives being put upside down by increased violence, racism towards specific communities, issues of identity, humiliating airport security checks, asking inappropriate questions; the artist see Gandhi as a human rights activist and a philosopher who tried moving from the centre to the circumference and back for self-knowledge. According to Gandhi, as human beings, our greatness lies not so much in being able to make the world- that is the myth of the atomic age- as in being able to remark ourselves, and the notions of Gandhi object to violence because when it appears to do respectable, the respectable is only temporary, the evil does it permanently. What interests Navjot about Gandhi and his philosophy is his idea of co-existence. The notions of law of nature in love, friendship, work, progress, and security is creative interdependence.

'*Mumbai Meri Jaan*' (2004)

13.30 minutes, 4 channel projection, colour, sound, loop

Three parts of the film – '*Mumbai Meri Jaan*' (Plate 1.6) is a psychological interpretation of narrated experiences of the three teenagers who came to Mumbai city for different reasons and how they dealt with the reality of their dreams. The film has been shot on locations where Navjot Altaf was taken by Sonu, Ganesh, and Saurabh (teenagers) – mostly by local buses and trains within the city of Mumbai. The fourth part of the video deals with the issue of migration, what makes/ compels people to shift from one space to another – in this case to Mumbai city – India's commercial and industrial capital and how migration is seen and reviewed by the people.

'*Briefcase*' (2004)
Single-channel video installation, 5 minutes projection, colour, sound, loop

The work '*Brief case*' (Plate 1.7) reflects: Despite the constant political tensions/ barriers between India and Pakistan and the security vigilance 'Briefcase' signifies the possibilities of connecting through the internet and music shared by the people from both the countries.

'*A Dog a Dog* ' (2001) (Plate 1. 8)
An animation shot: single monitor video installation, 4 minutes: colour, sound, loop

The subject deals with a sense of consciousness; the cycle of life and aspects of symbolising a dog represented in different cultures, for example, changing the colour of the dog interprets the diverse application in varying traditions. According to Plutarch – a Greek philosopher who lived in the latter half of the 1st century AD. *"...a dog symbolises the philosophical principle of life, a culture hero and mythical ancestor "*. Also, having been a companion in life, it continues as such after death and interprets between the dead and the gods.

'*Water Weaving* ' (2005) (Plate 1.9)
18.50 minutes; single-channel projection, colour and sound

The work is conceptualised on a myth about the creation of weaving characterised by a weaver Sukhman from Nagarnar and in Central India (Altaf,

2006). A hunter returning from the forest in the early hour of the day stops by a river to wash. That's when in the water the hunter sees a silver thread shimmering against the rising sun. Without knowing what it was, the hunter starts winding on his stick and returns to his cave. The hunter keeps it outside his cave. People from the village are startled by its shine, and some even touched it. Suddenly, there is a storm and a flood, and it gets destroyed. After some time, the hunter sees a flower glowing in his backyard and then the cotton emerging. Belief has it that those who had touched the silver thread became weavers. Nagarnar, a village in Bastar district is known for the weavers' community as Nancy Adjania writes that Navjot's meditative video-poem returns grace and dignity to the figure of the artisan, not by creating a work of art, but by indicating consciously on the act of labour itself. This lyrical account has a philosophical density that will outlive an anthropologist's limited scrutiny, a developmentalist's weakness for value judgement. The world is marked by many lines that need to be wiped out, many rips in the cloth that require mending. Like Navjot, we could begin by drawing the lines in reverse and in doing so, erase them (Altaf, 2006).

'Relational Sensibility' (2003) (Plate 1.10)

Double Channel Projection, video installation, 9 minutes and 18 minutes, colour, loop.

After spending considerable time in Bastar and travelling extensively in many parts of the world, Navjot Altaf very consciously questions whether in any given situation everyone knows everything or not knows enough. Does an individual look at things in relative terms and develop the sensibility of knowing how to communicate? For which one has to work towards exploring ways and possibilities.

'Catch' (2007) (Plate 1.11)

Three-Channel Projection; 50 seconds; colour, sound, loop

Regarding the video art; Navjot Altaf reflected that more than making one react to the virtual motion of the video image, it is to compel to physical movement, the viewer confronts the picture of the dog in shadow motion being trained to snatch or "catch" a ball on-screen one, as behind it on two facing screens the film shows in synchronisation a boy catch a bouncing ball on one, fall and pick himself again on another, the sound of a dog barking and the bouncing of a ball come up at intervals from two different films and different heights. The viewer has to shift attention, look, and then step and turn accordingly. Spectator's psychology leads him or her to the meaning of the image by evincing responses whose sensations are bodily embedded. The visual aspect of the work blending direct but blurred reality with a sparingly fine painter helps one realise that against the prevalent fixation with competitiveness and winning, life deserves to be enjoyed with spontaneity and sometimes irrespective of its outcome.

'*Images of Images and Images in Images*' (2001)

Three-channel projection, colour, sound, loop

'Images of Images and Images in Images' (Plate 1.12) is part of a multimedia installation *'Between Memory and History '*, an interactive work, consisting of audio, video, and text. The work is about reviewing and questioning the possibilities and problematic of the artistic representations of certain events and holocausts. These three films are created with the footage shot by the artist and the three films ' *I Live in Behrampada* ' by Madhushree Dutta, ' *Bombay A Myth Shattered* ' by Teestha Setalvad and ' *Blood Yatra* ' by Suma Josson made after the demolition of the Masjid in Ayodhya in 1992.

1.2.2 'Desire Machine Collective' in New Media Art Through the Exploration of Mriganka Madhukaillya and Sonal Jain's Multimedia Artworks

Desire Machine Collective (DMC) is a collaborative group of media practitioners based in Guwahati, between the artists Mriganka Madhukaillya and Sonal Jain since 2004. Mriganka Madhukaillya and Sonal Jain describe their work, exploring New Media Art and employ film, video, sound, space, photography, objects and in their multimedia installation; as an attempt to produce systems that resist the standardising drives of commodification. DMC's experiments with an extensive range of media techniques and approaches with the intention of analytical narratives and methods of depictions, infused with a political character advance them an individuality that contributed to their progress as one of the leading artist collaborative in India's contemporary art scene. DMC's art practice has been showcased at some significant international festivals and renowned museums.

1.2.3 The Journey of New Media Art Through the Works of Desire Machine Collective

Some of Desire Machine Collective's (DMC) projects that have extensively disseminated remain works entitled *'Trespassers will (not) be prosecuted'*(2008), and *'Nishan I'* (2007) and *'Residue'* (2011). *'Trespassers will (not) be prosecuted'* is an audio installation consisting of sounds from a sacred forest in Meghalaya. The work reconnoitres the realm of dematerialisation and transience. In practice, false memories of wood are imparted in the viewer's mind, and the work has a natural life which is reflected after the job. This soundscape was executed in a public space with subconscious philosophies of reminiscence, ecology, and geography qualified aurally, thereby retrieving it and interpreting it lively—it performs as an imperceptible involvement into time and space. By installing the work on the Deutsche Guggenheim's façade, Desire Machine Collective questioned whether sound could be regarded as a material thing as according to local belief it's prohibited to proceeds obtainable any object from Meghalaya's sacred forest. The thirty-nine minutes film, *'Residue'*, has images of a neglected thermal power plant near Guwahati that's gradually being believed up by the surrounding forest. DMC emphasises their interest in reviewing the changing aspects between machinery, nature and the relationship between images and how they can be perceived. The thought process of work also arranges with the cyclical process of creation, destruction and memory and how it is exchanged. In 2010 they first revealed *'Residue'* in the ambience of Deutsche Guggenheim also in Lyon Museum of France, Venice Biennale and Paris Triennial.

'Nishan I' remained explored in Srinagar, Kashmir. The work was executed with 4-channel audio-video installation along with four channels of sound. *'Nishan I'* catalogues the interior spaces of abandoned houses that were bereaved of their primary functions as bunkers for the army, with touches of the absences that are suppressed within them. The window in work determines the relation with the world, and this relates to the fragmented between the inner and external, the ego and the stare, public and private. Through this work, Desire Machine Collective appears at emotional and perceptual states that result from a disruption of organic flows, the point of leaving being a state of continual battle and the circumstances it executed. The work has been exhibited at Solomon R. Guggenheim Museum, New York. Another is entitled, *'Noise Life'*. The work is more personal than other works by them, the work opinions to extreme situations of perception happening in exceptional experiences of blindness or deafness. The work overpowers the viewer with a chaos of

sensations and attempts to convey how we make sense of our lives and express our experiences.

A few well known New Media works of Desire Machine Collective (DMC) are: '*Intense Proximity*' which was executed in 3rd Edition of the La Triennale, Palais De Tokyo, Paris (2012), '*Everyone Agrees: It's About to Explode*', a part of 54th International Art Exhibition of the Venice Biennale, '*India Pavilion*', Venice (2011), '*Indian Highway IV* '. Some of their other works are '*Almost Normal*' (2005), '*Alfa Beta*'(2005), '*Daily Checkup*'(2005), '*About Body Borders*' (2006), '*Aliyah*' (2006), '*Passage*' (2006), '*Untitled* ' (2007) and '*30/12*' (2009).

The following artworks of Desire Machine Collective (DMC) are to be discussed:

'*Noise Life* ': Desire Machine Collective At Basis-Frankfurt

In the central installation, noise, live sound, image and storylines are hard to separate from each other (Plate 1.13). This refers to work at the same time as running processes of perception, which we delivered to our everyday experiences. Psychological, political and social processes, history and now blur into a deliberately staged all-over, which combines semantic contents and subjective experience to a multi-layered structure sensation. The noticeable within the installation superposition of feelings and sensory experiences can result by recourse to Deleuze and Guattari as schizo-analysis are described. This term the overlapping, irrational and mentally dissociative experience of self and the surrounding world, it takes precedence over the rational, binary, and categorised experiences will be given. In the context of the installation, however, this term triggers out of his psychoanalytic function and can be read as a commentary against socio-political transformation processes. As the artists Sonal Jain and Mriganka Madhukaillya collaborating since 2004 under the name of 'Desire Machine Collective', when the study minutely go through with their artworks such as installations and films, the duo sets in particular deals with the political, psychological and historical effects of capitalist thinking power structures. In the artwork, through the artistic use of sound, often deconstructed image sequences and the rhythm of the images that are matched to each other , Jain and Madhukaillya open with their work an associative experience space. Conventional narrative forms, and thus the information content are at this moment significantly reduced, and the apparent linkages and tensions between India and the Western industrialised countries only suggest sketchily.

'*Being Singular Plural* ', Solomon Guggenheim Museum, New York (2012) (Plate 1.14)

Desire Machine Collective which is represented by Sonal Jain and Mriganka Madhukaillya, whose name arises from the viewpoint of Gilles Deleuze and Félix Guattari. The focus toward careful looking, watching, and listening, the collective has installed, on the exterior of the museum, an interactive, round-the-clock public artwork '*Trespassers Will (Not) Be Prosecuted* ' (2012), is inspired by sounds composed in a sacred forest in North-Eastern India. The exhibition also comprises two moving-image works on Annex Level 5: '*Residue*'(2011) which is a 35 mm film shot in an unrestricted power plant in the outskirts of Guwahati, Assam, and '*Nishan I*' (2007) which is a four-channel video installation analogous to a miniature painting in its microcosmic contemplation of time and space, as experienced in a neglected apartment in Srinagar, Kashmir. By reorganising aesthetic experience, Desire Machine Collective's artworks compel the viewer to shift from identifying the identity's first social being to considering its ethical-political imperatives (Poddar, 2012).

Subsequent to the Deutsche Guggenheim recapitulation of this exhibition-in- progress in Berlin, the New York appearance contains seven context-specific ventures, a majority of which have been specially conceived of or co-produced for this occasion. They are dispersed across three of the museum's Annex Level galleries as well as in the New Media Theatre and along the museum's outside. Philosopher Jean-Luc Nancy's concept of "*being singular plural* " offers the exhibition's structural framework. Identifying the interconnectedness of all beings, the selected films, videos, and interactive sound installations invite visitors to review conventional boundaries between such types as fiction and non-fiction, art and cinema, the still and moving image, documentation and poetry, and neutrality and subjectivity. By using sound, vision, and text in innovative ways, these practitioners shift viewers' situations from reflexive viewers to active participation—to places where the "we" of "being together" is in the immediate here and now. '*Being Singular Plural*' reveal viewers the unique prospect to encounter topical and innovative film, video, sound-based artworks by seven of the most ground-breaking and visionary contemporary artists, filmmakers, and media practitioners living and working in India today such as Shumona Goel, Shai Heredia, Sonal Jain, Vikram Joglekar, Amar Kanwar, Mriganka Madhukaillya, and Kabir Mohanty. The works included in this presentation reveal the quiet principles of practice, process, and perception while being grounded in a vital social consciousness.

This timely and discourse-defining exhibition is oriented toward co-producing new work, facilitating research, and assembling a community of practitioners (Poddar, 2012).

North-East India is a geographical zone comprising with an immense variety and heterogeneity in its cultural aspects as well as numerous identity formations in a multi-cultural community. This multiplicity has helped this region to develop its different forms of art and culture. In North-East India in comparison with national and international visual aspects, the artists are also exploring the creative matrix of tradition, spirituality, history, urbanisation and Western preferences to create a distinct India in New Media scenario where East is blended with the West.

1.2.4 New Media Artworks of Temsuyanger Longkumer: The Exploration of Socio-Cultural Traditions in Ethnic Societies and the Correlation Between Communities in the Microbial World and Our Own

In the New Media Art practices of North-East India; Temsuyanger Longkumer is a well-known artist to be discussed . Longkumer is a London-based artist from Nagaland. Longkumer's art practice comprises exploring concepts in the genre such as printmaking, painting, sculpture, video, installation and time- based art. Longkumer's art practice explores and emphasises issues connecting to socio-cultural traditions in ethnic societies and the connection between communities in the microbial world and our personal (Sen, 2019). His roots profoundly inspire Longkumer's works. Longkumer is born in Lapa, a small village in the Mon district of Nagaland where the artist spent his early years before he moved on finishing his school in Dimapur, and then moved to Assam then to Gujarat and Delhi to pursue an art education before moving to London in 2001 for further studies.

Regarding his concepts of art practice, Longkumer recalls in a way that his Naga roots have influenced him hugely. He is very attached to the land, its people and the culture. The artist expressed that the scenic region was untouched by industrialisation and filled with mythological tales and beauty of nature.

Temsuyanger Longkumer received his MA in Printmaking from Royal College of Art, London in 2003. Previous to this, he studied MA (Graphic Arts) at The Maharaja Sayajirao University of Baroda, India and BA (Graphic Arts) from Guwahati University, India. He was the recipient of the Drawing Award,

Royal College of Art, London and numerous scholarships including the 'International Students House Scholarship', 'Commonwealth Scholarship', UK and 'INLAKS Scholarship', India.

The following artworks of Temsuyanger Longkumer are to be discussed:

'*Gods Summit*': Temsuyanger Longkumer's Artwork at the Fourth Edition of Kochi-Muziris Biennale 2018

In Longkumer's artwork entitled '*Gods Summit*' (Plate 1.15), the installation conceptualised through imagining a conversation amongst the Gods and Prophets about the predicament of what humanity has done to it. In work a tent functions as the symbolic meeting place of the summit. The reveal of collaged sound clips from over forty films in multiple languages forms the Gods deliberation, with translation projected nearby through the artwork. This work highlights events from global history at some key pivotal moments where irreversible change has occurred and raises the question of what it means to have power, control, authority, wisdom, vision. Longkumer's work entitled '*Gods Summit*', being hosted at Aspinwall House in Kochi-Muziris Biennale 2018 familiarises spectators to the impression of an imaginary congregation of divine beings. Here, a selection of images is notable by the abundant forms and languages in which they have been apprehended , and imagined, over the sequence of civilisational history (Sen, 2019). Longkumer mentioned regarding the '*Gods Summit*' work that working with the implicit idea that these gods present different philosophical positions, Longkumer revealed that with it come varied interests, politics and lives. Anyone can observe the emergence of a cacophony of light-hearted and grave voices— agreeing, disagreeing and sharing.

'*Catch A Rainbow II*': Temsuyanger Longkumer's Artwork at Pepper House, The Fourth Edition of Kochi-Muziris Biennale 2018

Longkumer's Installation entitled '*Catch a Rainbow II* ' conceptualises as a symbol of hope after the recent floods that ravaged the southern coastal state. '*Catch a Rainbow II* ' is Kerala-centric , endeavours to make a rainbow that is visible both during night and day. This work, Longkumer says, also symbolises the Supreme Court ruling against the IPC's Section 377 that criminalised homosexuality.

'*Aye, Aye, my Suntanned Lullaby*'

'*Aye Aye, my Suntanned Lullaby*' is a video installation by Temsuyanger Longkumer which is another side-shoot of Longkumer's nostalgia for home. In this work the artist mixtures with it the rituals, tradition and the politics of Nagaland.

Longkumer explored the community's beating practice through visual language. From this particular vantage point, through the filter of a disappearing culture based on local wisdom, viewers can watch passers-by and glimpses of military occupation of the region (Sen, 2019).

In the New Media/ multimedia works of Longkumer entitled '*Portrait of a dance I* ' (Plate 1.16) and '*Portrait of a dance II* ' (Plate 1.17); the research study also finds the exploration of problems concerning to socio-cultural traditions in ethnic societies, and the correlation between communities in the contiguous world and our own which Longkumer mostly emphasised through conceptualising his New Media Artworks.

1.2.5 A Legitimised Analysis of Six Artists Who Make a New Genre in New Media Art of India

Here in this research, six artists have been chosen as significant figures to support the textual context of the video installation in the New Media Art practices of contemporary Visual Art of India. The artists are Nalini Malani, Ranbir Kaleka, Bose Krishnamachari, Jitish Kallat, Shilpa Gupta, Surekha and they are taken as they have given a notable achievement in the genre of New Media Art of the nineties . Through their art practices in the context of New Media Art, they have tried to incorporate specific images which go beyond the images.

Nalini Malani is an Indian artist of international repute who is well known as one of the experimental artists from the country. Nalini Malani was confined to the role of the artist and also as a social activist. The artist regularly practises her artwork on the narratives of those that have been ignored, forgotten or marginalised by history. Nalini Malani's art practice is influenced by her personal experiences as a refugee of the partition of India. She spaces hereditary iconographies and valued cultural niches under compression. Her point of view is firmly urban and internationalist and unforgiving in its condemnation of a cynical nationalism that exploits the belief of the masses. Here is an art of excess, going beyond the boundaries of legitimised narrative, exceeding the conventional and initiating dialogue. The characteristics of Nalini Malani's work have been the gradual movement towards New Media Art, international collaboration and intensifying dimensions of the pictorial surface into the surrounding space as a temporary wall drawing (Mural), installation, shadow play, multi-projection works and theatre.

Ranbir Kaleka, one of the well-known practising artists in the contemporary New Media Art practices, is born in Patiala, Punjab, in 1953. Kaleka's artworks, like mixed media, multimedia, are almost surrealist in their treatment of scenes from everyday life. Kaleka's interest, fascination in cinema also led to the advent of his video art, where the artist explores the effects of combining the physicality of the painted image with an image made out of light. The result is a 'sort of hyper image', which accomplishes a concentration and delicacy of colour. It permeates the motionless with the intelligence of crusade over the superimposition of sound and movement. The artist's measure into video art has been a vital endeavour for his further exploration of the psychological event, an occurrence that can only take place separate the physical boundaries of the mount of the painting, through the usage of light to form the image and the subsequent aura of the image. Kaleka has also developed and exhibited photographs and installations which contributed towards the New Media Art (2018).

Bose Krishnamachari is known as one of the contemporary Indian artists, who involved his art practices prominently towards the New Media Art practices. Fascinatingly, Bose emphasised as much kindness to form as he does to conceptual and contextual concerns. Startling planes of flat colour juxtaposed against skilful, almost photographic, representations of identifiable persona, imbue the work with an 'international' sensibility. Bose admits to combining Western image-making techniques (such as the installation) with the vernacular, in a proposition to attain an idiom that is entirely contemporary and brisk. Born in Kerala in 1963, Bose completed his MFA from Goldsmiths College, University of London. Krishnamachari's works, thus armoured by a here and today understanding and consciousness of contemporary culture, derives effortlessly from various disciplines, including literature and design, and periods.

Jitish Kallat was born in Mumbai in 1974, the city where the artist remains to stay and work. Kallat's huge oeuvre, straddling painting, photography, drawing, video and sculptural installations, divulges his tenacious enquiries into around of the fundamental themes of our existence. His works pass through variable focal lengths and time-scales; from close details of the skin of a fruit or the brimming shirt-pocket of a passer-by, it might develop to register impenetrable people-scapes or expedition into inter-galactic outlooks (Bhargava, 2019). Some works might be deliberations on the momentary existing whereas others influence back into antiquity and intersect the previous against the present through citations of momentous historical utterances (Bhargava, 2019). Kallat's works have been exhibited extensively at museums and institutions including Tate Modern in London, Martin Gorpius Bauin Berlin, Gallery of Modern Art in Brisbane, Kunst Museum in Bern, Serpentine Gallery in London, Mori Art Museum in Tokyo, Palais des Beaux-Arts in Brussels, Hangar Bicocca in Milan, Busan Museum of Modern Art and then Astrup Fearnley Museum of Modern Art in Oslo, ZKM Museum of Karlsruhe, Henie Onstad Kunstsenter in Oslo, Arken Museum of Moderne Kunst in Copenhagen, Institut Valencia d'Art Modern in Spain, Art Museum in Tokyo, Art Gallery of Ontario in Toronto, Jean Tinguely Museum in Baseland the Gemeente Museum in The Hague amongst many others (Bhargava, 2019) . Kallat's work has been a fragment of the Havana Biennale, Gwangju Biennale, Asia Pacific Triennale, Fukuoka Asian Art Triennale, Asian Art Biennale, Curitiba Biennale, Guangzhou Triennale and the Kyiv Biennale amongst others.

Shilpa Gupta is one of the prominent names in the contemporary New Media Art practice arena of India. Gupta's art practices have engaged with art in its participatory, interactive and public dimensions for over two decades. The artist has persistently mapped the defining power of social and psychological borders on public life. Gupta's work makes visible the aporias and in commensurabilities in the evolving national public domain in India, which comprise gender and class fences, religious variances, the constant power of exploitive state gears, and the seductions of social equality and deceptive ideas of public consensus enabled by emerging mediascapes. Shilpa Gupta was born in Mumbai where the artist studied her art leanings in sculpture in 1997 from the Sir J J School of Art. The artist's mediums vary from deployed found objects to video, interactive computer-based installation and performance. Gupta is concerned with human perception and how information, visible or invisible, gets communicated and adopted in everyday life. Gupta is consistently applying to how objects get definite, be it spaces, individuals, involvements and her art practice involve with precincts where these classifications get played out, be it borderlines, labels and ideas of censorship and security. Gupta's works focus on inter-subjectivity and phenomenology, repetitively reminding viewers regarding the interpersonal and highly intermediated surfaces of the act of observing, salvaging and memorising. Remain self-confidence labels, stamps, objects confiscated at airports, motion flap boards, or prohibited substances that pass through physiological and geographical chasms. Her practice accelerates the boundaries of how the art object is understood.

Surekha is a contemporary Indian video artist. The artist's art practices reveal concepts, including Indian identity and Womanhood. Surekha's works are known for the mix of video and physical presence, highlighting inherent experiences. Surekha has been discovering the possibilities of the video form, exchanging the public and private, finding the body as a site of dispute and annexation. The involvement of photography, video towards archive, document, and performance has an integral role in Surekha's New Media practice. Surekha was born in Bangalore and has studied art at Ken school of Arts and Visva Bharati University, Santiniketan. Surekha has shown her works both in India and many international shows. Surekha lives and works in Bangalore.

The six artists Nalini Malani, Ranbir Kaleka, Bose Krishnamachari, Jitish Kallat, Shilpa Gupta, Surekha through their practices significantly reveal how the New Media Art explores the contemporary Indian art scenario.

1.3 Operational Definition of the Term Used

Image Beyond Image: Image Beyond Image refers to a mental idea of a visual observation in a viewer's mind from observing a work of art that an individual looks to feel and that idea gathers a fresh concept into his/her account.

Implicated Imagery: Implicated Imagery refers to the concerned connection around an art image.

Image-making: Image-making refers to an art image in the making of the image.

Image-circuit: Image-circuit refers to a visible space within a frame as an art image.

1.4 Statement of the Problem

Visual Arts are ever-changing and unstable, which philosophically emerged and developed from the mid-sixties of the twentieth century. From that time, new art forms were confronted with different phenomenological problems of modern art theories. The gap between self-concern purity of modern art and pluralistic and transcendental postmodern art created a blank and figured space in the second half of the twentieth century. The different art movement started as the seventies carried out some new questions and critiques against the previous art practices. New Media Art was one of them through which the critical issue against modern art could revolve.

The research topic *"Image Beyond Image: New Media Art of Contemporary India"* has faced some critical questions regarding contemporary art- scenario of India. Such as:

i. How does society build art or construct the phenomenon of wholeness and Meta narratives in itself?

ii. What is the background concept of execution of New Media Art of contemporary India?

iii. Were the New Media Art exploring only for an extension of the Visual Arts milieu or giving support of conceptual representations to contemporary Visual Art practice?

iv. Were the New Media Artworks of contemporary India represent more interaction between the artwork and the viewer?

v. What are the conceptual dialogues of video installations in New Media Art?

vi. How did the digital effect reveal an impact only through visual interaction to give support in context to culture, history, society, politics and psychoanalysis?

1.5 Objectives of the Study

- To study the development of New Media Art in the late twentieth century.
- To study the historical background and emerging practices of New Media Art in India.
- To study the New Media Art practices in 1990s India.
- To focus on the socio-political emergence behind the development of New Media Art.
- To focus on the changes in art practices of the nineties of India through New Media Art.
- To focus on the six contemporary New Media artists of India and their art practices to project the arrival of a new genre in Indian contemporary art.

1.6 Scope of the Study

The study focuses on the New Media Art of contemporary India from 1990 to the till now. It also highlights the visual interaction of New Media Art with its conceptual aspect as an image beyond the image in context to contemporary art- world.

1.7 Limitation of the Study

The study limited to the evocation of New Media Art of late twentieth century to the till date highlighting the New Media Art of India since the nineties with studying and analyse the six artists' New Media Artworks as a referral to support the textual context of the video installation in the New Media Art practices of contemporary Visual Art of India. The artists are - Nalini Malani, Jitish Kallat, Ranbir Kaleka, Surekha, Bose Krishnamachari, Shilpa Gupta.

1.8 Data and Methodology

The data are collected from primary and secondary sources. The primary data are based on visiting the original New Media Artworks from various exhibitions and taking personal interviews from the artist himself/herself. Secondary data sources of the research study are based upon the reviews and references, published thesis, journals, books, periodicals, gazetteers and internet.

The methodology applied for the study was conducted by taking interviews with the artists that are considered as a referral of the research study and also from scholar/academician to support the textual context of the New Media Art practices of contemporary Visual Art of India. Along with the visual documentation of the relevant artworks of New Media Art are done through photography and videography.

1.9 Review of Literature

The entire literature available for the present study is divided into three broad areas. The first part focuses on New Media Art practices in 1990s India. The second part analyses in New Media Art of contemporary era and the third part is the miscellaneous/related referential studies.

1.9.1 New Media Art Practices in 1990s India

This part of the literature review is highlighted upon the New Media Art practices in 1990s India.

Sood (2003) features internationally acclaimed video works by leading Indian artists such as Nalini Malani, Vivan Sundaram, Navjot Altaf, Sheba

Chhachhi and a range of younger experimental video artists. The artists' works have been represented in a visual narrative to bring alive the experience of the installation within the gallery space. Conveniently written and yet as powerful and sophisticated as some of the works themselves. Video art in India simultaneously documentation, videography and an analytical account of video art. The author provides a lucid overview of the burgeoning New Media Art practice in India today. An exciting and informative resource book. The book includes essential additions to every library and a resource of inspiration for artists, art-lovers, critics, students, galleries and institutions.

Kumar (2014) describes the Fine Arts pedagogy in India and the impact of New Media Art in the contemporary Visual Arts practices of India. The role of a few galleries, museums, and art foundations is significant to enhance the quality practice of New Media Art in India in the nineties. The next decade also carries forward in a new high for practising art in the arena of New Media Art.

Rafi and Ahmad (2016) focus on the interdisciplinary as well as New Media Art practices of the nineties of Indian Visual Art. The inception of New Media Art practices in India can be noticed in the 1990s. Interdisciplinary art shaped a new dimension in the development of New Media Art in India in the nineties. The nineties have a significant shift in contemporary Indian Visual Art practices.

Evans and Gupta (2018) presents forty-eight contemporary artists and collectives working in discourse with the long history and growing future of India and its individuals. Its attention deceives on the contemporary moment through a range of approaches. The involvement of photography with New Media and also including installation, moving image, journalism and documentary photography reveals the reader a new vision about New Media Art. The author describes themes include caste and class, the partitioning of the subcontinent, gender and sexuality, activism, and conflict, racism, religion, nationalism, new technologies and development, the environment, human settlement, migration and integration. The author describes as a vast, multilingual subcontinent, India has always relied on images to maintain a cohesive whole across myriad subcultures, regions, caste and idioms. The overview of photomechanical imaging in the nineteenth century qualified the speedy faux and propagation of both spiritual and scientific ideas. Photography for most of its antiquity was too exclusive and procedural and was leftward in the hands of experts – until the birth of digital technologies. The author addresses the legacy of the twenty years, a period when photography and moving image media have been unswervingly composed within critical exhibitions.

1.9.2 New Media Art of Contemporary Era

This part of the literature review is focused upon New Media Art of the contemporary era.

Khanna and Kurtha (1998) describe that the present Visual Art scene of India is one of the most vibrant in the world, which is characterised by tremendous enthusiasm. The authors logically present how the current Visual Art practice derived in an old country immersed in traditionalism and the country which had suffered foreign rule for two centuries.

Rush (1999) presents Modern Art as radically prolonged the conformist intermediate of sculpture and painting. Subsequent on innovative ideas about representation and the free practice of resources in Cubism, Futurism and Surrealism - predominantly in the artwork of Duchamp - artists abandoned strict observance to a traditional chain of command of modes and incorporated any revenue, together with technological, which best assisted their resolves. Additionally, especially in the last fifty years, time and duration have reinstated narrative back in art: in filmmaking and video, the narrative theatricality of happening, performance and installation art, digitally manipulated photography and virtual reality. This book discusses both the most influential artists internationally, from Muybridge to Robert Rauschenberg, Bill Viola and Pipilotti Rist, and pivotal artworks which have radically transformed the map of world art.

Manovich (2001) describes the systematic and severe theory of New Media. The author presents New Media within the histories of visual and media cultures of the last few centuries. New Media works create the illusion of reality, reflect the viewer and represent a particular space, and the forms of New Media are unique.

Wands (2006) describes construction on the traditions of art history and using progressive machinery, digital artists push the boundaries of artistic appearance and discover some of the most critical social, political, and biological problems confronting humanity nowadays. Traditional practices, such as painting and sculpture, have been fundamentally transformed by digital procedures and media. In contrast, utterly new forms, such as internet art, digital installation, and virtual reality, have developed as recognised artistic practices, collected by museums, institutions, and individuals the world over.

All the various forms are presented here – digital prints, sculpture, and interactive installations; DVD and CD-ROMs; digital animation and video; websites and software art; New Media performance and music. The author describes an outline of the main characteristics of each category and discusses in detail about specific artworks designated by a board of curators as the most important of their kind. Quotes, statements, and other texts from digital artists, curators and theorists of New Media appear throughout the book to provide further illuminating insights. An introduction in the book outlines the history of digital art from its tentative beginnings in the 1960s to its full arrival in the 1990s. At the same time, the final chapter speculates on what the future might bring for the rapidly changing art form.

Tribe and Jana (2006) focuses on artists who have always been early adopters of emerging media technologies, from Albrecht Durer and his practice of the printing press in the 16th century to Nam June Paik's research with video projections in the 1960s. In 1994, the arrival of the internet as a popular medium catalysed a global art movement that activated to reconnoitre the cultural, social, and aesthetic circumstances of such new intelligence technologies like the web, video direction cameras, wireless phones, hand-held computers, and GPS devices. The authors label New Media Art as a specific art historical movement, focusing not only on technologies and forms but also on thematic content and conceptual strategies. New Media Art frequently involves arrogation, collaboration and the free sharing of ideas and expressions. The authors often address the political consequences of technology around issues of identity, commercialisation, privacy, and the public sphere. Many New Media artists are intensely aware of their art historical antecedents, making a difference to data, Pop Art, Conceptual Art, Performance Art and Fluxus.

1.9.3 Miscellaneous / Related Referential Studies

In this section, a few other studies, which are relevant to the current study, are reviewed .

Mago (2001) focuses on the different artistic and stylistic genres and Visual Art movements that enriched the contemporary Visual Art of India. Through the various ways of developments in Indian art, the process gradually developed contemporary Indian art.

Leyden and Dalmia (2001) present the work process of modern Indian Visual Art since its initiations in the nineteenth century. Without having proper resources, how the artists acquire their achievements and success.

Graham, Beryl and Lapp, Axel (2010) presents the practices of curators in the area of New Media Art in position to analyse the massive changes and developments over a relatively short period. They are also a celebration of many years that the online means for curators of New Media Art, CRUMB, has been publishing conversations on contemporary arts as well as New Media and research. The curators included in this book series beyond modern techniques. They have been accomplishing things such as not in the centre or the periphery but the junctions of this networked field of New Media Art.

Catricala (2015) focuses a series of theoretical contributions in which some perspectives of earlier and contemporary forms of media art, its histories and views and a few case studies of artworks by the new generations of Italian media artists' has been revealed. The crucial question is the definition of quintessentially European term media art that encompasses many media and art-forms nowadays, varying from film to interactive art. In the previous decades, the arena of individual artistic practices has been challenging to define such as post-media, inter-media, post-cinema, post video art? Whether media art is the best term among these categories. Whether media art indicates a technique that uses media or one that intersects all of them or one that is related to technology. Does the essay emphasise how in each instance, this notion could also be utilised to express traditional art mechanisms such as cinema and their avant-gardist activities, at the same period an individual can set the new generation of artists as media artists? Was Michelangelo a 'marble artist'? Contested by Fabrizio Plessis who refused the notion of 'video artist'. The section 'theory' helps clarify these questions—Sean Cubitt as Paul Thomas, authors of Relive. Media Art Histories (2014), explains for a media art history as a collaborative responsibility with a greedy approach blending experimental subjects and cultural history. Oliver Grau focuses alternatively on how media art performs a pivotal role in the representation of our information societies – he argues that media art is the art form that practises the technologies that fundamentally transform our communities. Within the perspectives, he also accentuates the importance of researching and archiving it. How media arts can be productively opened in education is the topic of Alfonso Molina's writings. Molina illustrated how the project associated with revelation and salvation is discussed in the last essay of this section where Valentino Catricala explores how such a perspective relates to 'media art'. Interesting analyses on cinema, video art, computer art, and media art compose the following section, 'Histories.' These contributions show how the flexible notion of 'media art' can be a powerful tool to re-examine the inter-realistic nature of both traditional and contemporary artworks. The next section, 'perspectives' finally looks at several critical topics in contemporary artistic debates such as 'post-internet' interactivity in the arts, the intersection of art, science, technology and society, sound art, and the democratisation of media art. To what extent the appearance of Italian media art is something that develops distinctively only in the very last section emphasising a series of artworks by Italian artists, can we define the boundaries of Italian media art.

Boden and Edmonds (2019) describe essays on computer art and its relation to more traditional art. Oscillating between practical and philosophical, the authors articulate the critical issues in the production and reception of computer art. The authors regenerate the dialogue of creative computing and in doing so, provide new insights on the computer arts and the opinion of creativity. The authors describe an enthusiastic artist and a philosopher observing computer art and how it has been both received and denied by the mainstream art world. In a series of essays, the authors grapple with crucial questions about the aesthetics of computer art. Other modern technologies – photography and film – have been recognised by critics as methods of doing art. Does the use of computers conciliate computer art's aesthetic credentials in procedures that the application of cameras does not? Is writing a computer program comparable to painting with a brush? Essays by the authors identify types of computer art, describe the study of creativity in AI, and explore links between computer art and traditional views in philosophical views in philosophical aesthetics. Essays by authors offer a practitioner's viewpoint, bearing in mind, among other elements, how the experience of planning computer art compares to that of traditional art-making. Finally, the authors present interviews in which contemporary computer artists offer a wide range of comments on the issues raised.

1.10 Organisation of the Research and Chapterisations

The research has been divided into six chapters. Such as

Chapter I :	Introduction,

Chapter II :	Image Beyond Image: New Media Art Practices in 1990s India,

Chapter III :	The Legitimised Narratives and the Web of Traffic: The Artworks of Nalini Malani and Jitish Kallat,

Chapter IV :	The 'Third Object'/ Urban Signs and the Vulnerable Body: New Media Artworks of Ranbir Kaleka and Surekha,

Chapter V :   Through the Ways of Memory and the Techno-

Images: Re-Interpretation of New Media works of Shilpa Gupta and Bose Krishnamachari,

Chapter VI: Conclusion.

The first chapter presents an introduction to the topic. The first chapter concentrates a general view of New Media Art. The study also highlights on the New Media Art of contemporary India since 1990 with particular reference to the video- installation practices of Nalini Malani, Jitish Kallat, Ranbir Kaleka, Surekha, Shilpa Gupta and Bose Krishnamachari. It is mentioned that the artists' artworks are taken as they have given a notable achievement in the genre New Media Art of the nineties. Each artist carries the distinctive characteristics featured in the execution of their New Media Art. The chapter focuses on the sub-topics like the evocation of New Media Art in late twentieth century, Nam June Paik and Bill Viola: significant contributors in the early development of New Media Art, the emerging practices of New Media Art in India, operational definition of the term used, some Indian artists who are working in New Media Art: a comparative analysis, study of some New Media Artworks of India, 'Desire Machine Collective' in New Media Art through the exploration of Mriganka Madhukaillya and Sonal Jain's multimedia artworks, the journey of New Media Art through the works of Desire Machine Collective, New Media Artworks of Temsuyanger Longkumer: the exploration of socio-cultural traditions in ethnic societies and the correlation between communities in the microbial world and our own, the artists who make the difference in a new genre of video installation: a legitimised study of six artists. The chapter also includes the statement of the problem, objectives of the study, scope of the study, limitation, data and methodology, review of literature and organisation of the research.

The second chapter discusses the New Media Art practices in 1990s India. The study highlights the Visual Art practices of the nineties of India. The chapter focuses on the sub-topics like inception of interdisciplinary art practices in India, interdisciplinary collective artist-run groups in India, the discourses of New Media Art of India in the nineties, the role of art organisation in the exploration of New Media Art of India in the nineties, role of art directorial in New Media Art of India through 2000s onwards: a connection to the discourses of New Media Art practices of India since the nineties, role of art institutes and Visual Arts pedagogy in India in relation to New Media Art.

The third chapter focuses on the legitimised narratives and the web of traffic: the artworks of Nalini Malani and Jitish Kallat, the chapter discusses the artworks of Malani and Kallat with a case study of both the artists' video-installations. The chapter focuses on the sub-topics like art practice of Nalini Malani: transition from traditional painting to New Media Art, Nalini Malani's art practice: the role of the bodily and the local, the role of Nalini Malani's technique into the artist's art practice: transformation to New Media Art, myth as interclass vocabulary into Nalini Malani's art Practice, the myth of Medea into Nalini Malani's Art Practice, the overhaul process in the work of Nalini Malani: an overview, the cathartic effect of Nalini Malani's artworks, New Media Artworks of Jitish Kallat, the artistic journey of Jitish Kallat: transformation from painting to New Media Art.

The fourth chapter discusses the 'Third Object'/ urban signs and the vulnerable body: New Media Artworks of Ranbir Kaleka and Surekha. The study concentrates on the artworks of Kaleka and Surekha with a case study of both the artists' New Media Artworks. The chapter contains different sub-topics such as the artistic journey of Ranbir Kaleka: transformation from painting to video art/video installation, Ranbir Kaleka's video art practice: exploration through co-founded film society, Ranbir Kaleka as activist in theatre and the artist's days during teaching in College of Art, Delhi, execution of monochrome into Kaleka's video installation: an analysis, narratives into Ranbir Kaleka's video installation, sound is fairly important and visuals border on 'fantasy' in Kaleka's video installations: an analysis, inspirations and philosophy of Ranbir Kaleka's artwork, video installation of Ranbir Kaleka: an overview, New Media Artworks of Surekha, Surekha's art practice: the body represented to recurrently re-emerge as a polyvalent site, Surekha's art practice: personifying beauty and pain, the nature into Surekha's New Media Artworks: forms/contents/processes.

The fifth chapter contains through the ways of memory and the techno-images: re-interpretation of New Media works of Shilpa Gupta and Bose Krishnamachari. The study discusses the New Media Art practice of Shilpa Gupta and Bose Krishnamachari with a case study of both the artists' artworks. The chapter focuses on the sub-topics like Shilpa Gupta's art and the narrativity of the body in space and time, Shilpa Gupta and Irit Rogoff's "inhibition ", Shilpa Gupta and Henri Lefebvre: Rhythmanalysis, Shilpa Gupta and Michel de Certeau "anthropological space", in conclusion: Shilpa Gupta, Michel de Certeau and Henri Lefebvre, New Media Artworks of Bose Krishnamachari, the artistic journey of Bose Krishnamachari: transformation from abstract painting to Multimedia interactive installation, reading and travel: the significant fragment of Bose Krishnamachari's art practice, the artist and the Mumbai: Bose Krishnamachari's art exploration, Bose Krishnamachari's works and the interactive audience participation: beyond the artist's taste, questioning 'the Idea of the formation of the canon in art': Krishnamachari as a curator, Bose's 3C theory: cricket, cinema, and curry, Bose Krishnamachari as an art directorial: the visionary approaches.

    The sixth chapter concludes the study and summarises the research. The chapter also highlights the research findings and suggests further research.

PLATES

Plate 1 . 1 : V S Gaitonde . *Untitled* **. 1963 . Catalogue Cover .
Courtesy : Asia Art Archive . Web . 21 February . 2019**

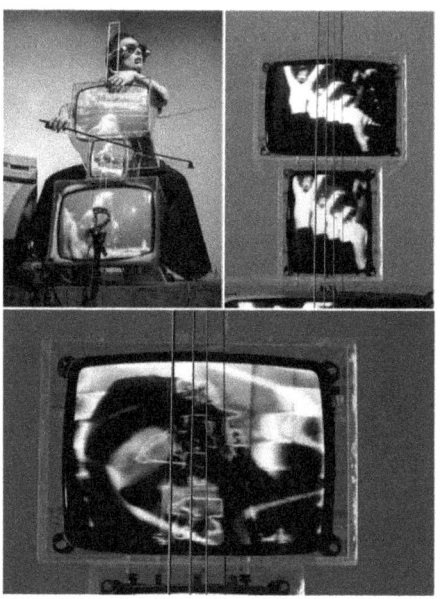

Plate 1 . 2 : Nam June Paik . *TV Cello* **(detail) . 1971 .
Courtesy : Art Gallery NSW . Web . 21 February . 2019**

Plate 1.3 : Bill Viola. *Quintet of the Silent* (detail). 2001. Video Installation.
Courtesy : Hermitage Museum. Web. 21 February. 2019

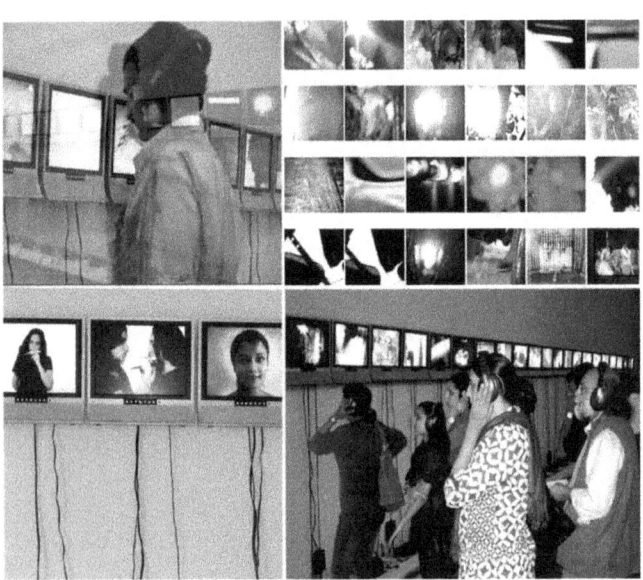

Plate 1.4 : Navjot Altaf. *Touch IV* (detail). 2010.
22 Channel Video Installation.
Courtesy : The Guild Art Gallery. Web. 21 February. 2019

Plate 1 . 5 : Navjot Altaf . *Minus into minus equals ?* (detail) . 2008 .
Single Channel Projection .
Courtesy : Navjot Altaf . Web . 21 February . 2019

Plate 1 . 6 : Navjot Altaf . *Mumbai Meri Jaan* (detail) . 2004 .
Four Channel Projection .
Courtesy : The Guild Art Gallery . Web . 21 February . 2019

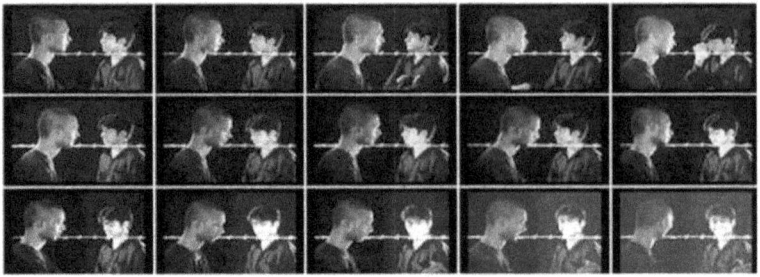

**Plate 1.7 : Navjot Altaf . *Brief Case* (detail) . 2004 .
Single Channel Video Installation .
Courtesy : Navjot Altaf . Web . 21 February . 2019**

**Plate 1.8 : Navjot Altaf . *A dog a dog* (detail) . 2001 .
An Animation Shot : Single Channel Video Installation .
Courtesy : Navjot Altaf . Web . 21 February . 2019**

Plate 1.9 : Navjot Altaf. *Water Weaving* (detail) . 2005 .
Single Channel Projection .
Courtesy : Navjot Altaf . Web . 21 February . 2019

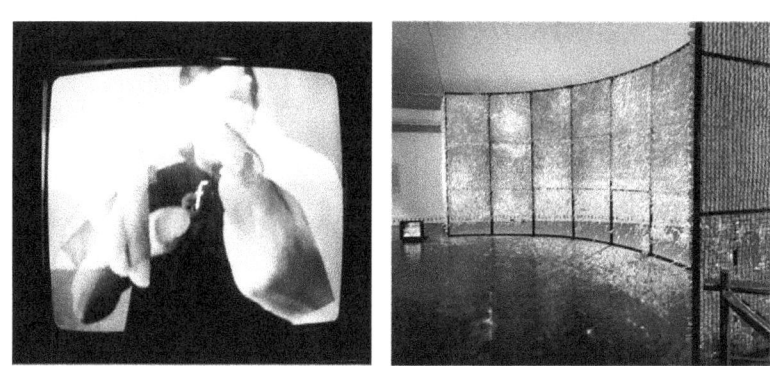

Plate 1.10 : Navjot Altaf. *Relational Sensibility* (detail) . 2003 .
Double Projection Video Installation .
Courtesy : Hakara . Web . 21 February . 2019

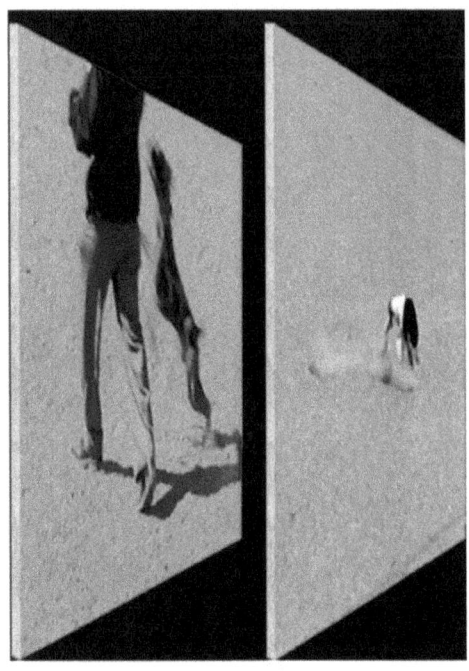

Plate 1 . 11 : Navjot Altaf . *Catch* (detail) . 2007 . Three Channel Projection .
Courtesy : The Guild Art Gallery . Web . 21 February . 2019

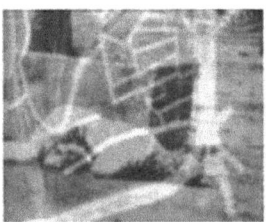

Plate 1 . 12 : Navjot Altaf . *Images of Images and Images in Images* (detail) . 2001 .
Three Channel Projection .
Courtesy : Navjot Altaf . Web . 21 February . 2019

Plate 1.13 : Desire Machine Collective. *Noise Life* (detail). 2015. Sound, Images, Elements of Plot.
Courtesy : basis-frankfurt.de. Web. 21 February. 2019

Plate 1.14 : Desire Machine Collective. *Being Singular Plural* (detail). 2012. Video Installation.
Courtesy : Solomon R. Guggenheim Museum. Web. 21 February. 2019

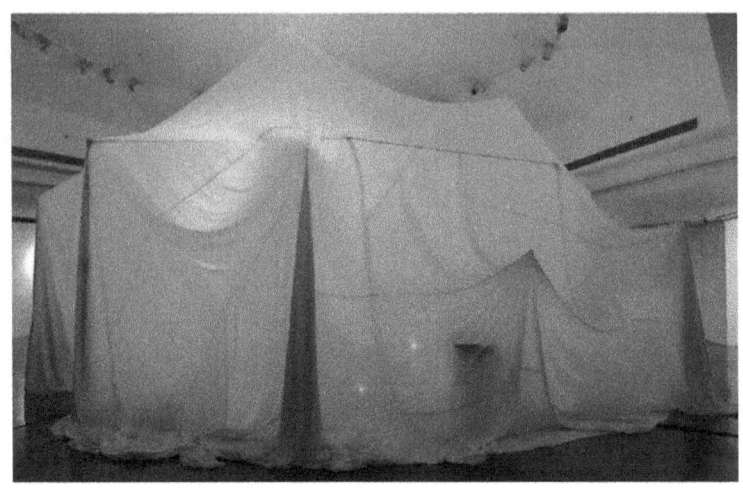

Plate 1 . 15 : Temsuyanger Longkumer . *Gods Summit* (detail) . 2018 .
Multimedia Installation .
Courtesy : Temsuyanger Longkumer . Web . 21 February . 2019

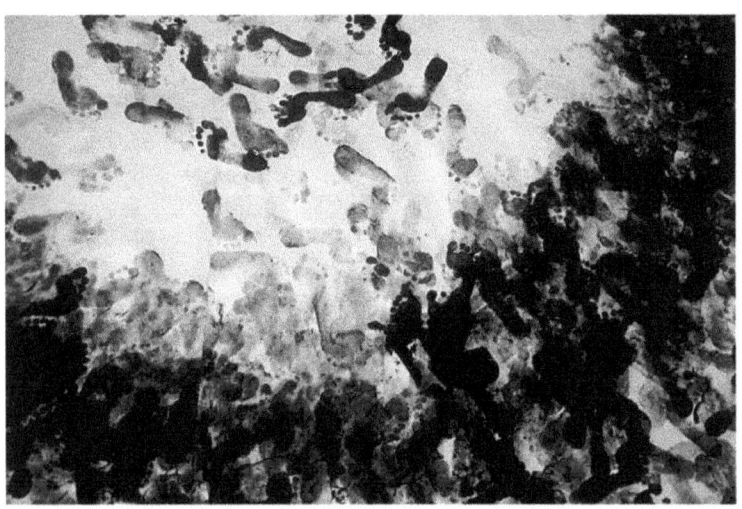

Plate 1 . 16 : Temsuyanger Longkumer . *Portrait of a dance I* (detail) .
Multimedia Installation .
Courtesy : Temsuyanger Longkumer . Web . 21 February . 2019

Plate 1 . 17 : Temsuyanger Longkumer. *Portrait of a dance II* (detail) .
Video Installation.
Courtesy : Temsuyanger Longkumer . Web. 21 February . 2019

References

"A Conversation with Desire Machine Collective." *Asia Art Archive in America*, 18 Mar. 2012, www.aaa-a.org/programs/a-conversation-with-desire-machine-collective/. Accessed 8 Feb. 2019.

Altshuler, Bruce. *Biennials and beyond - Exhibitions That Made Art History: 1962-2002*. London, Phaidon, 2013.

Bennington, Geoffrey, et al. *The Postmodern Condition: A Report on Knowledge*. Manchester, Manchester University Press, 2005.

Catricalà, Valentino. *Media Art: Towards a New Definition of Arts in the Age of Technology*. Pistoia, Gli Ori, 2015.

Cook, Sarah. *A Brief History of Curating New Media Art: Conversations with Curators*. Berlin, Green Box, 2010.

Cook, Sarah. *A Brief History of Working with New Media Art: Conversations with Artists*. Berlin, Green Box, 2010.

"Desire Machine Collective |Ocula." *Ocula.Com*, 2 Dec. 2015, ocula.com/magazine/conversations/desire-machine-collective/. Accessed 8 Feb. 2019.

Dewdney, Andrew, and Peter Ride. *The New Media Handbook*. London, Routledge, 2006.

Elwes, Catherine, and Shirin Neshat. *Video Art a Guided Tour*. London I.B. Tauris, 2006.

Fanning, Leesa, and Ladan Akbarnia. *Encountering the Spiritual in Contemporary Art*. Kansas City, Missouri, The Nelson-Atkins Museum Of Art, 2018.

Foster, Hal, et al. *Art since 1900: Modernism, Antimodernism, Postmodernism*. New York, Thames & Hudson, 2011.

Graham, Beryl. *New Collecting: Exhibiting and Audiences after New Media Art*. London, Routledge, 2017.

Graham, Beryl, and Sarah Cook. *Rethinking Curating: Art after New Media.* Cambridge, Mass., Mit Press, 2010.

"Jitish Kallat." *The Chopra Center*, 21 Mar. 2016, chopra.com/bios/jitish-kallat. Accessed 7 Mar. 2018.

Kastner, Jeffrey, and Brian Wallis. *Land and Environmental Art.* London, Phaidon, 2010.

Kumar, Vinay. "Fine Art Pedagogy in India And Impact of New Media Art." *Paripex- Indian Journal Of Research*, vol. 3, no. 1, 15 Jan. 2012, pp. 80–82, 10.15373/22501991/jan2014/23. Accessed 1 Mar. 2019.

Malpas, William. *Land Art: A Complete Guide to Landscape, Environmental, Earthworks, Nature, Sculpture, and Installation Art.* Maidstone, Kent, Crescent Moon, 2013.

"NAVJOT ALTAF (Mumbai, India)." *Groundworks*, 9 Apr. 2014, groundworks.collinsandgoto.com/navjot-altaf-mumbai-india. Accessed 7 Mar. 2018.

"NFB Pause: Chris Lavis and Maciek Szczerbowski Talk Gymnasia." *NFB Blog*, 18 July 2019, blog.nfb.ca/blog/2019/07/18/gymnasia-vr/. Accessed 4 Oct. 2019.

Paul, Christiane. *New Media in the White Cube and beyond: Curatorial Models for Digital Art.* Berkeley, Calif., University Of California Press, 2008.

Phaedra Shanbaum. *The Digital Interface and New Media Art Installations.* New York, Ny, Routledge, 2020.

Phaedra Shanbaum, Phaedra. *The Digital Interface and New Media Art Installations.* New York, Ny, Routledge, 2019.

Poddar, Sandhini. *Being Singular Plural.* New York, Guggenheim Museum, 2012.

Poddar, Sandhini. *Being Singular Plural: Moving Images from India.* New York, Guggenheim Museum Publications, 2010.

Quaranta, Domenico. *Beyond New Media Art.* Brescia, Link Editions, 2013.

Ratan Parimoo, et al. *Towards a New Art History: Studies in Indian Art (Essays Presented in Honour of Prof. Ratan Parimoo).* New Delhi, D. Kurniawan, 2003.

Ruhrberg, Karl, et al. *Art of the 20th Century*. London, Taschen, 2012.

Rush, Michael. *New Media in Art*. London, Thames & Hudson, 2005.

Rush, Michael. *New Media in the Late 20th Century*. S.L., London, 1999.

Sen, JD. "Naga Artist Longkumer Rechecks His Past and Present at Kochi Biennale." *News Expert*, 28 Dec. 2018.

Shanken, Edward A. *Art and Electronic Media*. London, Phaidon Press Limited, 2014.

Shu, Mei. *Thingworld: International Triennial of New Media Art 2014 /Thingworld: International Triennial of New Media Art 2014*. Beijing, P.R. China, The National Art Museum Of China; Liverpool, Uk, 2014.

Steiner, Wendy. *Venus in Exile: The Rejection of Beauty in Twentieth-Century Art*. Chicago, University Of Chicago Press, 2002.

Thomas C. *Art Appreciation Topic X: Art after 1945*. 17 Feb. 2011, www.slideshare.net/drthomc/art-appreciation-topic-x-art-after-1945. Accessed 10 Apr. 2019.

Tribe, Mark, et al. *New Media Art*. Hong Kong; Los Angeles, Taschen, 2009.

Wallis, Brian, et al. *Land and Environmental Art*. Berlin Phaidon, 2005.

Wands, Bruce. *Art of the Digital Age*. London, Thames & Hudson, 2007.

Zoya Kocur, and Simon Leung. *Theory in Contemporary Art since 1985*. Chichester, West Sussex, Wiley-Blackwell, 2013.

CHAPTER-II

IMAGE BEYOND IMAGE: NEW MEDIA ART PRACTICES IN 1990s INDIA

2.1 Introduction

"Man is a singular creature. He has a set of gifts which make him unique among the animals: so that, unlike them, he is not a figure in the landscape – he is a shaper of the landscape. In body and in mind he is the explorer of nature. The ubiquitous animal who did not find but has made his home in every continent."

(Bronowski, 1973, p.11)

The mainstream Visual Arts activities in India; since the 1990s can be categorised as an implicated imagery. The art before or till the nineties was considered as a purer or purist imagery and the discourse and institutional processes that occurred an irony between 'around it' and 'in the making of it' gave us an image of 'a visible space within a frame as an art image', by and large. Everything that happened 'around it' such as criticism, appreciation, sale, auction, hegemonic placing of 'one' work as superior to the other; hierarchy, awards, gallery-artist-work nexus and the like served as an appendix 'to' it, in the popular imagination of 'Art', even among about the specialists who wrote and spoke about it. The visionary glorification of mere static image minus its politics for art lingered by and large, till the nineties.

On a different perspective, this is how the aftermath of nineties art circumstances might be imagining its immediate past ! Further, did such a pronounced 'imagination' of its immediate happenings become an 'inevitable necessity' for the art after the nineties, or the art between the nineties to 2010, for its 'own' existence! Consequently; to imagine what happened to the concept of 'image-as-artwork' before that, in due course. In other dimensions, image-making was metamorphosed into image-circuit, as an optimist might wish to position it in a positivist mode. In this way, the art community closer to the ideal blend currently imagines the hierarchy between paintings and the New Media Artworks.

2.2 The Visual Art Practices of the Nineties of India

The nineties art practice in India has been a turning point for the Indian art practice scenario for the reason that most prominent artists of the country; whom we refer today in the context of curatorial projects, Biennales and triennials were emerging out of the institutional training in the early nineties. There could be a lot of anomalies as well such as the open economy system that occurred within the politics of Indian History, the artist-in-residency opportunities that took artists to unknown geo-political zones outside India, the hypertext and the world wide web that availed a bypass to the artists throughout the country deconstructed a clear cut hegemony implicated by the Academies and then by the white cube system, that earlier played a significant role in regulating – the visuals, the opportunities, and the choices of one artwork, artist, art groups over the others. Even International funding agencies spread the feeling that contesting the pre-nineties context of 'image-making' to stress on 'image- circuit' split the image-maker into two. For this reason; some artists traverse between the simple painterly grammar and the New Media, owing to the cajoling nature of the funding system.

Since the nineties, the three most important characteristics of art are – implicated imagery, image-making and image circuit. Through this, the process of circulating description has been behaving as if it is a part of image-making or vice versa. Residencies and workshops have replaced art camps, thus watering down a pre- existent hegemonic order, paradoxically evoking its hint of hegemony through a renewed usage of techno-suave media and an inflow of artists from wrong geographical premises. The result of this is that the notion of the nation has been divided, proving that the imagination of the imagery itself is subject to context-bound articulation.

The Indian art world before the nineties is aesthetically colonised to serve as a little thematic concern which finally amounts to its sophisticated outlook, which has been used as reserved themes differently for internal and international circulations. Hence the newly acquired aura of the post-nineties imagery does not shy away from its outlook, which is freshly built upon the older blocks. What the post-nineties imagery preaches is based on what is considered as banal, to begin with. What it addresses is a different story. If 'issues' like gender, queer, subaltern, contemporary- post colonialism and avant-garde are at the heart of the post-nineties, the way it seems is more important than it is.

In a different perspective, everything after the nineties has been and addressed are both not only constructs but duly acknowledges that they are constructs. Constructs that agree to be what they are can be dislodged. This is also the difference between the art before and after the nineties. Altogether the implicated imagery post-nineties is a construct that de-powers the rest of the art around it, yet being created. Surficial, it seems to be that the art in the familiar media is the one that is being de- powered. However a whole lot of practices, applications and institutional policies that stayed in the margin, before, owing to the priority to image-making (as different from image-circulation) have been empowered, and those that were futile have been disconnected, including, say, the nationalistic phenomena.

2.2.1 Inception of Interdisciplinary Art Practices in India

In the New Media Art practices in India, the research study observes that the last thirty years or so witnessed many exploring, significant development in the medium, depiction, and the whole process of art practising that changed the face of contemporary artists' philosophical crack upon art and its earlier verified history prejudiced the work of artists in diverse behaviours. Nowadays, art is evolving from previously laid out barriers and has become a cluster of media such as installation art, video art, performance art, conceptual art and the new buzz media art. Seemingly acting upon the original words of the French author Marcel Proust describes that the real voyage of discovery consists not in seeking new landscapes but in having new eyes, contemporary artists are employing a myriad of media into their works to express themselves (Lochan, 2010). This is because artists want to convey their message in a language that is prevalent nowadays and to create novelty in their stylistic manner.

Through this myriad of media, artists register their prominence in development does not happen in a vacuum, rather contemporary artists live in the society and respond to the events and issues of their time. Artists select their symbols, technique, medium and style for a work of art from the wide variety of equipment that is accessible currently.

The amalgamation of innovative resources and images with insertion at global biennales and galleries since the late 1990s has verified to be pungent. Paintings and mixed media sculptural installations made subsequently the new millennium reflect the changing face of the Indian art world: of older galleries refurbished into larger more expensive premises, in turn showing large masculinist formats in painting and installation (Sinha, 2010).

Interdisciplinary art commenced to appear in India since the inception of the 21st century. Still, the conditions for the growth of this art approach existed in the works of various New Media artists in the 1990s. The indication of Interdisciplinary art in India is apparent in the work of artist tactician M.F. Husain. Husain's artistic practices have intersected boundaries of traditional methods of art and made installations for the first time later on it became a common practice in India. Husain strewn newspapers at the Jehangir Art Gallery in 1992 showing great devastation to the mounting of the last supper in Red and the Last Supper in Blue in 1993, his expansive oeuvre moves seamlessly from one medium to the other. Husain has also made films. The artist had made a highly innovative installation, *'Theatre of the Absurd'* (Plate 2.1), an awareness of fierceness and its repercussions, at the Shridharani Gallery of New Delhi and in 1990 which created a stimulation among art enthusiasts in the capital city.

In the same decade of the previous century, Vivan Sundaram and Ved Nayar appeared as the most steady art practitioners of Installation art in India. Other artists who have been contributing towards creative Installations and conceptual art include Amarnath Sehgal, Satish Gujral, Gogi Saroj Pal and Ratnabali Kant (Mago, 2001). The art work of these artists cannot be defined as painting, drawing, sculpture, or Installation but has carved a niche for itself somewhere in between all these mediums. The artists' work is a temporary confluence of violence, nationalism, religion and femininity and questions each of other positions in contemporary India.

The 1990s became the compound for a standard shift in the context of contemporary Indian visual art. There seems a lot of expansion, change and a kind of upheaval in art practices. At that time, the century was facing a particular incongruity of expertise and its consequence transversely the nation. One segment of India was presenting the incomplete process of modernisation and the complicated role of technology, its various possibilities, and applications. The mobilisation of technology for political gain has acquired a large dimension (Sinha, Art and Visual Culture 1857- 2007, 2009). At that identical moment, contemporary Indian artists looked intelligently at the existing situation, and they started to use technology in their artworks.

From 1990 onwards, the sculpture has shifted a hugely developed horde of concerns, mainly regarding the application of varied materials concerning moving needs, and it grew progressively in synchronisation with novel shifts in philosophy and paradigm which is apparent in the art works of contemporary artists. Sculptors have widened the criteria for selecting the materials and technique up to the limits of their imaginations. The context and location of sculpture in India have considerably changed. This shift away from the unitary piece of installation, often incorporating other media, has brought fresh attention to bear on the use of material and form. The growing use of temporary content, light and sound with sculpture has redefined how a work is perceived. New locations like international biennales, art fairs, global institutional buying as well as international collectors have encouraged incrementally ambitious indoor projects, which has blurred the line between sculpture and sculptural installation. Traditional media like stone and metal transformed into new treatments, and unusual combinations and inventive techniques like site-specific installations and kinetic sculptures increased in popularity . Besides, boundaries between traditional disciplines like painting and sculpture were dissolved, with artists like Anita Dube, and Navjot Altaf, Sudarshan Shetty, Anandajit Ray, Jagannath Panda and G.R. Iranna, hybridising the two through their practices.

According to the Dutch curator Johan Pijnappel the artists in India began to practise with video art only after the 1990s, because of the established media of painting and sculpture remaining a dominant force in Indian cultural life. Initially, the video was employed as a component or element in a broader or supplementary diverse approach. For example, Nalini Malani produced a single channel documentary of her site-specific installation *'City of Desires'* (1992) (Plate 2.2), and Vivan Sundaram incorporated video screens into his sculpture and Installation *'House from House/Boat'* (1994) (Plate 2.3). However, since the mid-nineties, there has been an increasing number of younger Indian artists working with video art. Many of them first encountered the medium while studying abroad – mostly in the USA, the UK, and Australia. On the artists return from their education they continued to work with the medium. This group includes Ranbir Kaleka; *'Man with Cockerel '*(2002) (Plate 2.4), Subba Ghosh, *'Remains of a Breath'* (2001) (Plate 2.5), Sonia Khuranna,*'Bird '*(1999) (Plate 2.6), Tejal Shah, *'I Love My India'* (2003) (Plate 2.7) and *'What Are You?'* (2006) (Plate 2.8), Eleena Banik, *'An Urban Scape'*(2004), and Umesh Maddanahalli, *'Between Myth and History'* (2001) (Plate 2.9).

Video art in India sprang at the time of political turmoil and 1992/93 Mumbai disturbances. With the inception of New Media Art, the expansion and transformation necessitated a position in the content of Visual Arts practices. Artists like Nalini Malani who appeared as India's first video artist and Navjot Altaf thought that traditional art mediums like the painting, sculpture and losing the variety and would no longer conceive socially engaging observations.

Subsequently the younger generation of artists who had already become familiarised with video while cramming abroad found themselves in a dilemma at the time of the devastating Gujarat violence of 2002. The widespread riots, political conditions directly affected the society as well as artists and accelerated the demand for moving out of fame. So a large number of single-channel videos were created by the artists at that time. The artists, even first-timers, no longer focused the video camera on themselves, but the horrific world outside, while trying to make sense of the violent situation (Seid, 2007). Other artists such as Vivan Sundaram and Rummana Hussain broke out of the painting frame. They started to present their ideas through the medium of installation with all kinds of materials including video, photographs, ordinary building construction material, ephemeral wall drawings and more. Over time, video matured into the preferred medium (Seid, 2007).

The debate around issues of identity, indigenism, Indian social policy and political upheaval up to the new millennium affected the art practices. Indian art has become increasingly global in its address through the effects of New Media, international artists residencies, art fairs, biennales, galleries and a fluid globalised vocabulary to enter into the discourse. Through New Media and installation, there is a reworking of the personal/political space occupied by the artist. This matrix of highly interwoven political, social and economic conditions having new questions, different concerns borne the idea of vexing modernity in India. India's eager embrace of technology, the liberal and imaginative use of the photograph and an alliance with global modernities contribute to the beginning of interdisciplinary art practices. The blur between street and studio, traditional and contemporary media, ideologies and practices, feels back into the particular identity that Indian art has consciously created.

With the dawn of interdisciplinary art in India, the young generation of artists are producing their works by experimenting, combining, connecting, and involving different academic/scientific/ artistic disciplines. In this way, they are parting from conventional mediums into modern mediums of art such as mixed-media installations, site-specific installations, performance, kinetic sculptures, video art, interactive art, digital photography. Somewhat limiting themselves to the traditional mediums of art, they are frequently using metals, wood, glass, steel, plastic, light bulbs, fibreglass, concrete, stone, video and digital art, etc. These artists are undisputedly creating a hegemony in contemporary art.

2.2.2 Interdisciplinary Collective Artist-Run Groups in India

In the interdisciplinary/ New Media Art practices in India, avant-gardist art practices are going on from other artist-run groups: The Raqs Media Collective, a trio (Jeebesh Bagchi, Monica Narula and Shuddhabrata Sengupta) located in the city of Delhi, have been working since 1992, as artists, media practitioners, curators, researchers, editors and incentives of cultural processes. The artists' work, which has been exhibited widely in significant international spaces, establishes artists in the intersections of contemporary art, historical enquiry, philosophical speculation, research and theory often taking the form of installations, online and offline media objects, performances and encounters. The Raqs Media Collective have developed a theory and practice of documentary, video, New Media Art to generate extended allegories of subversion and cite them punctually in cyber-*mohallas* (neighbourhoods) and international expositions alike. Given the artists preferred tropes of migration, displacement and marginality, surveillance, the artists function across the trans-cultural zone of global art and bring a unique conceptual- discursive politics into the Indian art scene.

Open Circle, a Mumbai-based artist's initiative, is engaged in the activist genre of public art on the streets of Mumbai protesting/ 'performing' along with people's resistance movements or at sites such as the World Social Forum in Mumbai and other cities of the world. The artists addressed social and political issues in their local manifestations as well as in their global ramifications. The artists initiative organise transnational workshops to bring visual artists and theorists together to exchange ideas through discussions and praxis. The effort makes interpositions in public spaces in rejoinder to the current social and political happenings in India. They had concentrated on local and more immediate concerns.

In the development of New Media Art; youthful, many non-political organisations break ground with workshops and residencies hosting eccentric and transgressive artists from all over the world. New initiatives are also now being encouraged in the private sector where all art, even radical art, is subject to rapid commodification.

2.3 The Discourses of New Media Art of India in the Nineties

In most events of New Media Art, the self and self-attachment are imaged through a class of signifiers. In India, more effective technological progress was achieved in video art when digital editing equipment became available after

1990. Once again, it was a TV and non-fiction film that prompted development. Nevertheless, it came as a boon to the video artists.

Video equipment started being used in the fast proliferating TV channel productions, and government and non-governmental propaganda, in India, from the mid-eighties. Soon after, India made its entry into the world of IT with a big bang and by the beginning of the nineties started being recognised as a significant producer of programme software. All these were happening when the video technology was transiting from analogue to digital phase.

It was no wonder that soon, the creative artists in non-kinetic arts also, especially those keen to experiment with alternative media, would turn to this relatively easy to manipulate and manage technology and soon after the so-called 'liberalisation' of the Indian economy.

New Media in Indian art is comparatively the latest appearance. Its roots lie during the fifties and sixties in the experimental works of Krishen Khanna, where the artist accidentally used wide-angle projector and photography as a tool to execute the artist's artworks. Another contemporary Akbar Padamsee created a silent, black and white animation based work titled '*Syzygy*' a word derived from Greek technical term meaning the coupling of two things that might be alike or opposed. Unfortunately, these works could not receive critical recognition, but this experimentation somewhere reflects a new tendency in Indian artists to observe beyond the traditional practice of painting and sculpture.

The actual shift in Indian art can be noticed during the 1990s when some western curators started projecting works of Indian artists in a new paradigm, and the idea of globalisation started dominating the Indian society. New digital technological development became conspicuous in everyday life. This swift change provided the Indian artists with an exposure to the mainstream western art and simultaneously to various technological tools to experiment with artists vocabulary beyond the conventional painting and sculpture tradition to communicate their ideas with the global audience.

The early 1990s was the transitional phase for Indian artists with the opening of few private galleries with a vision to provide a venue for cutting edge artworks with the use of New Media as a tool for artists expression. This tendency developed a practice among artists to evolve a deep conceptual insight as they broadened the horizon for execution with new possibilities such as installation, performance and video art.

In the early nineties in India, some prominent internationally mobile Indian painters turned video/ installation artists, like Nalini Malani, Vivan Sundaram, and Navjot Altaf started documenting their installations and performances with a video camera. They soon graduated to combining projection of clips from films made by filmmakers – available in VHS tapes, in loop-run from TV monitors, with their installations and performances. The artists seem to have made use of these quotations from pre-existing cinema to exhibit their social conscience/political position/historical consciousness et al. as conscientious third-world individuals.

The earlier Indian video installations remained agglomerates of disparate object images, lacking integration towards meaning generation. The later converts to video art like Sheba Chhachhi, Shilpa Gupta, Shakuntala Kulkarni, Subba Ghosh, Subodh Gupta, Bharti Kher, Rummana Hussain, Anita Dube, Sudarshan Shetty, Tejal Shah, Atul Dodiya, Jitish Kallat, Ranbir Kaleka, Sonia Khurana, Kiran Subbaiah, Aditya Basak, Abhijit Gupta, Sanjit Choudhury et al., all who joined the first group.

In the decade after the turn of century, likewise did not do much to give to the technology of recording, reconstruction and reproduction of moving photographic images a new basic linguistic structure to merit it being called an original art, let alone defining the aesthetic identity of the modern art. It is not only the intention and the reasoning of the makers that legitimises the status of an entity, but it also has to be experienced as a significantly differentiated entity by the takers as well, for which an imposed terminology may not be sufficient. Fuzzy representation of objects, ill-differentiated light, shades, shadows, colours and tones, ill-represented projections and recessions which characterised much of the early video productions of the Western world and still characterised much of Indian video programmes, in the non- commercial sector, are incidental to art; these can easily be overcome by acquisition of skill and employment of proper equipment. Spatio–temporarily determined conceptual and attitudinal predilections like the autobiographical/confessional modes of explications, along with their linguistic baggage of use of shifter images, can also be overcome by jettisoning derivativeness and being true to the experience of here - and –now. These lacunae are of peripheral importance.

With contemporary Indian art making a foothold in the international art scene, video art by Indian artists has become one of the focal points of aesthetic debates (ML, 2010).

In India, pioneering endeavours towards making video art forms were undertaken by artists during the mid-nineties. Ayisha Abraham, Ranbir Kaleka and Sonia Khurana worked towards establishing an art language of video which was unfamiliar to the Indian audience/viewer. Artists like Shilpa Gupta took this art form to different dimensions by incorporating technological innovations in their artworks. Video art for Indian artists, like for artists from elsewhere . Where was it not just a technical medium? They used this technological medium not only for registering events and images but also for forwarding critiques through the registration of 'body in action' and the 'real people' (ML, 2010).

The rich and complex histories of New Media/video art, Indian artists who work with video as a medium, use their works as influential/significant devices to practise their politico-cultural concepts and analysis. Gigi Scaria is individual of those young Indian artists who have used video as a medium not only to extend the ideas that he deals within his paintings and installations but also creates a new visual language that could cut across the boundaries of documentaries , docu-fictions and performance art (ML, 2010). In one of his early video titles '*Lost City*' (Plate 2.10) Gigi Scaria outlines the daily visits of a young man living in a city. In his abode area, Scaria breathes like a visitor and engraves his trajectories on a wall as if the artist were creating a map of his consciousness. Gigi confers the idea of history as a fight against oblivion and loss (ML, 2010).

2.3.1 *The Role of Art Organisational in the Exploration of New Media Art of India in the Nineties*

In the transitional phase of Indian Visual Art scenario during the early nineties, different private art galleries and art events such as workshops, art fairs have a significant role to dimension Indian art practice in a new way. In the nineties; different galleries provided Indian practising visual artists with the dais to progress their artworks with the application of New Media for artists' expression and developed Indian Visual Art practice in the arena of New Media Art.

This is also important to intervene into the gallery circuit and other bodies which were formed to provide a platform for New Media practising artists because only with such platform New Media practice got impetus and exposure to the international art arena. During 1997 one of the critical figures Peter Nagy, an American artist who became a curator in India and established a gallery titled "Nature Morte" in Delhi, promoted innovative gallery practice with the display of photography, installation, video art along with the traditional domain of art practice. Another essential figure Pooja Sood who is an Art Manager and Curator emanated up with "Khoj International Artists Workshop" Khirkee Village in Delhi the same year and its first international exchange programme in Modinagar. This vision acquired art to the public sphere out of the white cube gallery practice and provided a dialogue between the artist and the local people. These two directorial giants curated several activities and displays based on New Media practice, including a cultural exchange with international artists in residency programmes. One of the memorable events in 2008 was the Public Art Festival, 48 degrees Celsius.

2.3.2 Role of Art Directorial in New Media Art of India Through 2000 Onwards: A Connection to the Discourses of New Media Art Practices of India Since the Nineties

Art Ecology which is a combined initiative of Goethe-Institut/ Max Mueller Bhavan and GTZ, an experiment set within the metropolitan capital city of Delhi. The ambition of this project was to cross-examine the teetering ecology of the city through the prism of contemporary art, and Pooja Sood was one of the team members to conceptualise the event. Sood is also a curator of the Apeejay Media Gallery, the first space in the country for the New Media works in early 2000.

Besides gallerists and art curators, the art collectors also showed great interest in New Media Art and were inspired to establish private museums in the country and raised a debate on the role of museums and their acquisitions. One of the first private museums set up by Lekha and Anupam Poddar named "The Devi Art Foundation." They consistently supported cutting-edge art forms and established a new philosophy of museums and questioned the role and position of a museum in a social framework.

In recent times of India "Kiran Nadar Museum of Art" is different private museum in the country opened in January 2010 focuses not merely on collecting art instead providing a platform for cutting-edge art forms and their recent acquisition a work by Subodh Gupta titled '*Line of Control*' an impressive sculptural installation, visually the giant mushroom cloud composed of steel utensils displayed in a public mall culture (Kumar, 2014). Since 2008 Art Fair in the country has increased the movement for art activities with a global vision, and such a fair provided a more significant platform not only for conventional art approaches but also brought forward the practice of New Media Art across the globe. In 2012 the fourth edition of India Art Fair which was earlier known as India Art Summit successfully concluded in New Delhi. India Art Fair is the country's premier platform for modern and contemporary art practice across the globe (Kumar, 2014). This edition featured most of the international and national galleries and leading artists to witness their first art practice of conventional and New Media Art also. India Art Fair provides an even more massive arena of art engagements featuring curated talks, video lounge, speaker's forum, New Media Art projects, book launches and other collateral events. Kochi-Muziris Biennale is also a very prominent platform for New Media artists of India to express the practising artists' thought process through the arena of New Media Art practice. Such art directorial across the country, providing art students, artists, curators, art historians, gallerists, art educationists a broader platform for art and cultural dialogue and debate and rewrite the definition of contemporary art. This coherence of art fairs, galleries, private museums, collectors and curators provide a mode of expression and somewhere suggest the root of New Media is firmly grounded in India at the end of the first decade of the twenty-first century (Kumar, 2014).

2.3.3 Role of Art Institutes and Visual Arts Pedagogy in India in Relation to New Media Art

In the development of New Media Art practice in India, different Visual Arts higher educational institutes have various roles. Different Visual Arts schools in higher education suggest a new vision of art practice in India through imposing a global view of restructuring the art pedagogy in the country and because there are quite a good number of Visual Arts higher educational institutes and universities in India which are offering an undergraduate, postgraduate and doctoral programme in Visual Arts. These schools of Visual Arts provide comprehensive knowledge on theoretical as well as practical disciplines under various specialisations and also provide extensive research orientation on multiple areas. It has been observed that most of these art schools work on the same pedagogical structure since their inception before independence. In India, the art schools were established even before independence by the British in cities like Bombay, Calcutta, Madras, Lucknow, Jaipur. Other independent organisations which promoted contemporary art before and after independence were The Bombay Art Society established in 1888, All India Fine Arts and Crafts Society established in 1928, The Academy of Fine Arts, Calcutta established in 1933.

It is quite noticeable today that there is a wide gap between the contemporary mainstream practices of art and the pedagogical structure of

Visual Arts schools in India. From a historical perspective the research witness various model for art pedagogy, firstly the colonial period witness art activities based on portraiture, landscape, still life in an accomplished academic style, which was purely based on British art pedagogy and schools of art in Madras, Bombay and Calcutta followed the same. Secondly, another pedagogic model we come across during pre-independence within the nationalist movement is the establishment of Kala Bhavan in Santiniketan based on indigenous ways of expression and methods and thirdly the most modernist radical school after independence during the 1950s is Faculty of Fine Arts, M.S. University, Baroda and other parallel art schools across the country on the same modernist stand always pursue to restructure its educational activities and objectives within the changing demand of time.

In recent time amalgamation of these pedagogical models exist in most of the art schools in the country at this juncture considering the fact of acceptance of New Media Art within the Gallery circuit, public spaces, museums, collectors and even within the art institutions and Visual Arts schools in universities. Some suggest that Indian art requires a new pedagogical model for Visual Arts in the country. Proposing a new model for art pedagogy requires training in varied new trends which are prevalent in mainstream Visual Arts practice. The conventional model imparts training under various terminologies such as Painting, Drawing, Portraiture, Composition, Printmaking, Photography, Mural and Sculpture et al. simultaneously the new vision should embark on multiple classifications such as New Media Art, public art, site-specific art, collaborative art projects, Digital Art, interactive art et al. The new vision will provide multicultural Art Education. Experimental and research-based practice in Artistic visual language, visual cultural studies and Art History will also offer thoughtful and innovative materials that challenge the narrative traditions of art education and traditional art history.

A new model for Visual Arts schools in higher education like universities can also include other specialised programmes such as Art Management programme, Curatorial programme, Experimental Media Art, Museum and gallery practices and New Media Art Programme et al. Such a new initiative can be seen in the sum of Art and Design Schools in India, like Srishti School of Art, Design and Technology, Bangalore already offering some of the programmes based on experimental New Media Art and Dr B. R. Ambedkar University, Delhi also proposes a new model for such programmes under universities looking in the same direction as they are in the position to conceptualise new programmes for study.

New Media Art practice is gaining momentum in various Visual Arts schools of higher education in India and that is evident in students' final year display/exhibition works. Although it is not part of specific curriculum as such as even than the New Media practice is visible, and that is due to more exposure to the students to the mainstream art practice through exhibitions, online galleries and international art fairs and other public art projects, which are motivating or inspiring them to experiment with the diverse mode of expressions. Students of various disciplines becoming sensitive to New Media Art approaches and showing high confidence and interest in their artistic endeavours, even beside the lateral movement of a routine framework of students syllabi do not restrict student/upcoming artists to work within the closed boundaries of the course structure. This approach is only visible in some of the leading art institutions in India and rest of the art schools are still into a mode of conventional pedagogy, and drawback for such schools lies in the teaching methodology which needs revival in research methodology, theoretical writings and exposure to the recent developments in art. But today such Visual Arts schools should not seem themselves in isolation because the impact of technology is far-reaching to every small corner of life, the need is to gain energy from such changes in society, and the globe is electronically connected; hence it is an exciting condition to aim at multidisciplinary and research-oriented approach with more emphasis on critical thinking, experimentation and active observer participation and to provide a new homogeneous pedagogical model for all Visual Arts schools of higher education in India.

2.4 Conclusion

The chapter "*Image Beyond Image: New Media Art practices in 1990s India*" researches the mainstream Visual Art scenario of India in the nineties. Along with how the nineties became a turning point in the Indian Visual Art practices and Indian artists establishing their language of art towards the New Media and revealed a different dimension in the Indian Visual Art practice.

The chapter concludes with the following analysis.

The New Media Art practices of the nineties in India dimensioned a new vision towards the development of Visual Art practices in India. By their conceptual thought process, the artists through their New Media Artworks reveal their expression what the practising artists perceived and by which portraying an image became an in-depth visual interaction within the specific image.

The nineties evolved many revolutionary art practices in the Visual Arts domain. Different art directorial also has significant involvement in providing a platform to the New Media practising artists of India.

Artists' run initiatives' have prominent roles in the inception of New Media practices in India in the nineties. Visual Arts pedagogy in higher educational institutes and universities in India also has a new vision towards the progression of New Media Art in India since the last two decades.

PLATES

Plate 2 . 1 : M F Husain . *Theatre of the Absurd* . 1989 . Water Colour on Paper .
Courtesy : MutualArt . Web . 21 February . 2019

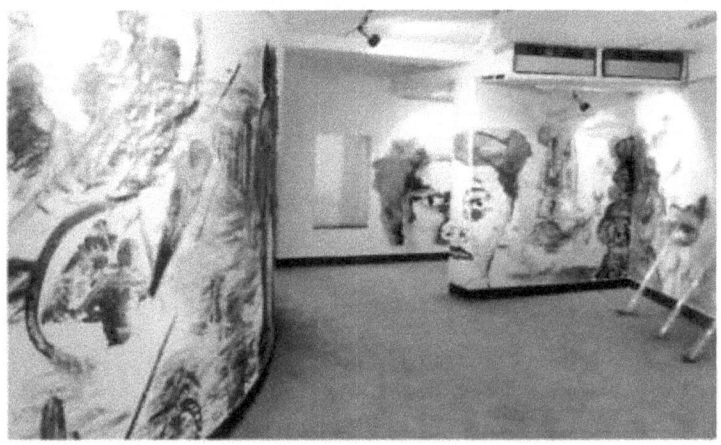

Plate 2 . 2 : Nalini Malani . *City of Desires* (detail) . 1992 .
Single Channel Site Specific Installation .
Courtesy : Nalini Malani . Web . 21 February . 2019

Plate 2 . 3 : Vivan Sundaram . *House from House / Boat* (detail) . 1994 .
Video Screen into Sculpture and Installation .
Courtesy : Vivan Sundaram . Web . 21 February . 2019

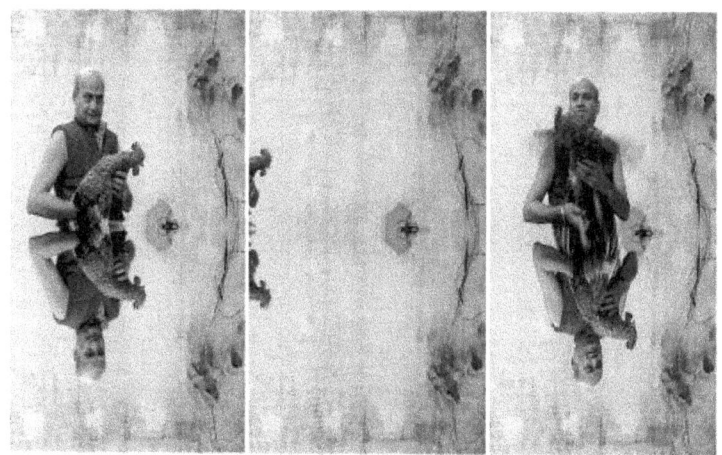

Plate 2 . 4 : Ranbir Kaleka . *Man with Cockerel* (detail) . 2002 .
Video Installation . Courtesy : Ranbir Kaleka . Web . 21 February . 2019

Plate 2.5 : Subba Ghosh . *Remains of a Breath* (detail) . 2001.
Installation. Courtesy : Talwar Gallery . Web . 21 February . 2019

Plate 2.6 : Sonia Khurana . *Bird* (detail) . 1999 . Video Art
Courtesy : Critical Collective . Web . 21 February . 2019

Plate 2.7 : Tejal Shah . *I Love My India* (detail) . 2003 . Video Installation .
Courtesy : Tejal Shah . Web . 21 February . 2019

Plate 2.8 : Tejal Shah . *What Are You ?* (detail) . 2006 . Video Installation .
Courtesy : Tejal Shah . Web . 21 February . 2019

Plate 2 . 9 : Umesh Maddanahalli . *Between Myth and History* (detail) . 2001 .
Single Channel Video Installation with sound .
Courtesy : Apeejay Media Gallery . Web . 21 February . 2019

Plate 2 . 10 : Gigi Scaria . *Lost City* (detail) . Video Art .
Courtesy : artnewsnviews.com . Web . 21 February . 2019

References

Adajania, Nancy. "New Media Overtures Before New Media Practice in India." *Domus*, vol. 04, no. 03, Jan. 2015, pp. 34–37.

Artville. "Artville Artist of the Day: Azis TM." *Artville Artist of the Day*, 12 Mar. 2015, artvilleartist.blogspot.com/2015/03/azis-tm.html. Accessed 18 Feb. 2019.

Dalmia, Yashodhara. *Contemporary Indian Art: Other Realities*. Mumbai, Marg; Hove, 2008.

Dalmia, Yashodhara. *The Making of Modern Indian Art: The Progressives*. New York, Oxford University Press, 2001.

Evans, Steven, et al. *India: Contemporary Photographic and New Media Art*. Amsterdam, Schilt Publishing, 2018.

Fernandes, Kasmin. "Is New Media Art a Fad?" *Times of India*, 12 Sept. 2012.

"Jamia - Event Detail - A Lecture On Contemporary Art & Art Practice: An Interdisciplinary Realm Artist: An Author, Curator, Educator & Social Activist By Prof. Nuzhat Kazmi." *www.Jmi.Ac.In*,.www.jmi.ac.in/ bulletin board /event module/latest /detail/2177/22969. Accessed 8 Mar. 2019.

Jhaveri, Amrita. *A Guide to 101 Modern & Contemporary Indian Artists*. Mumbai, India Book House, 2005.

Keenan, Thomas. *New Media, Old Media: A History and Theory Reader*. Routledge, 2015.

Khanna, Balraj, and Aziz Kurtha. *Art of Modern India*. London, Thames & Hudson, 1999.

Mago, Pran Nath. *Contemporary Art in India*. New Delhi, National Book Trust, India, 2001.

Mehta, Anupa. *India 20: Conversations with Contemporary Artists (Contemporary Indian Artist Series)*. Grantha Corporation, 2008.

ML, Johny. "Video Art of India- Gigi Scaria and His Videos." *Art Etc News & Views*, Sept. 2010.

Rafi, Saba, and Furqan Ahmad. "Interdisciplinary Art Practices In India." *International Journal of Research - Granthaalayah*, vol. Vol.4, no. Iss.8, pp. 168–168.

Sen, Jaideep. "Biennale Diary: Temsüyanger Longkumer Offers a Slice of Nagaland, Urges Viewers to Rethink Divinity." *The New Indian Express Indulge*, 7 Feb. 2019.

Sinha, Gayatri. "New Media Art in India." *Oxford Art Online*, 22 Sept. 2005, 10.1093/gao/9781884446054.article.t097944. Accessed 4 Mar. 2019.

Ulli, Beier. *Contemporary Art in India.* Port Moresby, Institute Of Papua New Guinea Studies, 1977.

Vadehra, Arun, et al. *Indian Contemporary Art Post-Independence*. 2nd Ed. New Delhi, Vadehra Art Gallery, 2000.

CHAPTER- III

THE LEGITIMISED NARRATIVES AND THE WEB OF TRAFFIC: THE ARTWORKS OF NALINI MALANI AND JITISH KALLAT

3.1 Introduction

Nalini Malani's art practice is inspired by her experiences as a refugee of the partition of India. She spaces inherited iconographies and precious cultural stereotypes under compression. Her point of view is steadily urban and internationalist and unsparing in its condemnation of a cynical nationalism that exploits the belief of the masses. Here is an art of excess, going beyond the boundaries of 'legitimised narrative', exceeding the conventional and initiating dialogue. Jitish Kallat is a well-known name in the contemporary New Media Art practices of India who is continuously exploring his working process in a multimedia approach to the subject matter; his works range from esoteric nature capes to political critiques of the socio-economic divine in his home country. Kallat often utilises popular Indian advertising aesthetics that he incorporates throughout his practice. His *'Dawn Chorus-7'* (2007) (Plate 3.1) series, for instance, depicts street urchins with hair that forms a 'web of traffic' and pedestrians.

3.2 The Video Installation of Nalini Malani

Nalini Malani's video installation comprises references to historical moments, but also myths because she finds that these are bridges; visual and verbal language bridges that connect to the audience. *Cassandra* for example reappears in various places within her work. People know the *Cassandra* myth, and through the tale, they can talk about more significant issues. Myths are like bundles, which have so much information about historical factors as well as vital elements. It's a connection that Malani would like to make. For a long time, Malani has been interested in bringing into the world the historical past into the contemporary because the sure thing is still operative. Certain aspects of those periods are still operative. In Malani's thought process, that's the only way by which we can move on (Malani, 2012).

Nalini Malani completed her education from Sir Jamsetjee Jeejeebhoy School of Art, Bombay in 1964-69. While still a student, Nalini had a studio at the Bhulabhai Memorial Institute, Bombay, where artists, musicians, dancers and theatre persons worked individually and as a community. In 1970-72, Nalini Malani achieved a French Government Scholarship for Fine Arts to study in Paris. In 1984-89, she received an Art Fellowship from the Government of India.

The characteristics of Nalini Malani's work have been the gradual movement towards New Media, international collaboration and expanding dimensions of the pictorial surface into the surrounding space as ephemeral wall drawing (Mural), installation, shadow play, multi-projection works and theatre.

3.2.1 Art Practice of Nalini Malani: Transition from Traditional Painting to New Media Art

Nalini Malani is one of the most substantial contemporary artists from India. She was born in Karachi in 1946, a year before the partition between India and Pakistan that followed the independence from the British Empire, what is now Pakistan (Samarth, 2010). During the partition, Malani went into exile to Calcutta in 1947 with her parents and moved to Bombay in 1954, where the artist still lives. The partition has manifested her personality and her work as she attempted to make sense of the feelings of loss, exile and nostalgia that have overshadowed her childhood. Thus far it was not until 1992, after the demolition of the Babri Mosque in Ayodhya by Hindu extremists, that interreligious violence became weaved into her work, indirectly through the performance '*Medea*', after Heiner Muller's play, and the actions which derived from that place; directly through a series of multimedia installations such as '*Remembering Toba Tek Singh*' (1998), '*Hamlet Machine*' (1999-2000),'*Stains*' (2000), '*Unity in Diversity*' (2003), '*Mother India: Transactions in the Construction of pain*' (2005), and the recent – and haunting – '*In Search of vanished blood* ' (2012).

The capacity of Malani's works to encourage audiences stems from three main elements. One is the artist's emphasis on the corporal and the local as vehicles for memories of sensations and emotions. The second is Malani's painting procedure reveal on reverse acrylic paper with acrylic and enamel, collective into installations with moving images, videos, and sound. The third element is the content she practises, based on myths taken from both Indian and Western traditions, that address the mind through metaphors long-established, playing with old patterns, to which she manages to give a contemporary relevance. Thus Malani convokes multiple universes, combining text and images, present and past, locality and globality into a kind of theatre in which facts are mixed with effects – anger and sorrow, fear and disgust, love and sacrifice – that relate to an individual and collective life story. The research study shall observe successively the role of these three elements in the reception of Malani's art practice and its power, asserted by the artist, to assuage inter-community hatred, by performing a catharsis.

Malani's work is constructed as a narrative that interweaves Eastern and Western mythologies and aesthetics forms to address interreligious violence in India, especially on women. Since the 1970s, Malani has displayed her emphatically feminine stance there, in a country torn between the effects of colonialism and the idealism of a Third World social democracy, as well as being seized by the political and economic changes brought about by rapid globalisation. Employing figures from myths, fairy tales, and the religions of diverse cultures, and reflecting on war, orthodox fanaticism, the effects of capitalism, and the destruction of the environment, Nalini Malani depicts the female position in scenes past and future. The artist's emphasis on the feminine figure as a topos of violence, both received and produced. As an uncertain figure, both caring and destroying locates her art within feminist discourses. Yet she privileges to be beyond this linkage and to be using mythical images of *Medea*, *Cassandra* or *Sita* as images of conflicts and violence within the human psyche, both feminine and masculine. In the early 1990s, Malani was one of the first artists in India to break from a painting by making ephemeral wall drawings, theatrical works, and video and shadow play. The research study purports to analyse her work and the mechanisms of its reception to evaluate its potential cathartic role on collective consciousness regarding communal violence in India and elsewhere, both for an Indian and international audience, a function which Malani prerogates for her art practice.

3.2.2 Nalini Malani's Art Practice: The Role of the Bodily and the Local

Malani executed a constant desire to link her work to a place, to the physical and to psychic sensations which inform peoples' experience of a site.

In 1980 the artist participated with five male artists – Vivan Sundaram, Bhupen Khakhar, Jogen Chowdhury, Gulam Mohammed Sheikh and Sudhir Patwardhan – in the exhibition conceived by the critic Geeta Kapur's Places for People, which focused on the indigenous and the local, in an anti-modernist gesture. It marked the first occurrence of postmodern thought in India. Malani contributed her life, a series of eight paintings started in 1978, recounting the presence of an ordinary man, the artist's personal and professional relationships, asserting the importance of the collective in the construction of individual identity and the fragmentary nature of it, made of juxtapositions of distinct "me", built by others. At the time, Malani lived and worked in the commercial district of Lohar Chawl, situated nearby the docks in South Mumbai. The vibrant location has involvement with commercial activity mixed with religious temples and service industry will later inspire Malani a series of monotypes, called *'Lohar Shawl '*(1991), in which an emotional map appears superimposed by various impressions from the *bazaar*. The space as if persistent on the inner biosphere of the artist's visual , olfactory, auditory sensations received from the colourful and noisy alleys. Accentuating the link between the individual and the collective, Malani hereby manifests the importance of living communities, as well as of bodily sensations and emotions, in the construction of a particular memory. The artist expresses in a way that memory is what an individual remains , previous is in the existing and in the forthcoming. Memory means the cooperative Memory – Memory of the race, Memory of the community. This twofold – individual and social – construction of an individual's identity, although a priori universally shared, appears in this quote as explicitly related to Hindu culture in which the real and the imaginary, the past, present and the future, the individual and the collective are enmeshed, mainly through the concept of *karma*, in which the physique is the vehicle of consecutive lives, made of meetings, exchanges, dividers, accidents (Kayser, 2015).

After many years of painting, Malani will turn to installations in 1998, with *'Remembering Toba Tek Singh '*, that plays precisely with this bodily, communal and mnemonic dimension (Kayser, 2015). The research study analyses that the Malani's images as a transitional object by which the artist brings back the collectively repressed, like Melanie Klein who used play to enter into dialogue with the unconscious of her young patients. In the year 2005, Malani responded to the theme of inter-community violence with the video installation *'Mother India: Transactions in the Construction of Pain '*(Kayser, 2015).

3.2.3 The Role of Nalini Malani's Technique into the Artist's Art Practice: Transformation to New Media Art

The research study needs to observe Malani's techniques and contents to understand how the technique-process is carried out into the artist's practice. Since the 1990s Malani has uninhibited oil painting on canvas. She paints with acrylic mixed with enamel on a transparent Mylar sheet, which the artist attaches to art or folds into a circular lantern, placing the painted side on the inside. This demanding technique does not allow correction. Malani drops a pool of paint on the Mylar, then extends and refines it with the tip of the brush to shape creatures . Because the enamel is adhesive, the silhouettes are frequently unclear. They appear to drift. The lack of viewpoint and bright colours are inspired by the Kalighat paintings which is a Bengali tradition of popular religious imagery of Goddess *Kali* – in an attempt by the artist to connect the present and the past. The research analyses that Kalighat is a significant moment in Indian art for Malani and for the artist to make her figure, but with a Kalighat stroke, the artist would like to make the viewer recall, the resonance of the past from that period in the nineteenth century, interjecting it into the present. These are the little things that Malani does; an individual meanders through it, like in a labyrinth the curiosity to understand why a figure has two heads and a tail.

The paintings are sometimes collective with numerous sound and light effects, sometimes with videos. The anticipated images spread and transfer slowly on the walls, floors and ceiling of the space, dominating the viewer who is absorbed in the interplay of forceful and redeeming pictures and sounds, and instantly stimulated by it. Malani thus builds a multifaceted experience based on storytelling schemes that continues a popular oral and visual tradition and indicates to abstain class boundaries. The paintings are like the surfaces of a book into Malani's thought process. She is also emphasising the influence of traditional *Pat* Bengali painting or *Patachitra*, a sequence of images on horizontal or vertical rolls, reflecting mythological or folkloric stories like a comic book style (Kayser, 2015). Using *Patachitra* as well as Kalighat painting style Malani hopes to involve the average Indian, less as the ease with contemporary art. Yet the artist wants to challenge the storytelling that has become "petrified". Malani's idea is not only to retell the stories in a new form but also new configurations.

The installation by Malani entitled '*In Search of Vanished Blood*' (2012), (Plate 3.2) presented at Documenta in 2013, represents this multimedia technique. Attended by the prosody of an Indian singer, followed by forceful voices announcing prophecies, the Mylar cylinders project on the walls large images of deities, as in Ajanta's caves. In a dialogue made of collages, Malani combines oral excerpts from several sources: '*In Search of Vanished Blood*', a poem by Faiz Ahmed Faiz, regarding the silence of women victims of the partition; *Cassandra*, a novel by a contemporary Austrian writer, Christa Wolf and *Draupadi*, by Mahasweta Devi, 1988, a short story about a Bengali raped by police even though defending the land of her tribe against the hunger of British colonisers. *Draupadi* is originally a mythical figure of the classic Mahabharata (4th c. BCE) that seepages rape appreciations to the fortification of *Krishna*. In Mahasweta Devi's short story, she stays an aboriginal, of the tribe of Santal, under arrest by *Senanayak* who is the educated head of the local police, reads anti-fascist journals. After being raped by her protectors, she walks naked into *Senanayak*'s office, like a monstrous spirit.

Draupadi pushes *Senanayak* with her two garbled breasts and for the first time, *Senanayak* is scared to stand before an unarmed target, terribly scared. According to Gayatri Spivak, *Senanayak* embodies the collusion of the bourgeoisie at the service of the British Raj, as well as of herself, as a well-meaning intellectual who has a tendency to ignore local realities. When we walk out of our own academic and First-World attachment, we share something like a connection with *Senanayak*'s doublethink. For the breather of the world's women, the sense of whose personal micrology is difficult (though not impossible) for them to acquire, they fall back on a colonialist theory of most efficient information retrieval. As Malani observes their photographs in women's-studies journals or on book jackets – indeed, as the artist looks in the glass – it is *Senanayak* with his anti-Fascist paperback that Malani behold. Similarly, Malani try to find to plug the breach of indifference that has opened between the globalised Indian bourgeoisie, to which she belongs herself, and the popular classes, victims of ethnic violence as well as "abject poverty", through mythical narratives.

3.2.4 Myth as Interclass Vocabulary into Nalini Malani's Art Practice

In the art practices of Nalini Malani, myth in an attempt to formulate a language "potentially shared" Malani uses mythical figures as myth is a universal language that creates a bond with the viewer, particularly in India where mythological narratives are performed every day. Yet the artist convokes exclusively female figures, taken from Indian and Western mythology such as *Medea, Cassandra, Sita, Radha*. In earliest and contemporary collective imagination they all represent abjection and folly, says Malani who uses those figures to address the violence of Indian society, but also all human beings transformed into "mutant" creatures by force. Among these various annexations, the character of *Medea* is distinguished by its multiple occurrences (Kayser, 2015).

3.2.5 The Myth of Medea into Nalini Malani's Art Practice

Malani started working periodically on *Medea* in 1974. The artist's first encounter with the Greek myth came through a stay in Paris where Malani attended the Sorbonne and visited the Louvre. But the tale of *Medea* became antenatal after 1993 when the actress and director Alaknanda Samarth presented the artist with the drama Medea-material by the German playwright Heiner Muller and invited Malini to paint the decor for her performance at the Max Mueller Bhavan Centre in Bombay (present Mumbai). *Medea* then developed for Malani the metaphor of a devastated woman. The staging was shadowed by the installation *Medeaproject*, 1995-1996, that presented the different stages of *Medea* from high priestess in Colchide, to bride, to poisoner, through three successive dresses painted on mylar with bright colours. On the walls, the '*Mutant*' series displayed black nude figures, of uncertain gender, enclosed with white gouache dots. The paintings collective with the dresses appear as the metaphor of the body inhabited by the poison of untold deeds, that cannot find any dwelling, as conceived by Muller. Malani wanted to break humanity in two and live in the empty middle, not specifically woman no man. They also resonance the unspoken words of the women violated during the partition were a silence that kept them in a dusk zone . When women's bodies were made the passive bystanders of the sickness of the separation in this manner, then how prepared women sorrow the damage of self and the biosphere? Now and then a woman would remember images of fleeing, but as one woman warned the artist's perception, it was dangerous to recognise the situations. These reminiscences were now and then compared to poison that makes the inside of the woman dissolve, as a solid is dissolved in a potent liquid. At supplementary times a woman would say that she is like a discarded exercise book in which the accounts of past relationships were kept – the body, a parchment of losses. The evaluation with *Medea* turns the process of deliberate alienation analyses the research which finds that the women use the comparison of pregnancy where one hiding pain, charitable it a home just like a child is prearranged a home in the woman's body but with a difference that as disparate the child, which the woman will be able to propose to the husband, this holding of the pain inside must never be allowed to be born. The juxtaposition of the metaphors used by women facing actual events, with

Malani's installation underscores her capacity to transform literary texts into images, that then becomes a metaphor for disturbances of various kinds. This is certainly the power of myths, which the artwork emulates (Kayser, 2015).

3.2.6 The Overhaul Process in the Work of Nalini Malani: An Overview

In work-related to '*Medea*', as in '*Mother India*', '*Stains*', and the '*Mutant*', Malani creates a communication between the feminine and the sacred, both divine and immoral. This method of female sanctity is present in Indian culture, but research study also evokes Western occurrences such as the figure of Isis and the "Red cow" of the Bible. Isis, the head crowned with horns, is uplifting. She picks up the fragments of the figure of her husband Osiris, murdered and disarticulated by his brother, thus becoming a deity of "Restoration " of life. The Red cow is a figure accompanying cathartic sacrifices after contact with the world of the dead. It comprises spraying the subject with water diverse through the ashes of a sacrificed cow. This mixture is called *mei niddah*, a term that is interpreted as menstrual water and water of separation. Thus the ritual reminds the healing power of menstrual blood and the feminine in general. The research analyses and compare '*Medea*', '*Stains*', the '*Mutant*' series and the performance body as a site , to a ritual cleansing of death, like the ritual of the "Red cow". The research further studies and analyses the Kristevan concept of "pregnancy" in regards to the role of women in purification processes, and it may be appropriate to convene this concept into the interpretation of Malani's works, who quoted Kristeva's essay "*Experiencing the Phallus as Extraneous*" in a recent exhibition at Kiran Nadar Museum. Kristeva said that the maternal body is in a situation to transmute the violence of eroticism into tenderness. The maternal body is the boundary for that transformation that authorises a human being to live, not to become psychotic, to not die in solitude, but to live. This gives a woman an enormous role; namely, the destiny of humanity is in the hands of women. Nevertheless, the study finds it more appropriate to refer to the concept of the amorphous, monstrous and archaic maternal body to which Kristeva refers in the "*Revolution in Poetic Language*" as the container of the subject before the subject, and which she compares to the Platonic chora. The chora is a period of uncertainty that of rupture and linkage, before spatiality and temporality. It precedes and inspires figuration, thus specularisation, and is only analogous to the vocal or kinaesthetic rhythm. It is contrasting to discourse (social, patriarchal) because it is never fixed. The chora is time and place without quarrel, without position; Plato refers to it as nurturing and maternal. Within it commences a structuring of the subject but an unstable, shifting structuring that temporarily articulates discontinuities and reshuffles them constantly. It precedes the cogito and the learning of language that aims to freeze the cogito and takes place in a negative process in a detachment from the mother's body and a rejection of the mobility of the chora.

The research analyses that the chora is the figure of the abject because a return to this stage threatens the symbolic order of the Law of the father embedded in language, and the integrity of the subject. This reappearance may nevertheless be a purifier. Reviving the borders between the conscious and preconscious subject, it participates in the process of purification. It is a return to an indeterminate phase (especially sexually) of the ego that occurs during an operation, be it ritual, psychoanalytic, or artistic, and allows a catharsis. The mutant women of Malani, black bodies pierced with white dots, these sexual and threatening bodies, painted on milk cartons, and stains can be unstated as a depiction of the wretched and the chora. Their deletion is akin to a purifying ritual that symbolically allows a detachment from the mother's body, from the kingdom of the dead to regain life. Their symbolic efficiency prays on their similarity with Western and Eastern ritual processes such as the Red cow, and also *tantric* practices related to *Kali*, an inner journey toward the indeterminate (Kayser, 2015).

Other works by Malani can also be realised as part of this arrival to a step before language and cogito. In the series painting unbearable the other, a Medea-like female figure drags two dead children, sometimes two brains, still attached by an umbilical cord, in a world populated by nightmarish characters, insects, larvae, monstrous animals. What is at stake, explored Malani, is to trace the source of the mutation, when *Medea* becomes a monster, and to erase her violence by internalising it that Death must be internalised to be deleted.

3.2.7 The Cathartic Effect of Nalini Malani's Artworks

At a conference entitled from the effect or the intense depth of the words, the research studies that Julia Kristeva positions that the move is a dynamic apparatus connected with desires of the human psyche. It ascends outside of the realm of reason, to the poetic process and allows an overhaul of metaphysical categories (body/soul, matter/mind, in / out, inside / outside). By endorsing a return to the unconscious self to an id where the categories are cut into pieces, it consents a reconvening of the smithereens in a different order. Such a proposal seems to clarify Malani's process on which she writes (regarding Stains) such as body solutions, secretions, self-lubricating, exudation, bubbles and tint living tissue. These morph into humans that act vaguely toward each other such as loving, hating, killing each other. Finally the physique of bones that remain form a pair of bloody hands that seem almost to come together but instead a bomb pops out from between the palms and explodes. The death excretions bubble out and are evacuated. The overhaul process conveyed by the work of art is distinct from the psychoanalytic treatment as it narrates to an archaic and poetic order.

Communication appears to transpire nevertheless between the image and the observer, in which the emotion is repeated and modified. This transference is understood in traditional Indian theatre, according to the theory of Rasa, as a correspondence between the physical manifestations of the eight first emotions, which the actors enact, and the spectator's emotional states. It takes place when the spectators are in an appropriate mood, which depends on both on him and the potency of the enactment. Those Rasa or emotional experiences are accompanied in twosome is one giving way to the other such as love/laugh; value/wonder; anger/sorrow; distaste/fear.

In Malani's works two associations are highlighted. These are anger and sorrow, distaste and fear. The research understands that her works according to the theory of Rasa as healing the fear of others triggered by distaste, and an atonement of the sorrow brought about by anger and finally a sense of value linked to an experience of wonder. The emotion of the observer in view of the abject presented in the image seems to be absorbed into an interstitial space, the no man's land opened by violence and the prohibition of its public disclosing, which the object mediates. The work reaches an international audience to its penetrating interpretation of a suffering physique and mind. Its juxtaposition of vehement and peaceful images, interceded by the gleaming semi-transparent painting or by the slowly moving images, reminiscent of inner fluids and of the mode emotions slowly take form in percepts. The installations are dramatic in a performative method, combining images, rhythm and sounds with the displacement of the viewer. This aurality reconstructs the real while it transcends it into a mythical narrative that can involve the average Indian. The inflamed and moving images accompanied by text read aloud, evoke the drama and contemporary trauma seen through the eyes of a frightened witness.

Through her art practice, Malani even wants to escape her own body and mind to identify herself with the average man and woman, in a desire of collective belonging. Therefore the work reflects a collective memory. It is consequently surrounded in a triple Indian tradition that of *Patachitra*, a mythical, religious or folk narrative illustrated with images animated by the narrator, that of the theatre, in which emotions are elicited and rearranged but also in that of the Indian autobiography of the early 20th century, in which the author expresses moods, not as an individual jammed in antiquity, but as an advantaged witness of a collective situation. In this tradition, the narrator's individuality happens only as a member of a group, and storytelling is a kind of participation in the public space as a show or performance. Therefore Malani's work is the countenance of a collective voice. It both establishes and compensates symbolically for the absence of mutual acknowledgement of inter-community violence in India. It echoes regarding mourning rituals conducted by women both in ancient Greece and in Punjab. The research differentiates good death from unfortunate silent death, without the support of loved ones, after which the spirit of the dead remains on earth as a ghost, unburied, whereas the objectification of the sorrow in the loved one – and in the community at large – demonstrates the admission of loss. It therefore provides a substitute body to the spirit of the dead that allows the ghost to become an ancestor finally. This deprivation is done by women while men standby that the task of mourning for the men was to hear this silence, to mould it by their presence. It appears to an individual that just as women drank the pain so that life could continue, so men longed for an unheroic martyrdom by which they could invite the evil back upon themselves and humanise the large looming images of nation and sexuality.

Malani's installations that manifest insanity in the public space are imbued with this feminine quality of collective mourning that distinguishes her work from the individualistic and solitary literary work of Manto, that lead him to madness and suicide. The inspiration of the artist branches from contemporary Indian history and culture but Malani's work conveys a transcontinental idea of a conatus, a value of collective life that of a world conquered by the values feminine of empathy and infused with a volume of catharsis .We are now in a non-Brechtian public and the knowledge of estrangement is not effective today. At this instant, we have to get into the Aristotelian argument of catharsis.

3.2.8 A Case Study of the Artworks of Nalini Malani

Some of the references of her artworks can be taken for discussion. Such as,

      a. *'Remembering Mad Meg'*
      b. *'Mother India'*
      c. *'Mutant'*
      d. 'Gamepieces '
      e. *'Unity in Diversity'*

f. *'Transgressions'*
g. *'Stains'*
h. *'Hamletmachine'*
i. *'Remembering Toba Tek Singh'*
j. *'Memory: Record/Erase'*
k. *'Medea Video'*

'*Remembering Mad Meg*' (2007)

Video shadow play, two single-channel animations, a series of lights and eight rotating reverses painted Lexan cylinders, sound, 3 min

Nalini Malani's '*Remembering Mad Meg*' (Plate 3.3) is a video shadow play, two single-channel animations. In her work , the researcher can notice that a series of light and eight rotating reverses painted Lexan Cylinders. The involvement of sound is also a viewer can visualise in her '*Remembering Mad Meg*'. The work of video shadow play is three minutes long .

'*Mother India: Transactions in the construction of Pain*' (2005)

Video Installation, 5 Projections, 5 and 1/2 mins

The work of Nalini Malani entitled '*Mother India: Transactions in construction of Pain*' (Plate 3.4) is a video installation. In this work, the concept explores how the imagining of the project of nationalism in India came to include the appropriation of bodies of women as objects on which the desire for nationalism could be brutally inscribed and a memory for the future made. The video installation '*Mother India: Transactions in the construction of Pain*' by Nalini Malani was inspired by an essay by the socialist Veena Das entitled "*Language and Body: Transactions in the Construction of Pain*". Apart from the fact that the independence of India and Pakistan was the scene of unprecedented collective violence, one thousand hundred women from both sides of the border were forcibly kidnapped and raped. Das mentioned that the bodies of women were metaphors for the nation, and they had to bear the signs of their possession by the enemy.

The language of pain as uttered by women who hurt the ferociousness turned into a zone of silence or the dialectal having all the phonetic excess of hysteria that destroys apparent meaning. It is this method that Malani uses in her work. Possession by perpetrating dangerous sexual fierceness on women has required a trajectory accurate up to current times. Malani's video '*Unity in Diversity*' which addresses the dissolution of this very concept that India as a nation-state started. Also, the woman as mutant, de-gendered, violated beyond imagination, has been an ongoing preoccupation in her work.

The video installation contains/companies, five projections, 6 DVD players, sound system amplifier, five directional speakers or five sound showers, DVD synchroniser for 6 DVD players, two black benches, Dimensions variable. The original size of the room is 7Lx11Wx4 H metres.

Regarding her video installation Malani acknowledged to Australian Centre for the Moving Image, Melbourne Gandhi Film Foundation, Mumbai; Indian Video Act Archive, Mumbai; Lucas Artists programs, Montaho Majlis, Mumbai; Sakshi Gallery, Mumbai, Shared footage, Mumbai special thanks to; icon India and Bose Pacia Gallery New York Text inspired by *"Language and Body: Transactions in the Construction of Pain"* by Veena Das from particular suffering, edited by Kleinman, Das and Lock. Oxford University Press in 1998.

'*Mother India: Transactions in the construction of Pain*' by Malini invites the viewer to confront the lie behind the noble by which the work got inspired and enchanting images of the motherland, given recurring interethnic attacks. On five huge screens images of the partition, she was followed by anti-Muslim assaults in Gujarat in 2002, alternative with the inaudible expressions of women involved in domestic duties, prototypes of gentleness and sympathy, collective with images of Hindu war spiritualities – such as Durga on her tiger. These images retell the viewer of the ambivalence of Hindu female deities, which are both protective and destructive, an uncertainty that Hindu fundamentalists, according to Malani, want to be erased, postulating that Hinduism is all peace. At the same time, Islam is violent and the source of evil. A hot mouth recalls the terrible deeds of the Gujarat incidents. At the same time, the voice of a woman and a man are heard in succession, recalling the reactions of women abducted during the partition and that of Indian parliamentarians who dismissed them. The shrill, panic-stricken voice of the woman shouts in a way that does anyone or anyone take her for a machine? The male voice replies that with a tone that the honour of the state is at stake as the research observes that the title is inspired by an essay entitled *"Language and Body:Transactions in the Construction of Pain"* of 1996 which queries the meaning of the snatching of women as markers of ethnic groups' comparative power during the partition. Through a complex intertextuality, Malani's installation also refers indirectly to Rabindranath Tagore's novel *"The Home and the World "*of 1916, which evokes the assumption by the Indian nationalist movement of the celestial status of women – observed as the supreme deity *Devi* who is believed as the mother of the world and its transfer to the image of the nation idolised as the "Great

Mother", "Mother India". This identity, according to Tagore, permanently deprived women of their subjecthood.

For Malani the traditional and nationalist patriarchal homily that acquaints women to divinities transforms them into insignia of endurance but at the same time into objects of use, in both cases into an inferior category of human beings without rights which explains their use as war take. The artist's art practice underlines and further complexifies this transactional game regarding the partition, suggesting that the silence which the women abducted and later returned have maintained regarding their suffering, is related to their self-espousing of this sacred role that in the work of grief in many societies it is the communications between language and body, especially in the gendered division of labour, by which the antiphony of speech and silence recreates the world in the face of tragic loss.

Malani's art practice concept explored the body of the reified Indian woman as the repository of fierceness, an object without rights but also the intermediary of an overhaul process, since women are, in traditional societies, in charge of howling formalities. They symbolically captivate pain through ritual songs. This impression of the female body as a position of the transaction of pain is expressed in the installation of Mother India, through its title.

'Mutant' (Plate 3.5)

Malani had earlier seen this theme in a hypnotic series called '*Mutant*', of 1994-1996. The latter comprises so-called "mutant" bodies, robust female figures in black and white dye painted on milk carton paper. Some face the viewer in a position of contribution, their arms prolonged and hands unlocked, or of threat, their sexual qualities undistinguishable. Mutant II Series A of 1994, reveals a masculine face completed with huge shoulders, its flat and hairy chest preposterously echoing the black threesome of the genital hair implanted between its colossal thighs. The left hand is concealed in the back. The index and middle fingers of the elevated right hand are enclosed with finger puppets. They appear to be moving to entice or divert an invisible subject, indirectly situated to the right of the painting in the way of its contemplation. These outrageous numbers, evoking ferocity and the wretched, first appeared in her *Medea*'s projects around 1994. The works were painted on milk cardboards to suggest tainted milk, and were related to undisclosed nuclear tests by the US in the Marshall Islands, leading to malformations. A new-fangled series called body as site-Mutant III series B of 1996 reveals among others a loud and fierce motherly body, equipped with a pistol, threatening the gentle figure of a child.

The paintings have been eroded away with milk by female performers at the 2nd Asia Pacific Triennial at Queensland Art Gallery of Brisbane in Australia. This performance suggests a ritual erasing of the abject painting (Kayser, 2015).

'*Stains*' (2000) (Plate 3.6)

Animation Video Installation, 8½ minutes looped, sound.

The work is single-cell animation constructed with accretions and erasures marking the trajectory of life and death pulling in the vagaries of the human psyche. A huge latex breast filled with milk hangs pendulously in the middle of a room. The milk receives the projections. The viewer steps up to the rim to look inside.

Regarding the work, Malani expressed that the body fluids, secretions, mucus, secretion, fizz and pigment are living flesh. These transform into humans that act ambiguously toward each other. Loving, hating, killing each other. Finally; the mass of bones that remain from a pair of bloody hands that seems almost to come together but instead a bomb pops out from between the palms and explodes. The death ooze bubbles out and is evacuated (Malani, 2012).

The research study analyses series conveys the topic of milk as an absorber of violence which is also staged in Malani's installation '*Stains*' (2000). Stains consist of watercolours representing blood, bones, internal fluids (lymph, plasma), filmed and then projected through a video projector on a screen of milk in the form of a gigantic latex ball/breast. To observe the images, the viewer must grow privileged in a circle that encircles the device. The title and the installation intimates both that milk purifies the blood and that it is blemished by it. Reducing the female body to an enormous udder that washes violence, the work creates communication between woman and society, in which her role is, according to the traditional association with *Devi*, to embrace and nurture.

Nevertheless, the blood that permeates this giant mass also suggests that this nurturing role is made at her expense, as witnesses of the partition indicate that what is there to be proud in a woman's body – every day it is polluted by being consumed which was said by a woman raped during the partition. The breast conveys the recollections of violence, which women keep within themselves, like a poison, to protect their families in a way that as a woman's body is made so that she can hide the faults of her husband deep within her. So she can absorb all pain then take the stance of peace which is said by another. Malani recommends that the body of women channel horror, by turning it into a large teat, tainted with the spirit of the dead. These installations are the symbol of the body as the locus of violence and a means to erase this violence (Kayser, 2015).

'Gamepieces' (2003)

Video/ Shadow Play, 4 minutes looped, sound

'Gamepieces' (Plate 3.7) is a shadow/video play. This low-tech structure of six mylar cylinders painted on the reserve with images of gentle, vulnerable creatures is constructed from two parallel iron rings. The rings are one twenty in diameter and one fifty cm in height and are lit by the video projections of the nuclear bombs and the mushroom clouds from 'Fat Man' and 'Little Boy' that distressed Nagasaki and Hiroshima. The calamitous images of loss and damage scorch the panoramic screens spanning up to twenty-eight metres (Malani, 2003). The images look as if to involve the spectator. At the two ends, fluffy white clouds excitedly spill out of a sapphire blue sky proclaiming their life was giving force. Single-cell animation scrapes graffiti of gods and demons from the Hindu pantheon impotently on the screens, of the shadow creatures attempting to erase the horrors. The work involves six cylinders, reverse painted mylar, iron armatures, four DVD players, sync with one remote sensor, four projectors, audio CD players, one amplifies, four speakers, dimensions variable.

Regarding the video/shadow play Malani communicated that mystical and quirky but gentle creatures glide past in slow rotations, almost nudging and attempting to erase, to obliterate with their massive soft shadow bodies the violence of the scenes in front of them. The creatures from shadows by the very same right with which they must compete to gain ascendancy over the massive destruction that scorches the screens (2003).

'Unity in Diversity' (2003)

Video Installation, 7 ½ minutes looped, sound

'Unity in Diversity' (Plate 3.8) is based on the figurative painting *'Galaxy of Musicians'* by the late nineteenth-century Indian painter Raja Ravi Verma. The work shows eleven musicians, all women dressed in different costumes of India portentous unity in diversity. This painting was revealed at the world congress of religions in Chicago 1893, where the philosopher Swami Vivekananda spoke of the menace of orthodoxy in faith. A promising concept

of nationalism was emerging at this time with strong reformist movements (Malani, 2003).

The video constructs this with later histories of the rise of fascism and the genocide in Gujarat in 2002 that shook the roots of this democratic country, leaving may them and despairs in its awakening. What flinches off as a visual fairy tale, where all parts of the nation play in harmony together, ends in a blood bath. The work contains a living room setting, flat-screen monitor of twenty-nine inch or back projection. The work comprises false wall painted deep crimson, ornate gold frame, black and white photo of Nehru and Gandhi, two wall lamps, two art deco chairs (Malani, 2003).

'*Transgression*' (2001)

Video-Shadow play Installation, 7 minutes looped, sound

In this video-shadow play installation, the reverse painted cylinders form an eternal movement of shadows on a wall that spans fourteen metres (Plate 3.9). The barrier has images from videos projected on it. Therefore, images appear in three registers, the painted image, the shadows and the projected image. These are the accretion of orientalism harking back to nineteenth-century British rule in India. But the soundtrack pulls one into the present period, with its postcolonial aggression of the WTO and the GATT, through a 'Sinister' sounding poem. The work contain three DVDs, four cylinders with armature, each bottle one twenty cms diameters x one fifty cms, four rods fifty cms, four electric rotating motors, reserve painted mylar/film, three LCD video projector (two thousand lumens) wide-angle zoom less parallax correction, three DVD players, one amplifier and four speakers ad two black benches (Malani, 2001).

'*Hamletmachine*' (1999-2000)

Video Installation, 20 minutes looped, sound

The work is based on the text of Heiner Mueller's "*Hamletmachine*" (Plate 3.10). The video play manifests the increase of Hindu fundamentalism in India, which reached its peak with the hyperactive violence of fanatics who brought down the sixteenth-century Babri Masjid (Mosque) in December of 1992. The rising conflict that followed this devastation provided the Hindu devotees with an opportunity to attack and pillage the shanty- towns of the minority Muslim population in a clear case of the loud clutch in Mumbai. Instant slum colonies remained burnt to embers. The railway stations were occupied with Muslims trying to catch any train that might take them away to the safety of their villages (Malani, 2004).

'*Remembering Toba Tek Singh*' (1998-99)

Video Installation, 20 minutes looped, sound

The work of Nalini Malani was inspired by "*Toba Tek Singh*", a short story by Saadat Hassan Manto. The video installation touches on the painful, horrendous and irrational journey of fierceness beginning with the piercing of India into two countries that is India and Pakistan, in 1946 to the aggressive pretension that led to the nuclear tests in 1998 (Plate 3.11). The work was executed in retort to the underground nuclear test in India on 11th May 1998, which is a significant day on the Buddhist calendar. The sizable cultural project consists of a single cell animation drawing by the artist, montage and layered with archival material of "*Little Boy*" and "*Fat Man*", the American bombs that killed millions of people in Hiroshima and Nagasaki during World War II. The installation work was explored as a video diptych. Two videos depicting two women owe each other crosswise the area of a room that has tin trunks containing monitors and bedding positioned in a framework structure. Specific is the kind of logs used by refugees to carry all their worldly possessions (Malani, 2004).

The images on the screens in the trunks portray people uncertainty away from their homelands, crossing borders, rioting, and misery. Many of these video images are taken from archival material from several countries. This installation contributes to the cleaving of countries and the irrational, in human use of technology (Malani, 2004).

The installation involves iron canteens covering small video screens, positioned at the centre of a room, creased with large screens. On the small display screens in work means archival images of the partition of the domestic life of refugees on the road of a deportee, including childbirth. They are labelled by a voice telling the short story by the Pakistani writer Saadat Hasan Manto, of 1955. The novel expresses the forced migration of a patient of Lahore psychiatric hospital who was a Sikh born in the town of Toba Tek Singh which the powers that be have categorical to refer to an Indian mental hospital, three years after the partition. Transported by bus to the boundary and enquired to annoy the no man's land to the other side, he refuses to choose a team and lets himself expire in the undeniable terrestrial. The intimate images in the canteens – an object related to affecting – clash with the "*big story*," these are expressed by the massive screens circulated the space, screening metaphors of worldwide nuclear struggle. The detonation of the atomic bomb in Hiroshima and Nagasaki, US nuclear testing in the Pacific atolls, conflict in the Balkans. The work has been generated by India's announcement of its possessing the atomic bomb, a claim that Pakistan will make a few days later. Malani practice of unconnected archival images avoids a direct observation, supporting the role of reminiscences and resentment in new clashes. In work, some images are blurred copies executed with a VCR. Between these displays, images captured by Malani reveal two women fronting each other, one Indian and the other Pakistani. They are busy completing the same domestic task, the folding of a *sari*. As Malani explored that the display of the same learned gestures reveals their kinship beyond political and nationalist rift, as in this vast double exile, rapes and abductions were committed, women exchanged as spoils of war and symbols of the power of each nation. With this chronicle, Malani desires to pay tribute to women that deliver food and care for their families in the time of wars and on the roads of deportee, without being permissible to contribute of decision making. The metaphor is transparent; perhaps too much madness and death are on the side of history – decided by men – life and restraint on the women's side . The mosaic of images in which some of them are blurred, some clear, conjures memories, a mixture of emotions and recollections, of intimate and collective visions, and purports to reconnect the collective consciousness.

'*Memory: Record/Erase*' (1996)

AnimationVideo,10 minutes, looped, sound,

The Job / Naukari: Theatre, Installation, Video (Plate 3.12)

This work is Malani's interpretation of the job by Bertolt Brecht, set by the writer in the period of the unhappiness in Germany. It conveys the memories of an impoverished woman who had to impersonate the dead husband to obtain his job as a night watchman. The woman has two little children and takes on a 'wife' to build the front. She is no longer permitted to move on with her work because, after an accident, her identity is discovered. So in a situation of joblessness , she is bound to walk the darker side of life to remain. The narrative is expressed in animation through the process of drawing and erasure on a parchment. The sheep skin acts as the memory membrane of the woman that gets overloaded and dies (Malani, 2004).

'*Medea video*' (1991 to 1996)

MedeaProjekt : involvement of paintings, installation, books, theatre, video, 1991 – 1996.

Medea is a project of Nalini Malani under the project '*Medea*' Malani has done paintings, installation books, theatre, video. Regarding her Medea video, Malani expressed that she executed a video of Medea material after the performances were over (Plate 3.13). In some sense, the artist guesses that she had to have a recording of it. But it was shot and edited as an autonomous piece (Malani, 2012).

'Now I See It Now I Don't' (2018)

Can a city ever be an individual's? Can an individual ever turn to it for assistance? Such are the questions evoked by Nalini Malani's video work, '*Now I See It Now I Don't*' in 2018, in which scraggly lines and superimposed images suggest an inevitable tragedy (Plate 3.14). The near-apocalyptic work shows a person floundering at sea, and a monstrous vision of the Gateway of India looming ahead.

The historic memorial arch, meant to welcome voyagers, seems to tease and tempt the struggling swimmer. The video work is displayed at Jhaveri Contemporary gallery's new space in Mumbai, as part of its inaugural exhibition, What's Essential. Malani describes the 58-second video work as "drawings in motion", and has gifted it to Jhaveri Contemporary on account of its relocation.

'*Can You Hear Me ?* ' is Malani's first solo exhibition in India in last five years and this marks her return home after winning the prestigious *John Miro Prize* in 2019 (Plate 3.15). The exhibition hosts in Goethe-Institut / Max Mueller Bhavan Mumbai previewed on October 19th, 2019 at Gallery MMB, and the show is on view till January 2nd, 2020. The exhibition juxtaposed Malani's first film animation '*Dream Houses*' (1969) with an entirely new. The exhibition room-filling video installation '*Can You Hear Me ?*' consisting of 11 projections with more than 50 video animations from 2018/2019 and spanning the same fifty years as when Goethe- Institut / Max Mueller Bhavan has established in Mumbai.

3.3 New Media Artworks of Jitish Kallat

Jitish Kallat is a contemporary Indian painter, sculptor, photographer, and installation artist best known for work that celebrates the city of Mumbai. Kallat was born on July 14, 1974, in Mumbai, India. He attended the Sir

Jamsetjee Jeejebhoy School of Art in Mumbai where the artist graduated with a BFA in 1996. Kallat had his first major exhibition in the United States in 2010 at the Art Institute of Chicago with a large installation titled '*Public Notice 3*'. Nowadays, Kallat's works are in collections of the National Gallery of Modern Art in New Delhi, the Museum of Contemporary Art in Los Angeles, and the Singapore Art Museum, among others. Kallat lives and works in Mumbai, India.

Much of Kallat's work has been constructed on his come across with the multi-sensory environment of Bombay/Mumbai, as well as the economic, political and historical proceedings that have contributed to its creation. Kallat's practice as a painter has frequently highlighted a concern that the artist shares with the founders of Indian modernism in visual and literary art. Kallat has couched his references to the "underdog" in a hyper-pop language to signal the ironies that attend the lives of migrant workers and menial labourers in India's megacities: people met on "second class" train compartments, people whose labour continues to keep the nation's aspirations afloat. In Kallat's installation and video practice, the artist has often revisited archival texts and museum displays intending to probe the production and dissemination of knowledge.

The research study analyses that in the essay, "*The Mumbai Syndrome*", Patricia Ellis vouches for Kallat's engagement with painting as subversively radical activity. In Kallat's art practice; the artist's approach has little to do with representation, abstraction, or formalism, but total mimesis of concept. Kallat's paintings are not localised images embarrassed within boundaries, difficulties of space and perception, or even commonplaces of self-defined development. They're considered as liminal gaps of peripheral mediations, metaphysical platforms of inter-connection .

3.3.1 The Artistic Journey of Jitish Kallat: Transforming from Painting to New Media Art

Jitish Kallat is one of the influential names in the contemporary New Media Art practices of India. Regarding Kallat's starting days of art practice, the research study analyses that art came to the artist in a way that the artist was incessantly drawing through his childhood. During these days, Kallat used to draw besides his sister, who is eight years older than the artist, who was struggling to make a drawing in her biology book. Kallat was around five years old at the time and volunteered to draw for the artist's sister and sat beside her, making the drawing on another sheet of paper. It appeared that the artist could do a better rendering, and this got Kallat's sister and the family all excited, giving a naive boost to the juvenile self-worth. In this way, the incredible alchemy happens when the artist draws, especially when the artist was a child then makes a mark and creates a space, adds a few lines, and derives depth. As Kallat adds more marks, a world begins to originate on a piece of paper, and feel incredibly empowered. The research study analyses that in these ways, Kallat's childhood explored thoroughly into the artist's mid-teens was persistently and obsessively drawing through which Kallat developed him as an artist since his childhood.

During the artist's early days; regarding Kallat's art practice inspirations, the artist had seen Husain's reproductions as a child before Kallat entered the art school. In Kallat's perception, Husain sort of symbolised the general public's perception of a modern artist in post-Independence India. Kallat wasn't profoundly aware of modern art movements until the artist entered art school, purely drifting from drawing to an interest in advertising billboards and how data gets both condensed and amplified on them. And so, Kallat landed up in art school not knowing whether his interest lay in the Applied Arts or Fine Arts. Kallat perceived that the epiphany was olfactory. The research observes and finds that Kallat recollects ambulatory in the Fine Arts department at Sir J J School of Art. Space where the smell of paint filled the high-ceilinged corridors lined with plaster casts. Kallat reflects that he subliminally knew that he was in the right place. This, in the year 1990 (Obrist, 2019).

At the time, the Sir J J School of Art was deeply oriented towards abstraction, something Kallat too inherited in his very early days. There was a very magnetic teacher, Prabhakar Kolte, whose work and Kolte's affinities with the Bauhaus school had a cast on the aesthetics of the school. By 1992, Kallat began noticing seismic shifts in his relationship with abstraction, wherein, emerging from a field of concept would be fragments of texts, notations or imagery. It was as if the external world was emerging from a ground of abstraction and seeking coherence as a representational form. In the earliest canvases during 1994–95 Kallat painted the figuration appeared by quarrying layers of paint. The forms were a result of peeling layers of colour as if time was acting upon the pigment, dislodging it and exposing the layers below. Such a process would reveal a self-image, and around this auto, the portrait would generate questions about time, ancestry, death, mortality, sustenance and all the themes that continue to surface in work (Obrist, 2019).

There is the persistent impression of time; there is the clock, the self-image in a watch in Kallat's art practice and regarding the concept behind Kallat travelled of pieces such as '*Flower Child Operates the Funeral of a*

Schedule' that the artist represented within a few days of completing art school in 1995. The painting good- humoredly memorialises the death of a six-year routine, ceremoniously portrayed as the death of a wrist watch, a transformed treaty with time, the self at once trapped and enlightened from time. At one end of the painting, ants hurry to demolish a watch in a Daliesque banquet; away, a watch transfers from a flute-bearer's wrist to a case/coffin. At the bottommost of the painting, the senses are shut down, enveloping one's head in a white drape. It's a question Kallat continues to ask himself today that if an individual obliterates every external marker of change, could time exist for that specific individual, would an individual's lungful and heartbeat be the only dial of time? These may have theoretical undertones but were always encoded and mischievously cloaked in the guise of the mundane narrative, such as the concluding rite at the end of campus life (Obrist, 2019).

In 1997 Kallat's first exhibition entitled '*P.T.O.*' (Plate 3.16) which was at Gallery Chemould, which is presently called Chemould Prescott Road, and at Prithvi Gallery which is now non-operational, used to be an inspiring conjunction idea for persons as of theatre and the performance. These very early images were made at a time when Kallat was about twenty-two years old. It was a time when the artist was asking himself existential questions like who the artist is, what has the artist here for, what is life and death, how do an individual merge moral and ethical uncertainties? And some of those questions developed the central pivot around which those paintings were made. A question that preoccupied the artist Kallat was this whole idea of ancestry, which was at once family ancestry, a more extensive cultural ancestry but also the specific artistic lineage that was propelling Kallat to make that exploration of art practice. While the artist (Kallat) was struggling to find a visual language that the specific thought process would help Kallat instrumentalise the act of picture-making as a tool to engage with life's questions, the research identifies that Kallat was also simultaneously questioning his (Kallat's) evolving pictorial language. Kallat perceived it was less apparent to himself at the time. Still, when Kallat looked back on his past experiences, it seems like the artist was asking himself: What does Kallat paints tell himself about who he is? And how does Kallat find clues to the coordinates of his existence (family, city, nation, planetary) in the piece that he has made? The artist-philosopher Kallat often thinks of the articles in the exhibition entitled *P.T.O.* (Please Turn Over) like a series of mysterious artworks. The pictures were like a battered public wall, like a collective pin-up board on which single images and ideas were decided and covered, similar palimpsests (Obrist, 2019).

In the initial nineties, an individual can be identified that the living room in India was shifting. Succeeding that the economic liberalisation in India such as the television set started to sunbeam a different soundscape, with diverse languages and varied information from across the globe. The material was organised otherwise on this renewed TV screen, and these codes of how 'the image' was configured started to affect the way Kallat art practised (Obrist, 2019). The paintings of Kallat at once appeared like a flaming TV screen and a weakening public wall where layers were peeled to reveal the underpainting. It was as if a city wall with layers of information pasted on had degraded with the passage of time and the sun, rain and wind acting upon it. The paintings seemed old at the very moment the artist would appear painting it, as if the act of painting was an acceleration of time. If Bhupen Khakhar's paintings were windows with images showing through, Jitish Kallat's artworks were walls with images plastered on.

And in the year 2000, something happens because there is Jitish Kallat's first installation, there is also Kallat exhibiting at the Havana Biennial with *Random Access Memory*' (Plate 3.17). The year 2000 is now the digital age. Information cultivates exponentially, but that doesn't mean that we have more reminiscence. One could say that forgetfulness may be someplace rooted as the very essence of the digital age. It's so exciting that artists protest against forgetting and work with memory.

These 108 drawings of Kallat, made using heat on fax paper, were an intertwining of memory and amnesia, materialisation of an image and its subsequent disappearance. '*Random Access Memory*' (108 Stopovers for a Pillion Pilgrim), exhibited at the 7th Havana Biennial, were made on exposed thermal fax paper by applying heat; thus, the tools and the medium were the electric iron, the incense stick, the candlestick, hot and cold water, and minimal use of pigment that adhered with heat. Titled '*Communication in Difficult Times: One Closer to the Other*', that edition of the biennial was being realised by Kallat with little or no budget. He was invited to participate grounded on his large canvases that the curators had seen. But when Kallat heard about the complex budget scenario and read the curatorial note, the artist felt the work must eliminate shipment from this artistic communication in uncertain times. Such was the journey from canvas to a transmission communication material such as fax paper, which collectively considered less than a container of face tissues but would unfold at the biennial as a massive double spiral of imaginings. At the centre of this giant reading was a self-image pretentiousness as a tourist-pilgrim exchanging the enormous twirl whose 108 stations were the ancient pilgrimage locations of India, art historical fragments and personal trivialities implicit as an image . The number 108 has abundant connotations in Indian and Asian traditions and spiritual approaches; it has astronomical significance and is also the number of beads on a seeker's chanting chain, a similarity one touched while continually returning to the identical arrangement of fax paper. After the biennial, the drawings were distributed amongst the several volunteers who helped pedestal the exhibition. Since these fragments were made on fax paper, the thermal stains were deemed to inevitably erase themselves in the homes of the volunteers in the course of six or eight months.

In the early 2000s; there's more and more connected to the city in the artworks of Jitish Kallat. Something that doesn't appear in the previous work that has less to do with the urban. It's interesting because we can't make a portrait of a city as it is far too complicated, so it's not a portrait of a town but captured through trajectories, through movements. But *Rickshawpolis 3* is a portrait of a city in a way (Plate 3.18). And then *Artist Making Local Call* (Plate 3.19) is also connected to the town, so are the 365 Lives. The research study identified that the executed works which Kallat painted in 1998, such as *Ordinary Recipe*, *Reading from My Old City Book*, *Mailing the Same to Good God's Cook*, or a painting the artist (Kallat) executed in 1999 entitled *CanisFamiliaris /A Dog's Life* (Plate 3.20), which was exhibited in Century City in 2000 at the Tate Modern. In *Ordinary Recipe*, the self- image is at the centre, but in the upper fringe, a people's cape becomes preserved like an abstracted map. In the three or four years that developed, this people-scape would become the central image in many of the paintings. But, as you point out, in the mid- 2000s, the city gets foregrounded, somewhat like a protagonist. The *Rickshawpolis* pictures of Kallat remained these impenetrable, distilled images of convergence, acceleration, ceaselessness; a painted collision-scape. Perhaps that is why they can be exhausting to look at . They are notations of every day that seem un- governed by gravity or time. In reaching for the momentary and the transient, they multiply, disorganise and get overlaid. If observing nature helps human beings/artists connect with our (human beings/artists) internal beats, finding cities perhaps helps access the turbulent top layers of our inner selves. After all, cities get moulded just as our bodies do. If atoms converging in particular configurations leads to complexity and sentience, human convergence rearranges "space" as a "place", injects it with meaning, temper, character.

In *Artist Making Local Call* in 2005 which is a Digital print by Jitish Kallat on vinyl mesh 241 x 1044 cm (95 x 411 in.), Kallat placed himself in the today extinct PCO (public call office) shop, endorsing the creation of a local call, while the camera makes a panoramic image. To make a view, the camera takes about a minute to comprehend its spin and record a 360-degree picture, ensuring that the motionless photograph has that much "period" preserved within it. As a consequence, a rickshaw and a taxi that both happened to be in the same advert, seconds apart from each other, appear in the picture as a virtual impact. The persons ambulatory on either side of this impact are the same; they have merely enthused crossways in the time that was accepted . In a different place, individuals moving against the direction of the camera's alternation troupe obscurities though their physiques endure imperceptible, suggesting ideas of death or non appearance. The Sun, positioned behind the PCO, appears to troupe shades in two directions, as if morning and evening were happening simultaneously. The portion appears to remember the irregularity established through a misregistered instant. It attaches with concepts that were predominant in the original artworks, whether it is the impression of time, humanity, the inattentive body and its gumshoe as death. But at this time, the city road is the pivot on which these ideas unfold (Obrist, 2019).

Looking at over thirty years of the artistic journey of Jitish Kallat, the research finds it is interesting that there is an expanded field where Kallat is walking after paintings interested in installations to photography and into the sculptures and video projections. But, in a way, drawing and painting do not ever go absent (Obrist, 2019). And while the artist work on all these video installations or these extensive research projects, of course, they are all large-format artworks such as those with the image of the commuter and the idea of travelling, works like the massive 'Baggage Claim' that the audience also showed at the 'Indian Highway' exhibition. As a working artist, all of these processes seem to continue parallelly in Kallat's mind and the studio. And indeed, as an individual observer , as such, the artist doesn't feel a hierarchy or preference of medium. In the best instances, the artist's strength says that the ideas and explorations have a seed of the intermediate entrenched in them, and in following the impression additional, it develops strong what form its capacity revenue, whether it remains a video or a drawing. But with painting, there is this implausible plea to the possibility of being able to fashion an image, to walk away from the conscious and tease out the unforeseen. Kallat has in the past many years enjoyed the process of working on substantial artworks. For a work such as *'Baggage Claim'* or the *'Allegory of the Endless Morning'*, a fleeting image, now and then from an ordinary photograph, can develop the preliminary opinion to start a procedure that would require the previous numerous weeks and months. And that pledge to an image through the time endowed to pursue it can be rewarding. The artist does frequently novelty that employed transversely diverse balances and media contributions a usual self-renewal of the studio procedure as, at a physical equal, one is unstable between dissimilar records. There was a degree of the artistic switch in the earlier paintings of Kallat, but with the most recent drawings *'Wind Studies' (The Hour of the Day of the Month of the Season)*, the artist perceived that he was letting go of some of it.

The research study analyses that once there is this conversation between Jitish Kallat and Homi Bhabha, and when Bhabha asked the artist that what does it mean for Kallat to provoke an act, an act of activity, which is at the identical period reliant on the destruction of that made act, It is by playing with fire – its distracting and negating effects – that the artist can do the work; and yet, Kallat initially lay down the lines of control with deliberation. The research analyses and finds that the new drawings of artist Jitish Kallat *'Wind Studies'* have allowed the artist a degree of letting go. Talking of the process, Kallat lay a few graphite lines on the paper while he involved himself within the studio, and then, the artist takes the drawing outdoors. It is positioned flat on a table in the studio backyard, and the artist then overlays an inflammable fluid on each line, one line at a time, exposing it to a small flame. The border ignites, and depending on the direction and intensity of the wind, at that instance, the smoke from the fire leaves its imprint, and the artist moves on to the next line. It is quite mysterious how our bodies are unable to process the shift in the wind, but the drawing becomes a field where the atmospheric variations of that moment get registered. In some ways, while working, the artist perceived like an eavesdropper in the presence of these more significant elements in interaction. And, once again, they are related to time, they mark the hour of the day of the month of the season. Kallat has said that the artist sees the burnt lines become a transcript of what transpired between wind and fire, and weirdly, it's also connected to *'Public Notice'*, because it's a transcript. The study finds that's true. The inflammable fluid is the same that Kallat used to render Nehru's speech twelve or thirteen years ago. So, if one is a transcript of a historical statement, the other is of a temporary natural process. Such repurposing of material or processes frequently happens in Kallat's work and are at times separated by many years. For instance, if in sightings the lenticular surface departs in context every time it flips and reveals its inverse, in a piece such as *'Death of Distance'* (2006), two very divergent narratives that entered the public domain at the same time continue to flip between black and white and white and black, depending on where one stands about the texts.

Regarding Kallat's artistic journey, the research study analyses that the artist-curated one of the editions of the Kochi-Muziris Biennale. The study observed that it also leads to the most recent work of Kallat, which is *'Covariance' (Sacred Geometry)*. When the researchers studied the *'Wind Studies'*, *'The Infinite Episode'*, these parts happened after the artist-curated the Kochi-Muziris Biennale. There is a long past of artists curating shows. Interestingly Kallat stopped all his work in the studio for the entire duration and made the Biennale as the artist's work during that time. The research has studied in detail and observed about this "Intermezzo", how it worked for Kallat to curate this massive show and then to start once again? The study finds that Kallat realised that if the artist were to curate the Biennale and make this process meaningful for himself, it would only make sense if Kallat completely exited doing his work for that duration so that the artist could funnel all his inquiries into this project. Kallat felt that the exhibition 'Whorled Explorations' must produce themes rather than reproduce a single preconceived curatorial idea. The artist's development is there one of mingling a rigid curatorial note, but to let a dispersal of reminders and instincts progressively self-organise as an exhibition. Two chronologically overlying historical episodes in Kerala between the fourteenth and seventeenth centuries developed Kallat's opinions of leaving. It was the period once the coasts of Kochi were carefully connected to the nautical episode of the phase of unearthing; a period when charts altered speedily with the influx of autopilots on the Malabar coast looking for spices and riches, modifications in topography and tries in antiquity, signalling a phase of conquest, coercive trading and colonialism, animating the early processes of globalisation (Obrist, 2019). It was also the moment when the Kerala School of Astronomy and Mathematics were making remarkable transformative proposals for determining human continuation within the broader cosmos. The exhibition projected the nautical exploration with the enigmatic travel of our planet itself hurtling at 100,000 km per hour in areas no individual recognises. The unrelated directions of these suggestions were intentional; one was a gaze directed in time, the other in space (Obrist, 2019).

Structurally, many have observed that 'Whorled Explorations' reflected aspects of Kallat's work, such as the recurrent overlaying of the terrestrial with the celestial, the re-visiting of particular historical episodes, such as in the *'Public Notices'*, that sit alongside cosmological expeditions that occur in earlier works from 2009, such as *'Forensic Trail of the Grand Banquet'*. As for the appearance to the studio after a gap of sixteen months, it felt somewhat seamless as the curatorial process was a transition of many of the ideas that Kallat has been grappling within the studio, delivered as a biennale through a different toolbox and in close dialogue with numerous, incredible artist colleagues (Obrist, 2019).

Some of the references of Jitish Kallat's artworks can be taken for discussion.

Such as,

'Forensic Trail of the Grand Banquet' (2009)

'Forensic Trail of the Grand Banquet' is a video installation by Jitish Kallat which has a duration of 00: 02: 20. The projection dimensions variable (Plate 3.21). The scaled video is a journey through an endless cosmic field where all the planetary clusters and stellar formations are made of X-rays of food. The video projection appears to be an infinite expanse of outer space in which galactic clusters , planets, asteroids and nebulae float. In the forecast, these moving celestial bodies occasionally drift towards viewers in a collision course drawing them into parallel worlds of perception – a meteoric vortex the research study analyses .

The work gradually becomes evident that the flying forms, which can equally invoke cellular processes or moving micro-organism, are X-ray images of numerous food types.

In the video *'Forensic Trail of the Grand Banquet'*, the cosmic view the artist explores is thus a mysterious floating banquet of nourishment. Here, in works such as *'Epilogue'* (Plate 3.22) (2010-11), Kallat inscribes the fundamental human impulse for sustenance and life into an image that invokes the eternal rhythms of the cosmos.

The video projection *'Forensic Trail of the Grand Banquet'* explores the legal and spherical perspective affirms a new and radical anthropocentric view of the cosmos. It is supposed that philosophy and art originate from the city. But which city? It was Cosmopolis. The research studies that Socrates selected Athens. He was a fierce protector of the city in the conflict in contradiction of Sparta. He had the prospect to outflow his death sentence through voluntary deportee. Thus far, although he knew of no better city, he still was not a blind patriot. In his essay *"On Exile"* Plutarch quotes Socrates's claim that he is not an Athenian or a Greek, but a citizen of the world. He supposed that he remained a "Cosmic" in the method that others were a "Corinthian" or a "Rhodian".

The seventh-century scientist and philosopher Blaise Pascal observed that whether we are staring out towards the cosmos or examining the realm of microscopic reality, we are "suspended between two infinities". The further out the study appears, the superior the prospect. The earlier we reproduce, the more multifaceted the feature. In mutually commands nearby is the knowledge of the unlimited. We have an expression to express the experience of infinity, sublime. The concept of sublime is an uncertain chunk of modern philosophy. The involvement of the divine is many preliminary opinions in art. These two worlds have not ever found a neat idea of rendezvous. Theory and practice are not so much postponed at conflicting ends of infinity but seem to oscillate between these polarities at a slight remove from each other. With this limitation in mind, the researcher would like to respond to the theme of the cosmopolis in the encounter with Jitish Kallat's exhibition 'Circa'.

Let an individual begin with the tantalising sense of starting a journey. Journeys begin in dreams. However, they also take a sharp turn when a person crosses a threshold and enters a carriage. The thought of a trip stimulates ambivalent arousal because it is between departure and arrival that there is the possibility of an unexpected encounter. There can be sadness of leaving and joy in the discovery. Hence, we would prefer to begin our journey with some assurance. Kallat loathes taking travel insurance, but the artist does feel better when the departure point is solid. The passageways of the Ian Potter Museum of Art in which 'Circa' is installed are all framed by what appears at first sight as the gawky bamboo poles that are used as scaffolding in Indian construction sites. Upon closer inspection, these poles are revealed to be pigmented cast resin, and they are held together with steel and rope. The poles also contain elaborately sculpted images of various animals, such as monkeys, snakes and birds. In many instances, these creatures are either violently attacking each other or are in the process of devouring their tails. They conjure mythological scenes, and artists also discover that the reference point from which these images were derived is the sculpted facade of the entrance to the main terminus of the Mumbai railway. Kallat wonders how many of the millions of daily commuters notice this allusion to the precarious nature of their journey. Of course, they already know of what we are now belatedly representing.

Rides shadow or create lines. These lines are rarely decent. Streams zigzag amid the hard and even contours of the land. Roads can turn brusquely, and railway tracks diverge along a smooth arc. The irregular line is a motif that recurs in this installation. This skinny and sprawling line is a distinct feature of the colonial maps of India on display – the faded and crumpled paper providing an echo to the vain pretence of administrative permanence, the jagged line also appears in the drawings on the vitrines that contain ancient Indian sculptures –

generating an illusion of the glass having cracked from pressure. Is the object trying to seepage, or the world-shattering from visible tremors? Finally, the extensive line is announced in the subtle blows that surface in tendril-like movement along with the pristine plasterwork of the museum's entrance. These mysterious new cracks are titled *'Footnote' (mirror 1)*. They are made of acrylic mirrors. They have an alluring effect. They were portraying us into an unexpected and dark negated that interrupts the level and unbiased superficial of the museum. Infectious the sky and artificial light on its reflective surface, they also rebound towards another horizon. The darkness has no bottommost, and the view is blindingly open. A footnote is also a belated byline of what a person already knows. It touches back the origin of the journey of discovery that an audience has just completed.

The installation also includes another suite of sculptures that are interspersed across the museum's polished wooden floorboards. The sculptures are of sleeping dogs. Climbing out of their backs are the sprouts of wheat. Again, the object and its location are in severe tension. The dogs are life-size and life-like. They are more familiar as companions to the homeless than they are as occupants of the contemplative corners of a museum. The sprouting of wheat seeds from within the unfired clay volume of the sculpture is in itself an incredible experience. How does wheat live and grow from such dead matter?

Nevertheless, what is most pertinent about these sculptures that are collectively referred to as 'Prosody of a pulse rate', is their conception in a spherical state of repose. These dogs are in a state of suspension, between exhaustion and rejuvenation. Sleep is a kind of rebirth. The dogs have surrendered into the surface of the earth. We would prefer to imagine that the ground is dusty and warm, rather than shiny and hard. Nevertheless, they surrender their muscular frame to a soft womb-like shape and allow the dynamic tension of the daily trot between hither and thither to realign itself into a rhythmic pattern of in-and exhalation. The image of an animal asleep in the spherical union, once prefaced with a title that alerts us to the poetic techniques of harmony, also exposes us to another mystic sign: the function of breath in the cosmic soul.

Jitish Kallat's video *'Forensic Trail of a Grand Banquet'* reveals face to face . Single comprises a material of 700 diet stuff that have been X-rayed. The other screen revealed the footage in reverse. Natalie King has perceptively defined the consequence of viewing this work as pulling us into a "meteoric vortex". Jitish Kallat has conceptualised that the microscopic organisms, nebula, or underwater formations that one sees flying around a specific person, are an X-ray of food items like *samosas*, *kachoris*, corn, et al. moving upon the essential for nourishment, once again. The idea of the banquet uploaded into the cosmos is quite bizarre in itself. It's how an individual chooses to look at it. This gesticulation of high-quality perspective by the artist is also a profound expression of a conceptual understatement. On the different, similar all the entitlements that Jitish Kallat brands, this one is obvious by a considered quality. To not make a big thing of something or suggest the particular viewpoint is to admit an interplanetary that has a sovereignty that is beyond the artist's range. To minimise the situation or scope to which a viewer 'chooses to look' is both necessary protection and a franchise to an involvement that surpasses human thought. It carefully circumvents a strange equal of self-assurance. It also recognises the individual liberty of the spectator. But what kind of freedom do we have previously this image of the cosmos that is from beyond including inside the video of the most precise method of days? On an individual level, if we are in the middle of this double space, there is no alternative. Such a manner of decision-making has either already disappeared as it has been absorbed into the universal ether or other the faculty for argumentation has acknowledged that it has been demolished in the confrontation with the sublime. The vortex sucks in all parts and separates the most detailed levels of knowledge. The little portions of diet and the most macro-ecology of the globe become indistinguishable. The simulation of an individual by the other has been a meaning of enchantment that remains from the earliest cosmologies to the most recent attempts by physicists like Stephen Hawking. The images created by the ancient philosopher and the visualisations composed possible by contemporary scientists are united not just by the illusionistic perversions that are conceived achievable with the most complicated camera, but also by a steadfast belief that the geometric laws that regulate the sector with the complex are valid principles for learning the source of the cosmos and the electric tautness that nurtures life and death. The combination of a legal and spherical perspective is in the research opinion an assertion of a new and radical anthropocentric view of the cosmos. It looks into the subtlest of details regarding everyday things such as the food that generates life and not only finds an image of the universe but also demonstrates a companionship between humanity and the most extensive spheres of our environment. It is one thing to try and make sense of the mystery of cosmic infinity by staring into the most microscopic details and finding a form that makes the incomprehensible slightly more comprehensible. However, beyond this, the neat and comforting illusion is another level of recognition of responsibility. The energy that is out there is also in here. Food, intelligence and the cosmos may all have a standard form. The point of putting two video screens to face each other and for one screen to reverse the footage is not confined to a principle of doubling. It also invites the viewer to stand in the middle and bear witness to the circumambient flows.

The general contention that the principle of creativity is intricately interwoven with the affirmative ideas of cosmos. How could an individual ever prove this? Let the person start with this primary capacity for seeing, sensing and imagining the world. When someone appears out at the globe, there is the horizon. The terrestrial curves are absent because it is part of a sphere and the skies open like an unlimited shade. On no account, the phrase is anything like the whole ever noticeable. Only part of the superficial of the globe skins another, and at any point, the vast bulk is always beyond our range of vision. The world as a whole is still hidden from any direct view. An individual's eyes always look up as much as they look out and across. Looking up, a person gains a vertical view as the cone of vision extends to the infinite depth of the cosmic screen. This gaze exposes an individual too far more than he/she can understand. This glowing darkness and sparkling murkiness inspire both dreadful awe and uplifting wonder.

In Jitish Kallat's work, the research finds the anthropocentric act of projection. It commences in the cosmology of small symbols. It conjures the incredible indecision in the contour of any voyage, the outcome form in the life-sprouting rhythm of a dog's sleeping breath. Diogenes the Cynic, who famously rejected Alexander the Great's offer of wealth and power, and whose name comes from his ambition to live in a state that could match a dog's cosmic harmony, would be proud to have made such an understatement.

3.3.2 A Case Study of New Media Artworks of Jitish Kallat

'Untitled (Two Minutes to Midnight)' **(2018)**

'Untitled (Two Minutes to Midnight)' is a sculptural installation by Jitish Kallat which is a plinth dimension 27.4 feet x 11.5 feet x 1.8 feet, the material explores the dental plaster, mild steel supports (Plate 3.23). Kallat's *'Untitled (Two Minutes to Midnight)'* revealed together two carefully chosen pointers, one from the prehistoric past and the other pointing to a prophesied future. The suite of sculptures derives their form from Palaeolithic hand axes and stone tools that were the first human effort to alter the planet. In work the primary stone tools mark the dawn of human ingenuity, augmenting physical capacities before future exponential innovations lead to uninhibited human supremacy and

indiscriminate manipulation of the planet. Numerous clusters of reptilian and mammalian, fish and bird eyes imbue the oversized tools with uncanny sentience. Kallat places these enigmatic sculptures on a plinth that derives its form from the hands of the iconic 'Doomsday Clock'. The 'Doomsday Clock', has been maintained since 1947 by members of the bulletin of the Atomic Scientists' Science and Security Board, a congregation that includes several Nobel laureates. The symbolic clock represents a hypothetical human-made global catastrophe as "midnight", and the bulletin's opinion on how close the world is to a worldwide calamity as several "minutes" to midnight. Its original position in 1947 was seven minutes to midnight. Since then it has annually been set backwards and forward twenty-three times. As of January 2018, the clock is set at "two minutes to midnight", due to nuclear threats, climate change, bioterrorism, and artificial intelligence. Kallat's sculptural installation explores together cyphers that link past and future, dawn and midnight to induce a contemplation on the many urges of our present-day existence.

'Public Notice' (2003) (Plate 3.24)

For the first in what would be termed as the artist's 'Public Notice' series, Kallat revisited the famous speech made by Prime Minister Pandit Jawaharlal Nehru before the stroke of midnight on August 14, 1947, to commemorate India's Independence against the British. Often recalled as the "Tryst with Destiny" speech, the historic address spoke of India's awakening into freedom after centuries of colonialism. Kallat hand-rendered the iconic text using rubber adhesive on five large acrylic mirrors before setting them aflame, thereby incinerating the words and producing mangled reflections that changed about the viewer's position against the burnt glass. The 2003 piece was a political statement Kallat was making against the carnage of the Godhra Riots in February 2002. Kallat has said about the work that the words are cremated, much as the content of the speech itself was distorted by the way the nation has conducted itself in the last six decades.

'Public Notice 2' (2007)

Created in 2007, Kallat's 'Public Notice 2' (Plate 3.25) is a large-scale display of letters formed out of 4,479 pieces of fibreglass bones installed on shelves against a background of saturated turmeric yellow reproducing the 1000-word speech given by Mahatma Gandhi on March 11, 1930, at the Sabarmati Ashram by the banks of the River Sabarmati in Ahmedabad a day before he along with 78 of his followers began the historic Dandi March to protest against the British-imposed tax on salt during which the virtues of Non-

Violence were repeatedly insisted on by Gandhi. The work reveals that the act of rehearsing a text from modern history and meditating on its relevance today is charged with revisionary historicism. Kallat simultaneously places the text within its particular historical moment and reinvigorates it for present purposes. In Kallat's this work the first activity, that of the historical situation locates the text securely in the past; the second asks us to reconsider it to glean an insight into present difficulties and possibilities for the future. The work represents the evidence of the past, scientifically gathered, enumerated, classified and sorted into significant units.

'Public Notice 3' (2010)

In 2010 Kallat executed his large-scale site-specific LED installation, *'Public Notice 3'*(Plate 3.26), at the Art Institute of Chicago. This installation was Kallat's first major exhibition at a US institution. The artwork links two disparate yet connected historical events, the First World Parliaments of Religions, held on 11 September 1893, and the much later terrorist attacks on the World Trade Center and the Pentagon, on 11 September 2001. Kallat's 2004 work *'Detergent'* could be seen as the prototype for *'Public Notice 3'*, a text-based work in which Swami Vivekananda's speech was rendered in the same way as in *'Public Notice'*. Kallat's *'Detergent'* came 'home' when as *'Public Notice 3'* it opened on 11 September 2010, at the Art Institute of Chicago. Swami Vivekananda's evocative words calling for universal toleration and the end of bigotry and religious fanaticism were presented on the Woman's Board Grand Staircase, a space approximating the stages of the two temporary halls in which he initially spoke: the Hall of Columbus, where he's opening address had been delivered; and the Hall of Washington-an area now primarily occupied by the museum's Ryerson Library-where Vivekananda spoke on other occasions during the World's Parliament of Religions.

The context of the work is September 11 but refers primarily to the meaning of 2001 being seen as a palimpsest overlaid on to the moment of September 1893, which was the first parliament of religions. The first attempt to create to sort of global confluence of faiths is classified a leap of imaginations which to the artist's mind seems to like an etoposide to locate possible future conflict within not nations but trust because this before the world was nation anxiety between each other and the whole colonial moment an so in a sense seen through the lens of September 11; 1893, 2001 could be a revisited with some different overlap themes and the primary Philmont that connects them is the primary speech that Swami Vivekananda- a religious leader from India delivered the opening in the moment of the parliament in the very sight where the museum stands today. The building was with the parliament place and then evacuated space came to the museum within the structure. In a sense '*Public Notice 3*' is a confluence of date and sight and over lake context and the artist progressed the work on the field notes 'tomorrow was yesterday' these notions of time and date that over lake tomorrow becoming yesterday and yesterday becoming tomorrow. The interplay of past, future and present as an individual can point out interestingly with natures notion of eternal recurrence which Kallat find fascinating and seems like the closest kind of parameter to look at what the artist looks within a space to visit a space's vigilance with historical past but also a space has gone through several layers of reincarnation.

The prehistory of the museum was very interesting for the artist—the year of the mutiny when the first museum opened not in space but another sight. But also the recent reinnervation of the museum undertaken in a way that it is unprecedented in India and is entirely dead space come alive and reincarnate and become accessible to the public again and that short story of rebirth the artist could find several concepts in an area which is otherwise very lush with imagery, context history, right from the cabinet of communities to the cabinet of cartography to the history of city street to artisan skills and all of these became area to work of concept to Kallat.

'*Covering Letter*' (2012)

'*Covering Letter*' is a video installation by Jitish Kallat, which is fog screen projection with dimensions variable (Plate 3.27). '*Covering Letter*' is the reiteration of an incredible work of historical correspondence. The video-installation reveals the brief letter written by Mahatma Gandhi to Adolf Hitler a few weeks before Germany invaded Poland, setting off the Second World War. In this letter, Gandhi makes an urgent appeal for peace, anticipating the depths of human savagery that the impending world war would unleash.

The work explored Gandhi, who is the pacifist and truth seeker begins Gandhi's note with "Dear Friend," addressing one of the most violent and deluded individuals ever to walk the earth. As the words ascend along with a video of descending mist, the audiences can walk through it, simultaneously inhabiting and dissipating the moving text. To Kallat, Gandhi's request to Hitler is an open letter which speaks as much to the present as to the past; a 'covering letter' to an endless resume of human violence.

The concept that exists in the '*Covering Letter*', Kallat conceptualised the video installation essentially is a dark room where the indignation itself becomes a piece of correspondence as the shaft of light interacts with the descending film of mist and mostly it is within this relationship with this light through which the alphabets, the letters which necessarily the absence of life. The work reveals the shadow of letters, the role on the floor towards an individual as an individual confronts the work peers in reverse and at the bottom of the video of mist. The work is relatively eligible and continues to gain eligibility as the letters rise within this video of discerning news. At some points it becomes evident that these collective letters, the alphabets, form a piece of correspondence written in the first person. So when an audience walks in, finds 'Dear friend' in work makes an individual very distilled seven-line plea to rethink what you might do with the world as stated in the letter save the world going to several countries. When the message rise sufficiently that an individual can realise the author of the word was Gandhi, and the intended recipient was Hitler, written at a moment when it was a crucial moment in world's history because it was a five weeks before the outbreak of the World War II and perhaps weeks before the concentration camps which until then really labour camps which extremes mortality rates was soon to become chambers of death. It was this kind of eminent moment, and yet the letters itself is almost like a Gandhian gesture and feels like the letter is meant to convey a fright of provocations not just to the intended recipient on a particular date but perhaps go beyond its delivery date and intended recipient to speak to any time, anywhere, and it is in that location that a covering letter the artist explored which is out today to any person who might inhabit the space of the message and also travel through walk to the letter, momentarily occupying the space of correspondence between possibly one of the greatest proponents of peace writing to one of the most brutal proletariats of this world that ever habitat this planet that point in time. The artist conceptualised that the location of the body between these two figures, these absent figures through the piece of correspondence, is the space of self-reflect that is revealed in the '*Covering Letter*'. The way the letter came to the artist was, of course, the interaction of the actual letter which hangs in the corner of the small beautiful Gandhi Museum in Bombay. The letter remained with the artist someway in the artist's mind in a long period but the way it explores as '*Covering Letter*' in the artist's concept is the mind is a video that anyone could occupy the momentarily and also could absorb these alphabets on their bodies when the audience leaves through interacting with the artwork. This is the image. But over time when the artist realise that it is capable with the relationship the cleansing images of mist but also the freight of historical experience of this descending wrapper that could be read in many ways and that's something emerge from the viewing of the works and others have experienced the work to people of had powerful visual experience of inhabiting the letter long with the history and through the work the research analyses that Kallat has experienced a lot of times into his work that images form in the making of the work. They didn't develop in the conception of the work, and this is being another experience to dimension the work.

'*Covering Letter (terranum nuncius)*' (2019)

In the Frist Art Museum of Nashville Kallat reveal his solo exhibition where the artist brings together two distinctly different types of communication entitled '*Covering Letter (terranum nuncius)*' (Plate 3.28) alongside Kallat's widely exhibited '*Covering Letter*' (2012) that collectively provoke a reflection on our world. The sound and video installation expressed and re-invoked excellent sound and images that were composed for an expedition into interstellar space as a planetary message to extraterrestrial life. Kallat executes from the Golden record hoisted onto the legendary Voyager 1 and 2 space probes launched by NASA in 1977. At present situated across 13 billion miles away from the planet Earth, the contents of this "time capsule" were gathered for NASA by a committee chaired by Carl Sagan. It is supposed to continue its cosmic journey well beyond the probable extinction of our species and our planet. In this work, Kallat executed the sound of greetings to the universe in 55 languages in a large round table with over a hundred backlit 3-D photographic transparencies placed on it. To place /execute the work in this manner, Kallat has referenced the images decoded by Ron Barry, who is a U.S based software engineer. Forty years later the images were first uploaded onto the Golden Record as sound files; Barry has covered the audio clips back to images as if the work were accessed by an extraterrestrial who would have to follow a similar procedure to view the images. In the work the images range from scientific to cosmological diagrams, representations of our genetic makeup and anatomy, as well as other life forms, architecture et al. frequently explained with dimensions, this is a significant portrayal of our world to an exotic other. At a time when we find personally in a deeply divided society, Kallat foregrounds these sounds and images for a collective meditation on ourselves as united residents of a single planet, where the "other" is an unknown "intergalactic alien." Also part of the installation is a bench that takes the shape of the hands of the doomsday Clock. This symbolic clock, presented annually by the bulletin of Atomic Scientists represents a hypothetical human-made global catastrophe as midnight, and the proximity of the world to the apocalypse as several minutes to midnight (Gupta, 2020).

3.4 Conclusion

Through the chapter *"The Legitimised Narratives and the Web of Traffic: The Artworks of Nalini Malani and Jitish Kallat "*, the research observed, identified and tried to find out the conceptual perspectives of the New Media Art practices by the Nalini Malani and Jitish Kallat. The research chapter analyses that the subject matters of Malani's art practices emphasise on the several episodes of Indian Hindu Mythology as well as the episodes of Greek Mythology. In her New Media Art practise the study finds that the subject matters that Malani explores the upper- middle-class Indian home. In Malani's subject matters, different prominent socio-political crises and conflicts that had faced the country India and also overseas, also a matter of concern through the artist's visual forms.

After her academic study days, Malani was interested in modernism and how it was manifested in India. The ideal reflected in the artist's work is that an individual is a famous person, from where he/she comes from, what is an individual's own identity. The artist tries to explore the modernist approach into her art practice. With the changing of times, Malani's works also reveal conceptual aspects of the country's situation such as in the transitional phases in the 1990s where the country wants to turn, whether remaining as socialist or moving towards the capitalist ways. The New Media Art practices of Malani reveals the different narratives through the artist's subject matters.

The research study analyses the artist Jitish Kallat through his New Media Art practices. The artist's works represent the prominent historical stories and episodes that have some dialogues with this planet. The artist's works also reveal a cascade of images, which begin to appear like self-similar images. Kallat very philosophically perceives his thought process, which shows the artist's body of works where there is a conceptual connection to work with an object. The executed works by Kallat also reveal the shift of identity through choosing an image to open to the public. The working aspect of Kallat also portrays the spaces of a progressive society, hidden historical stories where the research study finds a web of traffic in the artist's video installations.

PLATES

Plate 3.1 : Jitish Kallat . *Dawn Chorus -7 (+ 2 others, bronze sculptures ; 3 works)* . 2007 . Acrylic on Canvas with Bronze Sculptures . Courtesy : Artnet . Web . 21 February . 2019

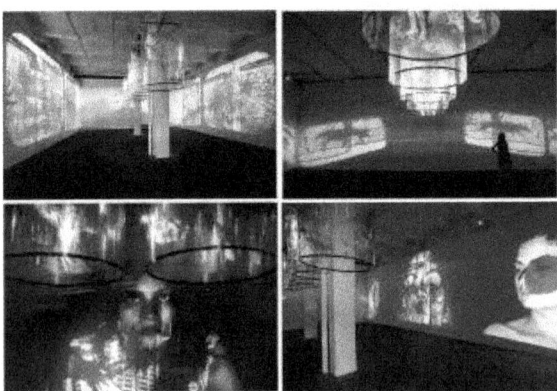

Plate 3.2 : Nalini Malani . *In Search of Vanished Blood* (detail) . 2012 . Video Installation . Courtesy : artsy.net . Web . 21 February . 2019

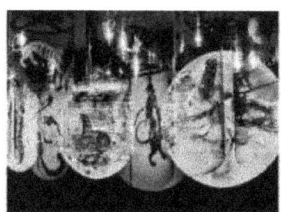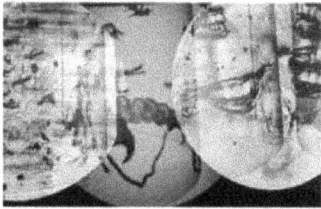

Plate 3.3 : Nalini Malani. *Remembering Mad Meg* (detail). 2007. Video Shadow Play, two single Channel Animations. Courtesy : artsy.net. Web. 21 February. 2019

Plate 3.4 : Nalini Malani. *Mother India : Transactions in construction of Pain* (detail). 2005. Video Installation. Courtesy : Kiran Nadar Museum of Art. Web. 22 February. 2019

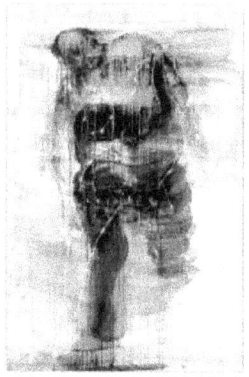

Plate 3.5 : Nalini Malani. *Mutant* (detail). 1994-1996. Black and White dye painted on milk carbon paper. Courtesy : Nalini Malani. Web. 22 February. 2019

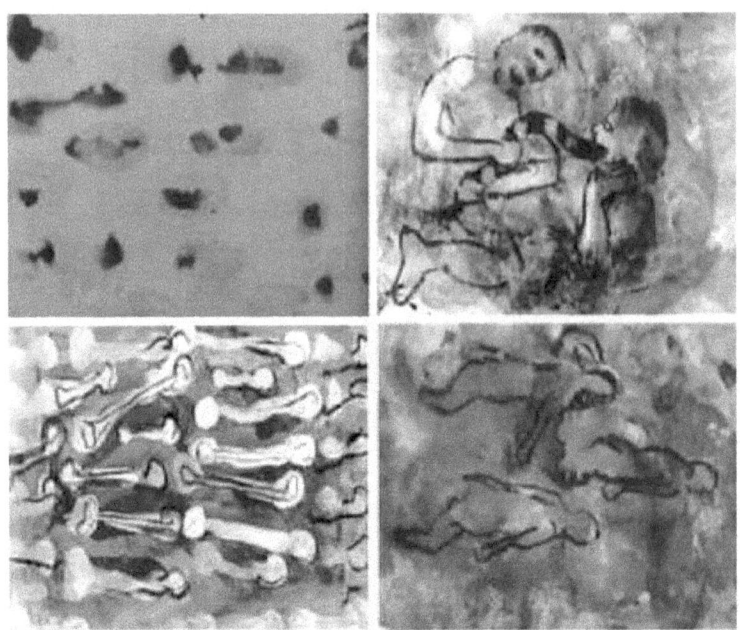

Plate 3 . 6 : Nalini Malani . *Stains* (detail) . 2000 . Animation Video Installation .
Courtesy : Nalini Malani . Web . 22 February . 2019

Plate 3 . 7 : Nalini Malani . *Gamepieces* (detail) . 2003 . Video / Shadow Play .
Courtesy : Nalini Malani . Web . 22 February . 2019

Plate 3.8 : Nalini Malani . *Unity in Diversity* (detail) . 2003 . Video Installation .
Courtesy : Nalini Malani . Web . 22 February . 2019

Plate 3.9 : Nalini Malani . *Transgression* (detail) . 2001 . Video - Shadow Play .
Courtesy : Nalini Malani . Web . 22 February . 2019

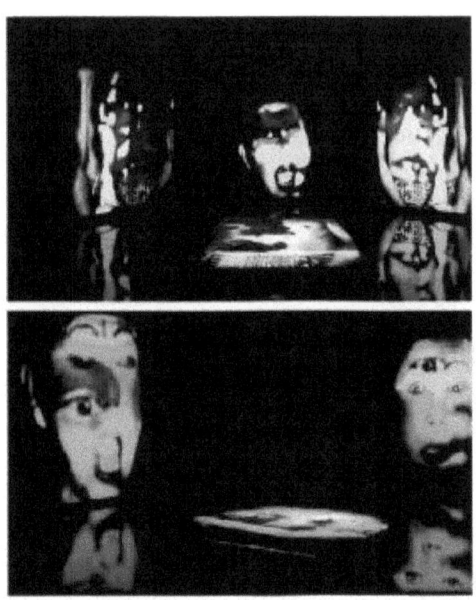

Plate 3 . 10 : Nalini Malani . *Hamletmachine* (detail) . 1999-2000 .
Video Installation . Courtesy : Nalini Malani . Web . 22 February . 2019

Plate 3 . 11 : Nalini Malani . *Remembering Toba Tek Singh* (detail) . 1998-99 .
Video Installation . Courtesy : Nalini Malani . Web . 22 February . 2019

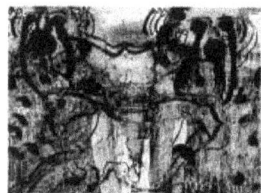  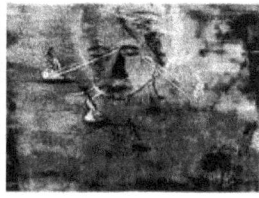

Plate 3 . 12 : Nalini Malani . *Memory : Record / Erase* (detail) . 1996 . Animation Video .
Courtesy : Nalini Malani . Web . 22 February . 2019

 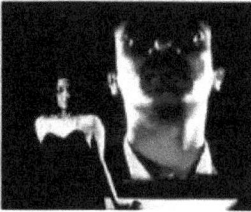 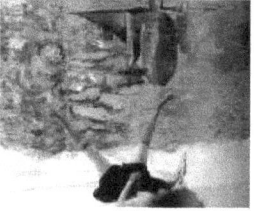

Plate 3 . 13 : Nalini Malani . *Medea video* (detail) . 1991 -1996 . Video Installation .
Courtesy : Nalini Malani . Web . 22 February . 2019

Plate 3 . 14 : Nalini Malani . *Now I See It Now I Don't* (detail) . 2018 . Video Installation .
Courtesy : livemint.com . Web . 22 February . 2019

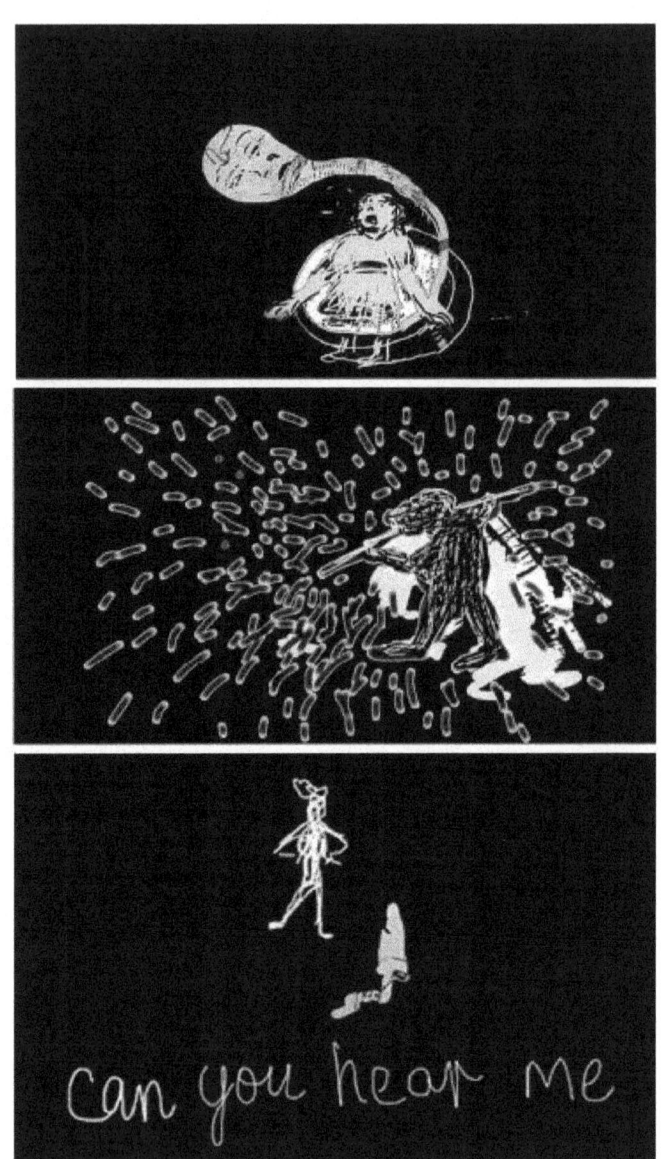

Plate 3.15: Nalini Malani. *Can You Hear Me ?* (detail). 2018/2019.
11 projections with more than 50 video animations.
Courtesy: sellevents.online. Web. 22 February. 2019

Plate 3 . 16 : Jitish Kallat . *P.T.O.* . 1997 . catalogue cover.
Courtesy : Gallery Chemould . Web . 22 February . 2019

Plate 3 . 17 : Jitish Kallat . *Random Access Memory* (detail) . 2000 .
108 works on exposed thermal fax paper , applying heat , water and pigments .
Courtesy : 7th Havana Biennial . Web . February 22 . 2019

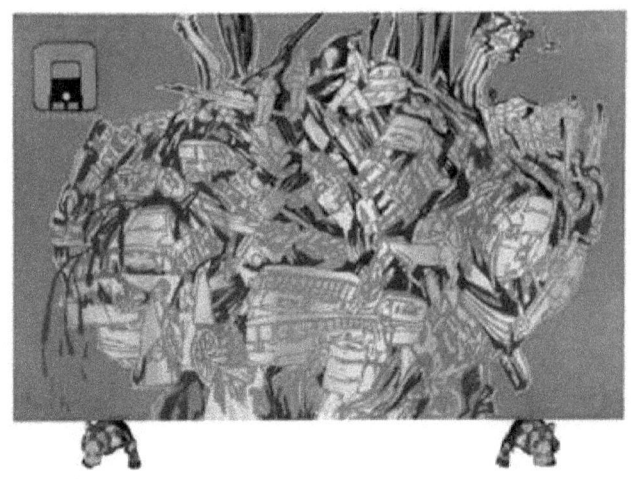

Plate 3.18 : Jitish Kallat . *Rickshawpolis 3* . 2006 . Acrylic on Canvas .
Courtesy : Sastchi Galley . Web . 22 February . 2019

Plate 3.19 : Jitish Kallat . *Artist Making Local Call* (detail) . Digital Print .
Courtesy : naturemorte.com . Web . 22 February . 2019

Plate 3.20 : Jitish Kallat. *Canis Familiaris / A Dog's Life*. 1999.
Acrylic on Canvas. Courtesy : Jitish Kallat. Web. 22 February. 2019

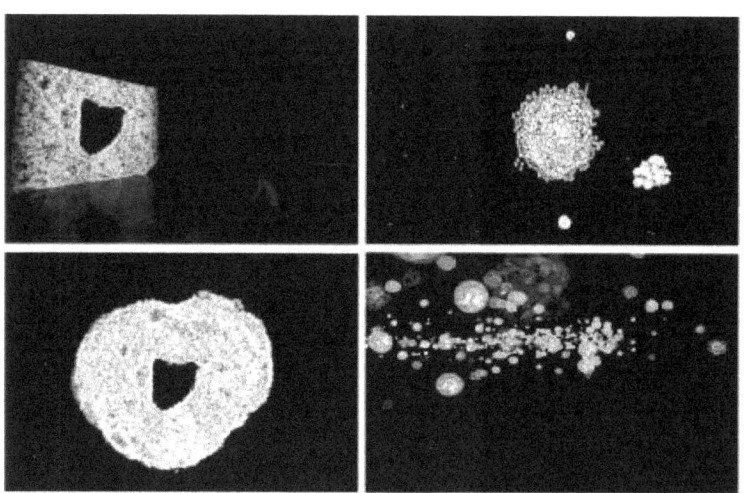

Plate 3.21 : Jitish Kallat. *Forensic Trail of the Grand Banquet* (detail). 2009.
Video Projection. Courtesy : Jitish Kallat. Web. 22 February. 2019

Plate 3.22 : Jitish Kallat. *Epilogue* (detail). 2010-11.
Pigment print on archival paper.
Courtesy : Jitish Kallat. Web. 22 February. 2019

Plate 3.23 : Jitish Kallat. *Untitled (Two Minutes to Midnight)* (detail). 2018.
Sculptural Installation.
Courtesy : Jitish Kallat. Web. 22 February. 2019

Plate 3 . 24 : Jitish Kallat . *Public Notice* (detail) . 2003 .
Burnt adhesive on acrylic mirror, wood , stainless steel .
Courtesy : Jitish Kallat . Web . 22 February . 2019

Plate 3 . 25 : Jitish Kallat . *Public Notice 2* (detail) . 2007 . Resin, 4479 sculptural units .
Courtesy : Jitish Kallat . Web . 22 February . 2019

Plate 3 . 26 : Jitish Kallat . *Public Notice 3* (detail) . 2010 . LED bulbs , wires , rubber .
Courtesy : Jitish Kallat . Web . 22 February . 2019

Plate 3 . 27 : Jitish Kallat . *Covering Letter* (detail) .
2012 . Fogscreen Projection .
Courtesy : Jitish Kallat . Web . 22 February . 2019

Plate 3 . 28 : Jitish Kallat . *Covering Letter (Terranum Nuncius)* (detail) . 2019. Installation . Courtesy : Chemould Prescott Road. Web . 1 January . 2020.

References

Bal, Mieke. *In Medias Res: Inside Nalini Malani's Shadow Plays*. Berlin, Hatje Cantz, 2016.

Bal, Mieke, and Nalini Malani. *In Medias Res: Inside Nalini Malani's Shadow Plays*. Ostfildern, Hatje Cantz, 2016.

Betting, Lotte. *Nalini Malani: You Can't Keep Acid In A Paper Bag, 1969-2014*. New Delhi, Kiran Nadar Museum Of Art, 2015.

Chadwick, Whitney, et al. *Nalini Malani - Splitting the Other Retrospective 1992- 2009; DVD Installations, Video Works, and Performances; [in Conjunction with the Exhibition Nalini Malani - Splitting the Other. Retrospective 1992- 2009, Musée Cantonal Des Beaux-Arts/Lausanne, March 20 - June 6, 2010]*. Ostfildern, Germany Hatje Cantz, 2010.

Christov-Bakargiev, Carolyn , et al. *Nalini Malani: In Search of Vanished Blood*. New York, Distributed Art Pub Incorporated, 2012.

Das, Veena. *Life and Words: Violence and the Descent into the Ordinary*.
   Berkeley, University of California Press, 2006.

David, Catherine . *Here After Here:1992 – 2017*. Delhi, National Gallery of Modern Art, 2017.

Desai, Amita, and Kamala Kapoor. *Nalini Malani: Medeaprojekt*. Bombay, Max Mueller Bhavan, 1997.

Ghose , Madhuvanti . *Public Notice 3*. Art Institute of Chicago, 2011. Chicago

Ginwala , Natasha . *Jitish Kallat* . Mapin Publishing, 2018. Ahmedabad

Hoskote , Ranjit. *Jitish Kallat: Fieldnotes: tomorrow was here yesterday* . Lad Museum Trust, Mumbai, 2018. Mumbai

Hoskote , Ranjit . *P.T.O.* Mumbai, Gallery Chemould and Prithvi Gallery, 1997.

Jitish Kallat: Covering Letter. Philadelphia, Philadelphia Museum of Art, 2016

"Jitish Kallat | Artnet." *Www.Artnet.Com, www.artnet.com/artists/jitish-kallat/.*
   Accessed 8 Jan. 2019.

Kapoor , Kamala and Desal Amita . *Nalini Malani: Medeaprojekt* . Bombay, Max Mueller Bhavan Bombay ,1997.

Kissane, Sean and Pinapp, Johan. *Nalini Malani. Catalogo Della Mostra (Dublino, 11 Luglio-14 Ottobre 2007). Ediz. Inglese* . Charta, Irish Museum of Modern Art , 2007 .

Malani, Nalini, and Robert Storr. *Nalini Malani: Listening to the Shades*. Milano, Charta Books, 2008.

Malani, Nalini. *Nalini Malani: Centre de La Gravure et de l'Image Imprimée, La Louvière*. La Louvière, Belgum, Centre De La Gravure Et Dl'image Imprimée, 2013.

Nalini Malani: In Search of Vanished Blood; [on the Occasion of the Exhibition DOCUMENTA (13), 9.6. - 16.9.2012, Kassel]. Ostfildern, Hatje Cantz, 2012.

Merali., Shaheen. *Jitish Kallat: Public Notice– 2* . Bodhi Art, 2008. Singapore

"Nalini Malani." Www.*Nalinimalani.Com, www.nalinimalani.com/*. Accessed 11 Mar. 2019.

"Nalini Malani - You Can't Keep Acid in a Paper Bag, 1969-2014 (2015) | Kiran Nadar Museum of Art." Knma.In, 2014, www.knma.in/nalini-malani-you-can%E2%80%99t-keep-acid-paper-bag-1969-2014-2015. Accessed 11 Mar. 2019.

Nath , Deeksha . *Jitish Kallat: Aquasaurus* . Sydney, Sherman Contemporary Art Foundation, 2005.

Kayser Via, Christine . *Nalini Malani, a Global Storyteller* . Romania ,Studies in Visual Arts and Communication: an international journal , 2015.

Obrist , Ulrich Hans. *The 30-Year Artistic Journey Of Jitish Kallat From Paintings To Installations To 3D Sculptures*. Scroll.in, 2019.

Papastergiadis, Nikos. *The Cosmopolis is the Starting Point*. South as a state of mind Art Culture Publication.

Shahane , Girish . *Jitish Kallat: Unclaimed Baggage* . London, Albion Gallery, 2007.

Sherman, Brian , et al. *Jitish Kallat: Public Notice 2* .Sydney,Sherman Contemporary Art Foundation & the Art Gallery of New South Wales, 2015.

Storr , Robert . *Nalini Malani: listening to the shades* . Charta, the University of California, 2008 .

"The Ghent Altarpiece: Adoration of the Mystic Lamb - Hubert and Jan Van Eyck - Google Arts & Culture." *Google Arts & Culture*, Google Arts & Culture, 2009, artsandculture.google.com/asset/the-ghent-altarpiece-adoration-of-the-mystic-lamb/6gE6DlMZF-OvSQ. Accessed 8 Jan. 2019.

CHAPTER- IV

THE 'THIRD OBJECT'/ URBAN SIGNS AND THE VULNERABLE BODY: NEW MEDIA ARTWORKS OF RANBIR KALEKA AND SUREKHA

4.1 Introduction

The media, the visual dialogue and its language are evocative of the way we live. India and its Visual Art have gone through a sea change in the last decade. This is as impressive as it is daunting. The artists behind the lens compel us to see ourselves as we are.

In the rich and complex history of video art/ video installation, Indian artists who work with video as a medium, practise their works as essential tools to establish their politico-cultural visions and critique. Ranbir Kaleka is one of those Indian artists who has used video as a medium not only to extend the ideas that artist deals within his paintings and video installations but also create a new visual interaction that could cut across the boundaries. The study of research analyses that through his body of video installation works, Ranbir Kaleka developed a unique technique in the 1990s and has been experimenting with the same for over three decades. The artist projects a video on painted canvas such that the painting 'moves', allowing for a narrative to develop, rendering the work a layered meaning. The physical attributes of painting, like weight and texture, and the accumulation of colour pigment, represent the work stability and permanence.

On the other hand, video—which has a spatial element as an image made of light—has opposite characteristics of being intangible, fleeting, and temporary. By mixing the two different mediums, the artist amplifies the inherent nature of each medium, at times layering or overlapping them, and forging a new image. By overlaying two different notions of time—the 'still' time in painting and 'transforming' time in the video—the artist devises ways of knowing and meaning- making. The essential focus in Kaleka's work is not just his unique methodology in working with video and painting, but the narrative of the work, which usually focuses on daily issues that arise across India.

Surekha is one of the well-known Indian artists who is a Bangalore-based, and her art practise includes video, photography, sculpture, documentary, digital and performance-based works centre mainly on the body within its gendered, political and historical context. The study of the research analyses that Surekha's *The Boiling Concept* and *The Burning Concept* (2006) reveal mental and moral qualities distinctive to an individual performed by the artist herself, abstracted from narratives uncovered in her research on unnatural deaths and domestic violence inflicted upon women throughout history in the city of Bangalore (Hazra , 2011).

In Surekha's New Media Art practice, the executing of restriction, veiling and silencing are taken up in more direct ways into the artist's work *Line of Control* (2003), *Between Fire and Sky* (2006) and *Three Fragmented Actions of Silence* (2007), which plays on the concept of veiling through positive and negative video visions and overlays of colour and external footage.

The artist's documentary works *Un-Claimed* (2010), and *Romeos & Juliets* (2010) executed at a sensory threshold space between artistic and everyday activities, accomplish an aesthetic observation of the rituals of burial and community involvements through speedups and slowdowns, muting and repetition while maintaining an intensified sense of their social significance (Hazra, 2011).

4.2 Video Installation of Ranbir Kaleka

Kaleka was born in 1953, in Patiala, in a Punjabi family. The artist is educated in art at College of Art, Punjab University in Chandigarh, he moved to London in 1985, where he completed his M.A in Painting at the Royal College of Art, London Charles Wallace Scholarship. Kaleka stayed in England till his final return to Delhi in the late 1990s. During that period, the artist also participated in the 'Contemporary Indian Art' showcase at the Royal Academy of Art, London during the festival of India. Kaleka's works were exhibited and taken from New Delhi to Los Angeles. It may be specified that this diversity of exhibitions of Kaleka's art practice will give the artist a recognition which may enable Kaleka as one of the most significant artists of the twenty-first century in India. The artist at present lives and works in New Delhi, India (Mukherjee, 2017).

The artist projects video on painted canvases. He superimposes the image of the same object or person already painted on the canvas. The superimposed is moving imagery, while that in the painting is static. The calculated movements, focal points, and theatrically take the viewer through a different experience of 'viewership'- an experience of surprise, bewilderment and psychological movements. Kaleka's narratives broaden the definition of the genre. While a viewer tries to find the artist's meanings, she/he is soon engaged in forming conjectural interpretations. A sense of unease and psychological unrest penetrates as one moves from one work to the other in the gallery, although each work stands individually. What is interesting to note, is the emphasis on actions, events and expressions that reflects on human nature, like - feelings of desperation, patience, change, dual and plural nature of thoughts and actions, desire, escapism, human struggles, memory and the gamut of the complex of human thoughts. The skill with which these expressions are executed in the paintings and videos are remarkable. The looped videos defy the notions of time, space, beginning and end.

In the New Media practices of Ranbir Kaleka the selection, sequence and placement of the works gave an understanding of the artist's practice over the years. The viewer engages with Kaleka's works that were perceptible, at the same time, loaded with possibilities of multiple interpretations.

4.2.1 The Artistic Journey of Ranbir Kaleka: Transforming from Painting to Video Installation

With over three decades of New Media Art practice, Kaleka is one of the most prominent representative artists of the Indian contemporary art world. In the artist's practice; combining painting and video, Kaleka's works have achieved significant international saliency during the last decade. Across the three decades of his artistic movement, Kaleka has formed both a remarkable body of paintings, vibrant with phantasmagoria and significant unrest, as well as a frame of trans-media works that combine conceptualist sophistication with a standardised opulence of image. The artist's works have been exhibited in various parts of the globe such as in museums, biennials, foundation and gallery contexts in Venice, Berlin, Lisbon, Vienna, New York, Mexico City and Sydney, among other centres (Kaleka, 2019).

In the late 1990s, Kaleka began experimenting with video and painting. Many contemporary artists have dabbled with technology after painting for years, but Kaleka took his experiments beyond the usual and the predictable. Not merely blending the two mediums or taking inspiration from one for the other, his works locate and focus on the print of the interaction of the two mediums, where painting and video intervene and synchronise with each other to create a narrative.

In the year 2019 in April, the researcher of the study visited the Kaleka's studio cum residence at SarvapriyaVihar, New Delhi to collect the primary source of data and also interviewed in a detailed manner about the artistic journey of Ranbir Kaleka. During the interaction between the artist and the researcher, the researcher asked about Kaleka's life and experiences as a visual artist, Kaleka very precisely discussed his body of works and then went through with the interaction that Kaleka started from his childhood memories from where the art practice came into Kaleka's life. The chapter analyses that Kaleka in his very early childhood grew up in a haveli. It was the feeling of a few people in a large haveli. The artist's father, mother, and two uncles, brother and himself lived together. In front of all of them, the family didn't talk about the violence of Punjab of that time outside the Haveli. In this presence, Kaleka's experiences of Haveli were also womb-like. All the artist's sensations became very strong in terms of his relationship with the outside world, Kaleka was living in a state of comfort that the artist within himself always felt that he could investigate more and would never be hurt.

The study of the research finds that it was actually where a work of art does come from Kaleka's childhood. In Kaleka's opinion, art practice comes from lived life, from what impacts an individual. In Kaleka's life, art takes its vibes from art history, cinema, literature, poetry, theatre or even stories told by people. This chapter analyses that Kaleka doesn't reflect there ever really were grand old times. That's why in some excellent literature and works of art, the involvement of darkness has been a significant source. It also appears from the possibility of reclamation, because one can't live utterly with dimness, and, if an individual could, one wouldn't be self- reflective when creating art (Kalra, 2019). In the interview between the researcher for this study of research and the artist, Kaleka highlighted about one episode of his life that the artist remember that when as a student in London, one of the artist's professors was looking at an oil painting of a hellscape by another student and the professor asked the student if his painted image scared him, and said that if it didn't, it was senseless to paint it. So, the fear has to happen to an individual. The desire to do the work has to come from within the artist (Kalra, 2019).

The first art practice came into Kaleka's life in a way that during his childhood there was a lot of coal in the house of Kaleka's for fuel and the artist would use coal to draw on walls and floors (Kalra, 2019). Kaleka has continuously practised painting and drawing from a very early age of his life, maybe almost about the age of three years, but without directions from somebody. There was a lot of coal around in the haveli where the artist grew up, which was used for firewood. With it, Kaleka drew things that he saw in the haveli — tractors, bicycles, animals, dancing women, et al. around the house and everybody seemed to appreciate that (Sarkar, 2014). Observing this; Kaleka's father used to say that when Kaleka grew up, the child artist's father sent him to an art school. And that was it. Kaleka hasn't stopped drawing and painting ever since. The artist used to bring a lot of donkeys. Kaleka's family owned a brick kiln, and his uncle would take Kaleka there. The artist would observe the donkeys stand in line, wait for their crossing and carry off pouches of clay bricks. They knew where to hold for unloading before returning for the next load (Kalra, 2019). The artist's uncle once commented on how intelligent they were, how they helped build towns and cities that became great civilisations. The interview of this chapter analyses that to Kaleka, they seemed to be mistreated. In a few of the artist's works, the study can observe that the disconnected head of a donkey which bleeds every time some cleared unguarded target falls to random but insidiously fired arrows (Kalra, 2019). Kaleka is working on another mechanised sculptural work with the donkey as a protagonist.

This chapter analyses that Kaleka takes a long time to execute a work of art and finds the fact that this thinking process as a result of his childhood when the artist had ample time to contemplate. The conversation between the researcher and the artist, Kaleka, interacted in a way that as a child, the artist hardly stepped out of the haveli. Kaleka had a small family in his childhood— the artist's parents, brother, grandmother and two uncles — but it at no time felt that time was strained. Kaleka never felt uninterested. An Individual can think of it as 'slow time', but it is a time that allows for contemplation. Even as a student of art, Kaleka would take up to a year to finish work (Kalra, 2019). For the artist, it is about getting it right. The artist doesn't have to do many works; it's fulfilling when the work gets closer to how the artist wants it to be. Kaleka works with a lot of preliminary material — sketches, research and reference material — and, in his video installation and digital works, Kaleka does not start until the artist finds the right people to be his protagonists in the subject matters of Kaleka's artwork.

The study of further research analyses that the artist started to think of combining painting and video in the late eighties but the first work of video implementing with a painting entitled '*Man Threading A Needle*' explored in

1998. Regarding that, the artist interacted with the researcher that Kaleka was genuinely interested in looking at paintings, and the artist could spend hours with a single work of the masters. Similarly, Kaleka was fascinated by cinema. The artist wanted to combine both and yet keep them separate. Kaleka wanted to play with how time sits in both painting and video. Combining the two allowed the artist to work with the extensive — the corporal foundation of a painting — and the imaginary — cinematic image, made of light. Video allowed the artist to disrupt the surround of the canvas; the figures could accurately move out of the arena of painting and onto the wall. There was an immense tonal range that Kaleka could have as his palette, from the darkness of the painted pigment to the white brilliance of the video projection. The artist showed '*Man Threading A Needle*' at the British Council (Kalra, 2019). By then, Kaleka was so vibrant about the medium that making it was effortless. When one speaks of some art that 'this looks difficult', it means that a specific individual needs to be longer with it. He/she has to reach a state of ease with the medium (Kaleka, 2019).

4.2.2 Ranbir Kaleka's Video Art Practice: Exploration Through Co-founded Film Society

The study of research also analyses that Kaleka had co-founded '*Patiala Film Society*' in the seventies of the twentieth century. The artist interacted with the researcher about that in a way that Kaleka was about twenty-three in age then. The artist had just completed his graduation from Chandigarh and was teaching art at the Patiala Women's College. A few of the artist's friends and Kaleka decided to screen films. The artist and his friends had a small projector and were registered on the circuit of the '*Indian Film Society*'. One of the artist's groups would move to the embassies in Delhi to collect/ receive films. It isn't effortless to explain precisely how that exposure impacted Kaleka's work, but movies and literature do rewire the artist's art practice process (Kalra, 2019). Kaleka highlighted that the artist's video practice comes less from the history of video and more from the history of cinema.

4.2.3 Ranbir Kaleka as Activist in Theatre and the Artist's Days During Teaching in College of Art, New Delhi

The artist was also active in the theatre and did his teaching even in the College of Art, New Delhi. With the researcher of the study, the artist discussed that the years were like there people Kaleka knew who were doing theatre. Kaleka devised annual theatrical performances in his school in Patiala. The five years (1980-85) the artist taught in Delhi were incredibly fulfilling. Kaleka had several older friends such as Krishen Khanna and J Swaminathan who would drop in to look at the artist's work. VS Gaitonde was a neighbour of Kaleka at that time. Vivan Sundaram along with the Baroda artists as well as other Bombay artists were friends of the artist during that time, most of them because of the Kasauli artist camps organised by Vivan, where the whole lot from cinema, theatre, literature to music was discussed (Kalra, 2019). Manjit Bawa was also a close friend to Kaleka. Tyeb Mehta was very inspiring to the artist during those days. This is also the period when (Sufi singer) Madan Gopal Singh introduced Kaleka to (filmmaker) Mani Kaul, and the three of them would often meet (Kalra, 2019). The artist interacted with the researcher of this research study during the interview that Kaleka feels that people don't meet each other much these days. The artist remembered that he was still in Patiala at that time when the artist had written a few scripts that he shared with Kumar Shahani. Shahani asked Kaleka to send the texts to Akbar Padamsee, who had been working with video art at that time. When Kaleka did the same, Padamsee asked the artist to come to Mumbai. Kaleka interacted that he never went, but both Kaleka and Padamsee interacted regarding this later. Kaleka also discusses that a few days ago, he heard from Padamsee that while archiving his works, Padamsee found a letter that Kaleka had written in the late seventies (Kaleka, 2019).

4.2.4 Execution of Monochrome into Kaleka's Video Installation: An Analysis

The research study analyses that a lot of Kaleka's work is explored and executed in monochrome. Regarding that, the artist expressed with the researcher that (Henri) Matisse had said that drawing is our observation of the surroundings and colour is an emotive rejoinder to it (Kaleka, 2019), which means it can emotionally take an individual somewhere a specific individual did not want to go (Kalra, 2019). Kaleka said that he does not use colour unless it is necessary, not only in painting but also in the artist's sculptural and video works. Though, when Kaleka went to England, all the paintings became very colourful for some time. The artist was interested in kitsch, and so Kaleka pushed the colours to the edge before they became too loud to bear.

4.2.5 Narratives into Ranbir Kaleka's Video Installation

The study of the research analyses that storytelling is a critical aspect underlying all of Kaleka's artworks. The artist grew up with stories. The research studies discovered that when Kaleka was very young, the artist's family were living in the big *haveli* in the village of Patiala, and there wasn't very much to do. So even the tiniest of things would engage Kaleka a lot, which is something that continues until today (Sarkar, 2014). The artist tends to focus on one thing very intensely. In addition to this aspect, Kaleka's father and the two uncles of Kaleka were all imaginary storytellers. They would invent stories and sometimes endorse them as well. One of them would practise a lantern to accompany his stories by casting huge shadows on the wall (Sarkar, 2014). Kaleka believes and also explores that the interest in a moving image came from there into Kaleka's art practice. Kaleka even likes inventing stories too. And though all accounts have some meaning, the artist prefers to keep them open-ended (Sarkar, 2014). There shouldn't be a conclusiveness to them. And they should get an indication of some aspect of life. The study analyses that if Kaleka completely understands them himself, the artist loses all interest. It has to continue to elude the artist as well. And most significantly, it has to be right. And that is a very compound entity. There are an entire lot of functions happening in the head for an individual to touch right. It means that it's associated with life, but it contains some of those mysteries of life as well (Sarkar, 2014). Those are the kind of stories, events if Kaleka could call them that – which the artist likes to create.

4.2.6 Sound is Fairly Important and Visuals Border on 'fantasy' in Kaleka's Video Installations: An Analysis

The study of the research analyses that in Kaleka's work sound has a significant role in revealing. The artist also contemplates through his art practice that sound is a particular piece that the artist is nowadays working on, someone's going to write music to it. But there are a few works of Kaleka which are without any sound (Sarkar, 2014). The chapter also analyses that at times Kaleka's visuals reflect border on 'fantasy' the way they come out all bright, colourful and engaging into the artist's video installations. There is an absolute 'kitschy-ness' in the colours because Kaleka does explore that there's a lot of possibilities in Kitsch and the Popular Arts, like the bizarre painting, for instance. Kaleka's psychology through his art practice expects that kitsch still has the possibility of sensing a viewer to it, and there can be subtlety in it. There's something we can react to as sophisticated kitsch, as it were, although they are contradictory terms. But it's possible that interests Kaleka's art practice (Sarkar, 2014).

4.2.7 Inspirations and Philosophy of Ranbir Kaleka's Artwork

The study of the research analyses that the inspirations and philosophy of Kaleka's art practice develop along with the artist's sketching and painting, Kaleka's art practice comprises video and sculpture too. The source of inspiration is not always obvious, thoughts; ideas emerge from a pool of events: The event is more or less a psychological state which employs images that have a universal familiarity and tap into a sort of collective memory. The 'pool' Kaleka refers to has submerged in his early childhood stretching up to contemporary events around the artist. Great books, cinema, theatre, storytellers and art history too nurtures this pool. Kaleka explores that curiosity about the self and the world is an integral part of the work of an artist.

His first solo exhibition *'Sweet Unease'* (2010-11), (Plate 4.1) evokes Kaleka's childhood in Punjab, where traditional wrestling is a universal sport, with no distinct beginning or end, the video depicts a perpetual cycle that doesn't give viewers the satisfaction of watching complete events. Kaleka's works in various mediums like oil, watercolour painting and mixed media on different shapes of wood and board, digital photographs and video installation. His New Media works, particularly his painting, installation have been developed recently in his career. His paintings , both on paper and canvas, in oil as well as mixed media, are quite surrealist in their behaviour of passages from everyday life. The lines are suggestive, instead of being sharply traced, and the colours are deliberately used with care restraint. During the discussion between the researcher and the artist, when the researcher asked him about the concepts of surrealism, trauma and eroticism in his paintings. Kaleka interacted in a way that the artist likes the idea of surrealism as in art history. Kaleka's paintings have been described as surrealist, but the concept of trauma comes from the stories of people the artist knew, the stories of cruelty, torture and murder related to them. As an individual knows Punjab can be very violent, which Kaleka has always seen from a distance, but physically it never happened to the artist.

Regarding eroticism, Kaleka expressed that the artist was thinking of his painting which is sexual, of frontal nudity- for example, Kaleka's work *'Long sleep of the storyteller'* (2012) (Plate 4.2), or *'Family Picture II '* (Plate 4.3). The artist would mention that the body was thought of as that which contained violence along with the sensuality. But, the characters in the painting are situated within a kind of complexity which gives these characters a 'mental life'.

Kaleka started working with different mediums such as oil, mixed-media. The artist continued experimenting in various areas like digital prints such as '*Urban Utopia, Done Undone, Menaced by dragonflies*' (2014) (Plate 4.4), and '*A- Panoramic-Spectrum Ground*' (Plate 4.5), as video installation like '*Kettle*'(Plate 4.6) and since the transition from painting to video in the 1990s, Kaleka has practised video as a tool for material innovation.

When the researcher of the study interacted about Kaleka's process through which the artist introduced images leading-edge technique. Kaleka expresses and elaborates regarding the evolution of his work over the years with the changes in direction, primarily his foray into working with video. Kaleka interacted with the researcher in a way that over the years, what has not changed as what the artist wants from his work is that there is a process of meaning-making where Kaleka reaches an 'event'. The 'event' is more psychological, which employs images that have a universal acquaintance and blow into our collective sense of reminiscence. In painting the 'event' may be executed through a conformation of persons and substances. The stance of the body, the trajectory of the eye, the texture of surfaces, the vigour or otherwise of the painter's hand all contribute towards creating what the artist called an event, the reading of which is not rectilinear and not necessarily temporally or geographically specific but carries the physiological tinkle of familiarity or an emotional twinge of recognition (Shahane, 2009). One significant visible difference from the early work of Kaleka as a student to now has been the practice of colour, from a range of greys; Kaleka started to push colours to the threshold of garishness. The artist felt that it was possible to produce a kind of sophisticated kitsch, which is complex and nuanced. Earlier nearly all works of Kaleka appeared as if it fitted to an 'enclosed interior'. Those breaks began to slowly open up wider with access to the 'outer space' although this 'enclosed interior' continues to interest the artist very much (Shahane, 2009). Over the years, Kaleka has been looking at art forms of other cultures and acquiring a more extensive visual repertory. Kaleka explains that the artist likes inventing metaphorical events as well, which are not culturally specific.

Kaleka's interest in video arose more from the artist's interest in cinema than from video art. Kaleka wanted to see what would happen if the artist combined the physically painted image and an image made of light. The artist arrived at a sort of hyper-image which had a quality different from both painting and the cinematic or video image. This became another tool with which to create 'events'; for creating meaning and telling stories.

4.2.8 Video Installation of Ranbir Kaleka: An Overview

The study of the research analyses that Kaleka can explain the video through the artist's painting entitled *'Man Threading A Needle'* (Plate 4.7), which was done in 1998-99. This is a painting on the board size 23.3 X 35.8 inches. The painting shows a 'man threading a needle.' The painting is spot-lit and sits on an easel. As the individual /audience observes and sees the man suddenly blink or gulp. The person in the painting occasionally makes a desperate attempt to thread the needle. At various moments the person perceives the sound of a peacock, a passing train and a police siren, this makes his persona nervous, his body drags with hefty consciousness. The painting most of the time lingers still. This impact is achieved by projecting a video of a man threading the needle on a painting of the man threading a needle. Oil colours give the surface of the painting a palpability, a weight of an object, whereas the videoed image gives it the aura of light and we arrived at a kind of hyper-image (Kaleka, 2019).

The researcher's interpretation after seeing this artwork *'Man Threading A Needle'* (2008) is that in this work, the artist reveals a middle-aged male threading a needle. The man is typically still, penetratingly focused on the needle, which the person in the artwork occasionally attempts to tread; the research study also noticed some twitches and jerks in a cycle where the past and the present sun into each other in a phantasmagorical flow. The works were to test the conventional approaches of learning art and life (Kaleka, 2019). The surprising sensation of the intelligence shifting gears to accommodate a moving man and then the still painted image is almost palpable when it is looked at in the piece. At one point, the painting on canvas that the installation is lit by the projector light alone evacuated of any video image. In another phase, illusory depth of the painting is destroyed by the silhouetted flat shadows on the canvas, which confirm its flatness and establish the installation as an object, a metafiction, beforehand the loop commences its spell of movement and depth again (Kaleka, 2019).

The artist's another video installation titled *'Fables from the House of Ibaan'* (2007), that was also one of the terrific works (Plate 4.8). His other extraordinary works are *'Man with Cockerel'*, *'Crossing'* (2005) (Plate 4.9), *'Cobbler'* (2003) (Plate 4.10), *'Reading Man'* (2009) (Plate 4.11), *'Cul-de-sac in Taxila'* (2010) (Plate 4.12), *'Conference of Birds and Beasts'* (2010) (Plate 4.13), and *'The Great Topairist's Astonishing Dilemma'* (Plate 4.14) and many more all of them are most crucial examples of his ingenious skills in the field of art.

The essential focus on Kaleka's work is not just on his unique methodology in working with video and painting, but the description of the work, which usually depicts daily issues that occur across India. Kaleka's work has been widely exhibited in India and abroad. He organised more than 12 solo shows and participated in more than 24 group shows such as 2012 Volte Gallery & Saffron Art Gallery, Ranbir Kaleka "*Fables*", Delhi "*2010 Volte Art Gallery*, 'Sweet Unease', Mumbai " "*2009 Bose Pacia Gallery, 'Reading Man', New York*" and many more. Kaleka's work continues to be exhibited and collected from India as well as abroad. He is a recipient of the National Award in 1979, Lalit Kala Akademi, New Delhi and in 1986 Sanskriti Award, New Delhi, all these shows his recognition at international level.

The research study finds Kaleka's works with absolute sincerity, a different kind of complete awareness with his creative process and technique. Using imprecise description, he speaks to what he describes as 'impressive themes' that explore endless subjects like 'life, death, loss, and aspirations'. He throws full light on a difference between spatiality, temporality, sensation and significance, making us intensely alive to the various reactions of viewers.

4.2.9 A Case Study of the Video Installation of Ranbir Kaleka

Some of the references of Ranbir Kaleka's video installations can be taken for discussion. Such as,

a. '*Sweet Unease*'
b. '*Cul-De-Sac in Taxila*'
c. '*Not From Here*'
d. '*Kettle*'
e. '*Man with Cockerel*'
f. '*Fables from the House of Ibaan*'
g. '*He Was a Good Man*'
h. '*Wall*'
i. '*Forest*'
j. '*Consider*'
k. '*Crossings*'
l. '*Man With Cockerel -2*'
m. '*Man in Water*'
n. '*Windows*'
o. '*Music Room*'
p. '*Video Lounge*'
q. '*Powder Room*'

r. *'Man Threading A Needle'*
s. *' House of An Opaque Water'*
t. *' Fearsome Acquiescence of A Monotonous Life'*
u. *'Not Anonymous_ Walking to the Obscure Fear of A New Dawn'*
v. *'Bound'*

'Sweet Unease' *(2011)*

Single Channel video projection on painted canvas mounted on fractured wall 11:11 minutes loop. 294 cm x 53.5 cm (115.7 x 21.1 inches)

Ranbir Kaleka's *'Sweet Unease'* provided an opportunity to observe selected works by the artist, mostly video projections on paintings, done over the last decade. These works gave a whole new experience in the ways of viewing and engaging with Ranbir's art.

'Sweet Unease' is Kaleka's debut solo exhibition in Bombay which was exhibited from 16 December 2010- 15 February 2011 at Volte Gallery. The New Media Artworks constitute a significant research-based artwork of a decade of Kaleka's video installation practices. The work that gave the show its title *'Sweet Unease'*; comes across as a complex work-packed with layers painted and projected images, objects, characters and narratives. The work has multiple total points, where movements/events take place, at many times, simultaneously. The work depicts violence, nudity and carries a dream-like feel at various points in the 11 minute and 11- second loop. Science, fiction and reality merge densely and intensely in this narrative that can also be analysed . The *'Sweet Unease'* exhibition projected Kaleka's seven video projections/video installations from the earliest works shown here dating back to the early 2000s; the latest was released especially for this juncture. The works those who have already savoured Kaleka's art practices have observed *'Cul-de-sac in Taxila'* that was the stand-alone avatar of the chapter titled *'Man with Hammer'* from *'Crossings'* which was a 2005 installation that mobilised a four-channel projection with corresponding acrylic paintings, as well as *'Fables from the House of Ibaan'* (2007) and *'He was a Good Man'* (2008). And while *'The Kettle'* and *'Sweet Unease'* (both 2010) embody Kaleka's most recent inquiries during the exhibition time, the early work, *'Man with Cockerel'* (2001-02), was also on view in an enclosure parallel to the exhibition. The study of the research finds that through the artworks Ranbir Kaleka celebrates the poetics of the liminal moment: that threshold of potentialities at which the self becomes transitive, poised to metamorphose into any of several others (Hoskote, 2010). During the last one and half decades, Kaleka has composed

several preparations of the painted image and the projected image, settled to cohabit in the same space. However, Kaleka does not embrace the simple juxtaposition, super imposition or mixed-use of media to achieve a pluralising effect.

On the contrary, the artist produces a meticulously calibrated adjacency of media, with which to disrupt the civilities of the layered image. Kaleka's images are only apparently simultaneous and palimpsest. In knowledgeable certainty, they are asynchronous: they lag behindhand one another, the problem at one another, hold together in a spectral sparkle only to split apart in brief eruptions before regaining deceptive stability. In the subtle break between the appearances of these images, Kaleka breaks open alterations of spatiality, temporality, sensation and significance, making us penetratingly alive to the criticism of viewer reception.

The video '*Sweet Unease*' encompasses two paintings, one on the left and another on the right, and there is one man in both of them but in slightly different ambiences. One figure is warmer in psychological mood, and another one is chiller; one is more suitable, the other is more rested , one of them drinks his tea differently while the other drinks with his little finger stuck out (Sarkar, 2014). The video projection not only revealed the expressions of dancers but also involved wrestlers as well. Through the video, the projected figures are just eating and wrestling. So both the events/actions become metaphorical. The video '*Sweet Unease*' has revealed to a similar viewer individual be seated consumption in the left and the right-hand canvas. They have a slightly variable mannerism. Each room has a different mood. They eat continuously at the table and infrequently get up, leave behind their painted personalities on the canvas and encounter on the wall where they involve in continuous wrestling captivating on different personas. Food sustains life, and in this installation 'eating' is a metaphor for it and 'wrestling' the struggle with life's questions (Kaleka, 2019). The overall gesture of the video expresses a psychological interpretation.

'*Cul-De-Sac In Taxila*' (2010)

Single Channel Video Projection on Canvas (video still) 3:55 min loop with sound, size variable

In the work of Kaleka, the study of research analyses that *'Cul-de-sac in Taxila'* is 3 minutes 55- second loop with sound. In work, a white horse appears on a white background in front of a man seated on a chair. The event seems sinister as the man tries to hit hard on the head of the horse, but results in nothingness. The video work '*Cul-De-Sac in Taxila*' which is the whimsicality of the exhibition, '*Sweet Unease,*' attracts upon Kaleka's childhood in a village in Patiala, Punjab. The work reflected painting of a man contemplating space where video disappears in, giving him breath. He attacks the air in reverse of him with a hammer; at the opinion of influence, a white horse appears who begins to disappear as rapidly as she seems. The unified loop is interrupted by dwindling water drops in the pan behind him, calculating time. A Kuon is played in an affirmative Sisyphean cycle of desire, mental effort, labour, loss and momentary attainment.

The research analyses that in work the existing person's self-mental presence is static at the same time, the other image of that specific individual is continuously shifting within his identity and ideology. The study finds that in different aspects of a person's life situations, there are many dilemmas to face. Still, it depends only up to that particular individual towards which directions he/she continues himself or herself to overcome the situations. The work reveals that conceptual interpretation in the process.

'*Not from Here*' (2009)

Installation shot, Astonishment of Being, Birla Academy of Art and Culture, Kolkata 4 Channel Video Projection on canvas, 6 minutes loop, sound Size variable, projection size at Birla Academy: 243.8 x 1371.6 cm (96 x 540 inches)

Another intricate work, '*Not from Here*' (2009) (Plate 4.15), is projected on an eight feet long canvas. Here, a migrant family waits at a train station, along with their belongings. The 6-minute loop involves the sound of the train and a busy street merging with sounds from the other works in the gallery.

The study of the research analyses that '*Not from Here*' explores a journey. The video-projection reveals if an individual departed to the ridge of the house, at just under a kilometre away, beyond the flat open meadow with a smattering of brown bushes and dispersed *kikar* trees, a person could observe a picturesque train station. Miniature, it was more like a guard's room, beautifully proportioned. The work reflects that the train appeared from behind the distant houses and continued in a half- circle, stretching a kilometre to the small train station. On bright days the simple track was a red curve of white heat, a kilometre wide. The train brought in migrant labourers to the more massive station in Patiala. The season for harvest. Local farmers crowded the platforms to pick up farm-hands, jostled to have a first pick of the more robust. The artist reflected that in their childhood days, people often went fishing in ponds and a canal that ran close to the little station. Trains stopped only briefly at this station, sometimes for less than a minute. The small station had no platform. Occasionally, people saw a bundle thrown hurriedly from the train followed by a scrambling family getting off; women hastily passed a trunk or a child to their man below on the ground. When the train left, they always formed a huddle. In its wake, the train left a family looking forlorn, appearing strangely defenceless, abandoned in a landscape of barrenness accentuated by lonely *kikars*.

At the Birla Academy in Kolkata, '*Not from Here*' was projected on a 14-metre full canvas screen. A family group is painted in one section of the canvas screen in acrylics. Three thin columns with struts are also depicted in acrylics. These columns intersperse the screen. Since 1998, Kaleka has projected videos on paintings. The palpable 'thingness' of the painted images fused with the 'aura' of images made of light makes for a kind of hyper presence. The image speaks with a different eloquence. In work the luggage shows on the ground are painted in such a manner to receive a hyper image; on the other hand , the painted family group has only a tenuous relation to the videoed image.

The narrative has no clarity in the video; only a sense of the 'imminent' is there. The loop in work starts with a blue cast of early morning before sunrise. Day appears, and a life-size train thunders past (Sinha, Puri, Khanna, 2014). The new arrivals stand self-conscious and stiff as if lining up to be photographed. Their belongings lie on the ground. From their looks, they appear to be from a slightly indeterminate background. Their exact relationship to each other is a little ambiguous too. Momentary body shifts and nervous gestures increase as trains roar past behind them. One by one, they begin to walk out of their painted shelves , leaving their bodies as mere traces on the canvas. The luggage on the floor is painted in detail. These belongings acquire a hyper-real presence, but the family group is painted in a sort of line wash. In the family group, after a video-image walks out of its painted-image, what is left behind is an insubstantial imprint. Visitors to the city are almost invisible, without a record of their presence, just a spectral presence in the city's vision. As the family group gets spent, only two are gone, one each on the extreme edges of the crowd, a woman and a small child who is a girl. The two do not go off anyplace, they do not walk out of their tinted images. Other members of the crowd never return. Eventually, the woman and the child disappear in the place where they stood (Sinha, Puri, Khanna,2014).

Stories of labourers' lost children are plenty. In all, over several thousand children have gone missing in Delhi in the last two decades. Whatsoever the providence of this group in the video installation, the traffic of immigrants has continued and will continue. Nearing the end of the loop: a whistle announces new arrivals, and to the strains of a song, a ghostly procession of past and future trains come in and out bearing new travellers. The grey of the video transforms into a melting, rolling rainbow of colours as the trains arrive attended by happy sounds of the travellers and the hosts.

Migrants have faced violence, while others have found their dream of a better life fulfilled. Ongoing engagement with the subject of immigrants and visitors to the city will evolve into further events in the video.

'Kettle' (2010)

Single Channel HD Video Projection on Painting, (video still), 3 minutes 35 second loop. 90.5cm x 68cm (35.6 x 26.8 inches)

In India, everything is recycled. In the country of tea-drinkers, the study of the research analyses that *'Kettle'* is the story of a little Kettle's journey to a decent kitchen from a shop. After serving the first proprietor, the kettle is abandoned, demanded, abandoned over and reclaimed. At pauses, illusionary depth of the painting is devastated by the silhouetted shadow of a hand stalling the videoed image of the kettle to confirm the flatness of the canvas and establish the video installation as only an object before the loop starts its 25 frames-a-second spells of movement and depth again (Kaleka, 2010).

The *'Kettle'*, a 3 minute and 55-second loop reflects notions of change and stability. While a kettle remains static, the changing background of the canvas shows urban and rural landscapes with commotion, chaos, people and buildings. In daily life surroundings, there are a lot of swings into an individual's sphere. In this video, the kettle can be identified as a symbol of identity. In the day -to -day life of India, the kettle has a very symbolic existence. In a morning; in the standard class people, when an individual starts his/her day with a *chay*, whether it is in the room-homely ambience or a roadside corner, there are lots of ideas and stories are there with the flavours of *chay* which is kept in a kettle. The research study finds that in the video, the kettle plays that role of identity to hold and breathe of an individual which is conducting lots of happenings within the locality of a common men's culture of India. The video projects kettle as a medium to interact with various people of typical class through their daily life situations. People share a lot of closed things, exchange their thought process, and discuss how to overcome the harsh conditions. In so many, that kind of process kettle became a medium of approach in the flavours of a sip of *chay*. The video conceptually projects such to the audience.

The kettle is the central image in the video which shifted by a black hand-palm reflection which carries a dimension into the video, which creates a shift within space between space. The black hand diversion in the frame of the video created a duel of the kettle, which is once shown as a real image and as a still life study of a real kettle in another sequence. There are different ambiences that can be identified in the work which is sometimes viewed as different characters in different landscapes-cityscape spaces as part of the video. The research study finds that there are various conceptual subject matters with philosophical aspects revealed in the work of video. Various performances played a role in the different amalgamation frames into the video. Psychological elements are also there in work by Kaleka.

'*Man with Cockerel*' (2001 – 2002)

2 Channel Video projection, 29 seconds loop, size variable

The video entitled '*Man with Cockerel*' is a well-known artwork of Ranbir Kaleka. The video started with a man entering carrying a cockerel. He pauses, looks at the viewer and suddenly dissolves into nothing. He reappears as the cockerel tries to escape. The superimposition of the reflection on the man breaks as the man chases the cockerel. Kaleka observes the videos as mapping nuances of dual desires- one to hold and the other to escape. A bald man with an easy-going, Buddha-like face, clutching and letting go then clutching and letting go a plumed fowl reflects in '*Man with Cockerel*'. This rhythmically repeated, soft-grey image proposals a tantalising grasp of desire, an allegory on dispossession.

Kaleka's subject-matter is representational and still, by the form and compression of its videoed execution, by a method of durational deception, by sheer transience, it dispatches its implied meaning. The imaged figure – at the verge of extinction and disappearance – reads like an index of mortality. Its quotidian identity is subordinated to a fragile sense of being where no assertion, no action is necessary except that which trusts in a minimal continuum of survival. The language of representation enters the liminal zone and the encounter, sanguine, serene, evanescent, resembles a haiku where the hypothesis offered about a lived life needs no backing of proof (Kapur, 2005).

In the video, the central image reveals a man holding a cockerel which is continuously appearing and also disappearing for a period of the gap in the video. The space of the screening mostly shows monochromatic work. The sound plays a vital role to perceive the work to the audience. The breather of the surroundings explored mysterious and psychological narratives to an individual who became an audience in the video. Whenever the central image of the work went disappear in the video, the exciting part to analyse that lower part image of the figure which is explored as shadow is disappeared little delay from the screen and within this shifting of image the amalgamation of sound started to create a dialogue to the observer in the work of art.

The mostly monochromatic space in work sometimes also becomes a mysterious reveal of coloured interaction by screening different atmospheric gestures of climate. Whenever the central figure in work is shifting his area from the projection, the cockerel is the reason, which is slipping away or trying to escape from the central figure which is always appearing held by the middle-aged person in the video. The study of the research analyses that Kaleka explores a spontaneity in the images existing in the video which appears and disappears with a conceptual impact into the mind of audiences of the work. There is no systematic plan but spontaneous essence which created a dialogue between the images of the video and to the observer of that specific work. The work interacted with situations that come around into the life processes of creatures and dilemmas faced by a human being and the consequences reflected.

'Fables from the House of Ibaan' (2007)

Single channel video projection (video still) on painting, 5 minutes 24 seconds loop, sound

The video work by Kaleka the study of this research analyses that a man thoughtfully seated on a table. Bordered only by a milk jug and supplicatory candle holders, the static image represented as the front piece for a projected film. The central scene unfolds in an unconcerned entry among the easy home life of a central family component. The son turns in and out of the horizontal, as the mother carefully refills the symbolic glass jug. Kaleka's deft handling of time quickly solidifies this sense of comfort. The artist disassembles and reassembles the viewer's mind of space by playing with the concept of indoor versus outdoor. Also, his precious attention to detail underscores the work's sublime quality and transports the viewer into a suspended realm (purohit, 2008). In practice, there are various kinds of performances which can be continuously projected. There are different spaces interacted variety of interpretation which carries multiple sequences of symbolic/conceptual aspects through the video.

In the work of video, there are fables one can identify through the play of characters. Role of images reflected a vital conversation into the mind of observers. When the boy ran and opened the door to look at the outside from the inside of the house, the images of the video revealed that the boy's observation after opening the door transforms into the cityscape of a geographical location. The interior space of the video reflected various visual interpretations through the visual-fables. The still image of the figure sitting in the right side corner in the frame suddenly reveals as he is unfolding the jug of milk which was previously shown to be refilling another woman. There are a lot of psychological conversations happening in the video. The surrounded picture plane shifts into lots of dialogue as well as monologue between the observer and the work. The interior space sometimes created black waves and sometimes also shifted into tones of chromatic as well monochromatic which creates a visual-interaction and is bound to stress in an individual's brain what is going on in the frame of video art. There are also reflections of frames just beside the central subject that start to create another dialogue between the work and between the audience/observer of the work '*Fables from the House of Ibaan*'.

'*He Was a Good Man*' (2008)

Single channel video projection (video still) on painting, 5:3 minutes loop, stereo sound

This chapter analyses that Kaleka's video works combine the period and light of the moving image with the dependability and materiality of the painted image. In '*He Was a Good Man*' (2008) (Plate 4.16), Kaleka revisits another exploration titled '*Man Threading A Needle*'. The work reveals a middle-aged male threading a needle. The man is regularly still, intensely focused on the needle which he irregularly challenges to the thread, shadowed by some convulsions and jolts in a cycle anywhere the previous and the existing run into each other in a phantasmagorical movement. The work's critical tone examinations the conventional approaches to reviewing art and life. The astonishing feeling of the brain shifting components to accommodate a moving man and then the motionless painted image is almost tangible when looking at the piece. In work at one opinion, the painting on canvas in the installation is ignited by the projector well-lit alone, an expatriate of any video image. In another passageway, the deceptive depth of the painting is demolished by the silhouetted evenglooms on the canvas, which settle its flatness and establish the installation as an object, a metafiction, before the loop starts its spell of movement and depth again (Kaleka, 2019).

The video reveals the appearance of the central figure in black and white, which is later transformed into layers of colours into the frame of the video. There are reflections of various ambiences in the negative space of the video which interpret the dimensions of the visual language of a work process. The central figure revealed that trying to stress into threading a needle besides parts of the frames created a psycho-visual interaction between the work and the viewer. In the work process, the sudden sound of a train along with the visual reflections of the same creates an impression of the journey of life .

In the work process, different layers of the video reveal spontaneous exportations that the artist represented through his narratives of visual interaction where a third space has prominent involvement. A lot of philosophical aspects also Kaleka expresses through his work process. There are lots of layers that created the artist conceptually and philosophically in the work that reveals a volume to analyse the video also to observe by an audience. The research study finds that the '*He Was a Good Man*' reveals the central figure's eyes were continuously in a mood of over- conscious which sometimes also creates a dilemma in common man's daily life situations by which an individual cannot solve his/her everyday things in a smooth way. The work also expresses the ideas of philosophical phases emphasised by Kaleka.

Kaleka, through his work, reflected prevalent things which an individual came across and conceptualised these points and revealed into his New Media work process in a very thoughtful way. The application of sound, moving images emphasises a very prominent approach in a third space/object where work becomes a reflection of spontaneity.

'*He Was a Good Man*' (2008) shows a man trying to thread a needle projected onto a painting. The excellent play of light and reflection and emphasis on the expressions of the protagonist are the highlights of this work. The artist observes this work as extracting the notion of time out of painting and light out of the film, creating a third thing - a hyper image, where events are not linear.

'Wall' (2009)

Single-channel video

7-minute loop, sound

'Wall' (Plate 4.17) is one of the video works by Kaleka, which is a monochromatic reveal of expression. The work explored the terror events, believed to have a locus in West or South Asia and enacted in different parts of the world come to be known in media and academic parlance as the "failed plot". At various times, London, Washington, New York, Hamburg, New Delhi, Lahore, the Philippines – and so on – have become the new, explosive location for the failed plot. In every case, the system, the network has been unable to connect or ignite. As research gets underway, the truth remains elusive, and its quest is abandoned. Fragments of the plotters live, little bits of narrative float and beam through global media networks. Yet the whole plot is never known, and the narrative remains partially uncovered. In a million unrecorded ways, these narratives are completed, abandoned, denied, until they uneasily subside in the residue of public memory.

The work appears with a person trying to cross a wall with a bamboo ladder. Gradually the figure turns to disappear in the space and again the appearance of the identity of a person with the same pose but another arena of a frame. The gradually progressed with more figures trying to climb a wall with a ladder and also trying to the crossing and reach another region of the wall, which is towards the audience space. The projection developed with more figures appearing on the wall with sitting, and standing postures and some figures at a glance also placed on the forward region of the space. In the later part of the video, the artist explores the sound of chaos where more numbers of gatherings reveal with a layered and overlay gesture of figures.

The video further explored that more figures in layers with various postures easily laddered down their footprints towards the forward part/region of the wall. Then after crossing those gatherings into the foreground space of the frame with their smooth landing with the helpings of the ladder, a chaotic situation arrives. The video explores those conditions to conceptualise a work of projection/ New Media Art.

'Forest' (2009)

Video projection (video still) on a painted surface, 16 min loop with sound

The study of the research analyses that *'Forest'* is full of metaphorical events which belief have universal resonance (Plate 4.18). The art practice can be merely labelled as exposed overwork regarding rejuvenation in a period of confusion and strife.

A meadow of flowers unveils burnt area under where a man beats himself as an act of penance. Sign of burnt-ground has in modern moments involved 'hidden atrocities' and simulated contacts as well as deforestation. The flagellant grows up and walks off, turning into an animated cartoon. He arrives at different features in the video. He protects some books from a burning library. He trains himself with the books. He confers the power of knowledge by regrowing lost limbs. He pours the 'water of knowledge' into a hole dug by a child. From the void, fountains rise, and we see a city born underneath.

Book counters in the forest symbolise a library of knowledge. I have shown a lion as the keeper of wisdom. The lion is thrown away by the forces of destruction as the library is burnt. In the end, we see a little cub return to the new city.

The work reflects the artist's meditation on 'regeneration' amid a period of confusion and turmoil. Operating with the themes of destruction and rebirth, loss and gain, knowledge and power, '*Forest*' encapsulates a world displaying our own. Black, burnt-down ground is revealed underneath the flowers on the range, on which a man lashes himself. Shelves of books seem and a lion, custodian of knowledge, guards them. Nature is provided to humankind's ends. The library is fired, and the lion is driven out, but some books survive in the ashes.

'*Consider*' (2007)

Two-channel video projected on two canvases,11 feet x 7 feet 6 inches each canvas, mounted on a 30- foot atrium wall, 9th floor

The work by Kaleka is a permanent installation commissioned by the Spertus Museum in Chicago. Memorials have conventionally obtainable the viewer an imposing, inspiring and eternal artwork upon which to anticipate actual damage. Think of the towering, unspoiled pillar that attitudes as the Washington Monument or proud . The fixed sculpture of Abraham Lincoln that be seated inside the Lincoln Memorial. Visualise walking through one of the monumental conventional arches that inhabit cities across the globe, remembering French soldiers who battled in the Napoleonic wars. The Indian soldiers who fought in the Afghan wars and so many others boldly lost to the world's actions. Image sitting by the two reflecting pools proposed as a tribute to those who perished in the attacks on the World Trade Center (Kaleka, 2019).

Ranbir Kaleka's *'Consider'* is not a memorial like any of these (Plate 4.19). Though commissioned by the Spertus Museum in remembrance of the Holocaust, it does not provide consolation for this most horrific of historical events. Instead of materials like marble or stone that will weather the seasons and the decades, a stable and permanent reminder of tragedy, it is a video-painting made of partially painted canvas panels and digitally projected light. Refusing to tell its story plainly and graciously, so that the viewer may respectfully and correctly observe it, it presents discontinuous, open-ended narratives that raise more questions than answers. Far from being prominently displayed, it is hidden around a corner and pushed to the far end of an unapproachable light well. Most startling of all, its visual content presents neither the emaciated figures that are the personal record of the Holocaust nor an abstract form as a symbolic stand-in; instead, it pictures a multi-generational, upper-middle- class Indian family at home, focusing on the adolescent daughter of the house.

Only the intangible audio component of *'Consider'* bears the clear trace of the Shoah, amid a soundtrack of secondary noises and twangy Chinese and Aegean music, a woman and a man narrate first-hand accounts of how human hair was used in place of animal fur as an industrial material during the war. The testimonies have implications that are as obvious as they are unbearable, indicating that a body part readily associated with beauty and care—long women's hair, sometimes braided or strung with pretty coins—was transformed into a valuable commodity, dehumanising the bodies to which that hair belonged. Archived by Polish scholars and heard here in English for the first time, these two oral histories exemplify the gross uniqueness of the Jewish genocide: the exploitation of human beings beyond the grave.

How then does the study of the research make sense of Kaleka's pairing of such disparate audio and video components? Why layer the recollection of heinous crimes over the projection of boisterous family life? And what does it mean to do so in such an ephemeral medium? To begin sorting out these questions, it is useful to note some moments of overlap between *Consider*'s seemingly mismatched soundtrack and visuals. The links hide in the details, the Indian grandfather's transistor radio echoes the narrator's explanation of how factory workers discovered, through clandestine broadcasts from London, what was going on in the concentration camps. His grand daughter hangs clean laundry on a rooftop clothesline; the voice- over tells of wet hair hung like laundry for drying. Most saliently, the girl's long dark hair, lovingly plaited by her mother, decorated with gleaming coins, swung this way and that, soaked in a rainstorm, evokes every strand of hair brutally stolen from millions of degraded Jewish heads. These and other associations weave throughout *'Consider'*, subtly connecting the normal and every day with the tragic and the horrific—an appalling but not unrealistic comparison. By picturing that quotidian space as an Indian one, Kaleka abstracts the Holocaust from its European Jewish context into a broader human language; he achieves this too through the fact of being not a Jewish artist of European descent but a Punjabi one based in New Delhi.

In work for all the universality that arises from this layering, so does incommensurability. Between these two poles pulses a potent tension worth struggling with, one that lies at the very core of vanguard memorial art today. Artists as diverse as Jochen Gerz, Shimon Attie, Art Spiegelman, and Rachel Whiteread have over the past three decades reinvented what it means to make art about the horrors of the past. As James E. Young explains in At Memory's Edge: After Images of the Holocaust in Contemporary Art and Architecture (Yale, 2000), these post-Holocaust practitioners have used an array of non-traditional means—from conceptual art to site-specific slide projection to graphic novels—to make work about a past that they can only know vicariously, through the mediation of others' memories and research. Their projects refuse to redeem the catastrophes of the past through aesthetic pleasure or to present tidy historic visions by leaving out the messiness of dissemination and interpretation. They heed the obligation to remember while exposing the difficulty of doing so.

Kaleka's *'Consider'* expands on this contemporary mode of memorial-making, transposing its hyper mediated memory work into the medium of video- painting that he pioneered in the late 1990s. It is a technique uniquely well-suited to the purposes of critical remembrance: unstable, ethereal, and time-based, it makes meaningful demands on the viewer, who must continuously labour to make sense of the disjunction between audio and video; to register the torrent of information colliding across two screens and a complex soundtrack; to negotiate the discrepancy between painted and projected image. This last tension, between paint and light, challenges the very qualities that have traditionally made large-scale painting a premier recorder of history: by literally painting with light, Kaleka transforms the medium from one of permanence to one that refuses to be still, and that disappears with the flick of a switch. A debate is established between the animate and the inanimate, as the girl's projected image floats atop her painted one, bringing it to life while simultaneously revealing its ghostliness, which haunts the work's entirety.

Painting—and its weighty, unbearable subject of the Holocaust—is thereby demystified, brought down to earth where we mortals of today must grapple with it, denied the promise of a history that stays neatly in the past and allows for transcendence in the present, refused any secure—or final—solutions. Instead, *'Consider'* offers us something that works much more like memory itself, full of after-images, blurred recollections, and uncanny repetitions grafted onto the present day, where memory truly lives.

'*Crossings*' (2005)

Four-channel video projection on painting, (video still/installation still), 15 min loop with stereo sound 190 x 250cm, (75 x 98 inches).

The work of art is a proposal for India in Venice 2005/tentative title: Liminal Passage. The video made a series of events/ conversations in a landscape of immense proportions. This video has projected on four 190 x 250cm, (75 x 98 inches) acrylic paintings.

The research study analyses that the video installation stylistically shifts the landscape hauls and transforms about the proceedings dramatic in the landscape. The numbers of four 8 feet x 6 feet paintings determined in parts are painted in great detail with an extensive range of colours. Other areas being monochromatic (Kaleka, 2019). Some projected images have crystallised with the painted images rendering them largely immobile. The occasional animation in these images amplifies their stillness. In cinematic terms, the immobility has existed within the actual course of time. It will psychologically stretch time, enhancing, other video images have run/moves and move freely between the four paintings. The static video images have on juncture move absent from their painted personalities leave-taking behind a colourful or monochromatic ghost, an 'after-image'. The characters visit other paintings and return to inhabit their 'painted shells' revitalising them with their 'breath'.

The video is based on a script written by Kaleka, a magic realist drama of private lives and authentic engagement with a smudging of boundaries which brings reality into fantasy and fantasy into our reality. The sound (Madan Gopal Singh) which is a composition of everyday noise blended with primarily Indian music and a range of other musical idioms.

The script includes an episode with the ritual of a Sikh tying his turban. He first dyes his turban a specific colour (dipping it in a village pond turning the entire lake into a giant vat of iridescent colour). The turban is then dried by two people holding it at either end and running into the wind creating a bulbous sail.

There is then the specialised rolling of the cloth and finally the slow 'tying' on the head.

The village pond transformed magically into another colour as the long piece of cloth (the united turban) is pulled out, the Sikh finds himself standing on the shore of a differently dyed pool in a foreign land (America) with his turban now dyed in many colours. He carries in his suitcase the turbans rolled into colourful bundles like so many flowers which he offers to strangers.

Occasionally the projection will, in certain areas, fade out revealing the painting underneath and then slowly flicker back to life, intensifying and reanimating the painted surface (This is painting living within time and time living within the painting). The painted image will be a play between stylisation and verisimilitude. Charred or slimy, ephemerally tinted or layered with material substances (iron filings et al.), surface articulation will suggest space, weight and formal authority, a presence as a 'thing', autonomous, with its laws, unpredictable in its 'becoming'.

The 'thingness' and palpable presence of the painted images fused with the 'aura' of images made of light will create a beautiful texture intimating a new eloquence. The study of the research analyses this work as a hybrid or a composite, but productive image-structure breathing to the rhythm and beat of one heart. There is an inner connection, logic between the video-movement and the painted/sculpted surface. The video image is tied to the concrete and the material (literally). The work is possessing a kind of wholeness, observing one aspect of our discovery of surrounding verities. It is 'time' pulsating in the flesh of the painting. A moment is reproduced in its fluid mutability. In the time's rhythms, the image falls into infinity, exceeding its limits. In the exhibition space, the work is adorned in a sheen of light, in a cave-temple like semi darkness, glimmering in a self-willed concreteness.

'*Man With Cockerel -2*' (2004)

Single-channel video, (video still), 6 min loop with stereo sound Back projection on a screen fitted in a constructed wall, (size variable)

The video by Kaleka explored that a man is caught in a circle of endless pursuit and capture of his escaped 'cockerel' (Plate 4.20). The viewer's day dream is jolted by a play with diegetic and non-diegetic conventions of sound - domestic, industrial, every day and the environment . The only comfort is the long silent lapping of the waves on an empty screen at the end of the loop before the man again finds his 'cockerel' and arrives at the frame (Suri, 2015).

'*Man in Water*' (2003)

Two-channel video (video still). Installed as projections on a wall and object. Room open on three sides, 396.2 x 305.8 x 1219.2 cm (156 x 120 x 480 inches) (variable). Water dye black 152.4 cm (60 inches) deep (variable) 13 min loop with stereo sound.

The work '*Man in Water*' (Plate 4.21) explored sculptural shapes in water that can be read as a mountain/ mound/rock (painted fibreglass). The projection at the back is 13 ft wide x 10 foot high (size variable). These are the exact dimensions of the room/enclosure built on the pool. The pool water was dyed black to get a good reflection. The back-projection shows a traffic junction in old Delhi from dawn to the afternoon. People are going about their chores. The work eventually gets extremely jammed and busy with *tongas* (horse carriages), pedal rickshaws, pushcarts, buffalo-carts, trucks, buses et al. and even a 'caravan' of elephants. At critical moments the traffic gets speeded up and even begins to rush furiously backwards. The entire traffic from time to time is submerged under a sea of water.

In the video work, the man who is dressed in a burlap-sacking cloak (not unlike Indian labourers on building sites) looks/ appears like a monk who is carrying a sack over his shoulder. As we hear the constant traffic sound combined with various sounds of stock-market reports, medical advice, commentaries, television advertisements et al. the man goes through different emotional states and transformations. At one time a burning book passes through his body (instantly we see a swarm of burning books shooting over the traffic). He lurches forward and fades into the rock behind him. A cave mouth appears in his place. In it we see a 'beetle struggling on his back', a 'vulture circling the sky', a 'man balancing on a fallen tree in a forest' and finally 'children playing on dunes'. The audience can hear their laughter, and the man re-emerges. He shrugs and roars like a lion and changes into 'gold'. The mountain/mound changes into gold as he fades into it. The sea behind changes into gold as well as we hear strains of a *Sufi* song.

'*Windows*' (2002)

Single Channel video-sculpture, 244 x 122 x 122 cm, (96 x 48 x 48 inches), 6 minute loop, sound. The work explored and revealed with single Channel video, 6-minute loop with sound.

'*Windows*' conceptualised free upright sculpture of 244 x 122 x 122 cm (96 x 48 x 48 inches), high kiosk-like wood/board construction on wheels, collapsible to facilitate transportation (Plate 4.22). The work of video projected on the 'kiosk' making a 6-minute puppet-theatre/Punch & Judy, comic strip, kind of cinema-show: an enactment seen through and outside two windows. The installation requires and explores total darkness of ideally a tent, (size variable), in the open with black or dark blue interior and a colourful design on the outside (Kaleka, 2019).

'*Music Room*' (2002)

Single-Channel video, 13-minute loop with sound.

Conversion into CD-ROM, commissioned by Artpix, Houston.

In work, a piece of Punjabi music is traced in a surreal room from old folk to skyscraper Bhangra. The '*Music Room*' (Plate 4.23) executed a tiny man sleeping in a nook of a room and woke up to the strains of old Punjabi folk music. He floats down to the floor and witnesses the Spatio-temporal changes happening outside his room through an opening in the wall and a door. These changes are accompanied by the evolution of Punjabi music and his stature, where he gets uncomfortably large in his tiny room.

'*Video Lounge*' (2002)

6 Channel video loop with sound. Alliance Française, New Delhi. The work is executed in collaboration with 'Silen TV' (Michel Mallard, Olivier Reneau, Denis Chevalier).

The work by Kaleka is Collaboration with 'SILEN TV', France Multiple projections cover the maximum space of a room creating an ambience composed only of moving images (Plate 4.24). In work, a visual environment is created which does not impose any single story on the viewer. Still, multiple narratives link-up between different projections, breakup and relink creating re-figurations of meaning. The audience can enter the video installation at any time as any point can be the beginning of one narration or an end of another, inviting a 'different' kind of intimacy with the moving image. The study analyses that the video projections are in work on different screens are continuously shuffled, and new ones added.

'*Powder Room*' (1999 – 2000)

Single-channel video-sculpture Installation, 3-minute loop with sound

The work by Kaleka is a single-channel video-sculpture Installation (Plate 4.25). There are two-way functional washroom, (size variable), with mirror (size variable), light bulbs, washbasin/running water, lipsticks, face powder, ribbons, *bindis* (the mark *Hindu* women wear on the forehead), comb, tissues and other articles of adornment—3 minute loop with sound involved in the video- sculpture Installation.

The work analyses that when an individual/observer looks at his/her reflection in the mirror of the work and is free to use any of the make-up items in the room. Suddenly he/she is disturbed by a piece of melancholy music emanating in the work which is from the mirror and an observer's reflection in the mirror is replaced by other images. The faces in the mirror replace his/her face at precisely the same distance from an individual as his/her reflection. Thus in work, an observer's eyes do not re-focus to engage the intrusive images. The images tell stories / open narratives.

One possible reading suggests a dysfunctional family that comes together in another sort of reflection - the reflection on a photo-sensitive film: a family photograph.

'*Man Threading A Needle*' (1998-1999)

Single-Channel video projected on 59 x 91 cm (23.3 x 35.8 inch), oil painting, 6-minute loop with sound.

Kaleka's '*Man Threading A Needle*' is one of his earlier video projections . The work is reflected in an oil painting on board which is 59 x 91 cm (23.3 x 35.8 inch) in dimension and of a man threading a needle sitting on an easel. The painting is spot-lit (Kaleka, 2019). The work reveals as one viewer understands the man unexpectedly blinks or swallows . He infrequently makes an anxious effort to thread the needle. At various instants he catches the sound of a peacock along with a short train and a police siren, this makes him nervous. The man's body drags with heavy breathing, and the painting stays still almost all the time . This effect is realised by projecting a video of a man threading the needle on a painting of the man threading a needle (Kaleka, 2019).

In the year 2019, the researcher of the study visited Kaleka's latest solo exhibition entitled " *Fear of A New Dawn* " which was exhibited in Vadehra Contemporary in New Delhi from March 8 to April 6. In this exhibition, Kaleka's five artworks have been displayed in which four of them are New Media Artworks by Ranbir Kaleka. The study of the research also analyses them by interviewed artist Kaleka.

'*House of An Opaque Water*' (2012)

3 Channel projection with sound on three panels

The work '*House of An Opaque Water*' in the exhibition "*Fear of A New Dawn*" has explored a three-channel video projection in a three panel where video reveals a village under water and sometimes also above the water (Plate 4.26). The waves of water sometimes float over the images, which have the reflections of villagers. The video also reveals a portrait of a man along with different elements under water; sometimes, images also show flames on the boat. The boat appears without any person floating on water.

The video also reveals the appearance of fishers who are looking for their business. There is the appearance of hands in the video who tried to make circles in the arena of the riverside. Along with the reveal of the village home reflections, the projection also has the appearance of the artist himself in the video with the presence of urban house reflections. The video creates a mysterious ambience with the involvement of various sounds with the monochromatic approach. There is conceptual analysis in the work the artist explores through the representation of the video projection.

'*Fearsome Acquiescence of A Monotonous Life*' (2019)

Two-Channel video installation with sculpture. W 196 x D 138 x H 82 cm / H 164 cm with shaped pedestal. Channel A: 1-minute loop, channel B: 10-minute loop.

The work is a video installation by Kaleka which is displayed in the exhibition entitled "*Fear of A New Dawn*" held in New Delhi (Plate 4.27). In this work, there is an involvement of sculptural architectural form, and inside this, there are projections progressed on. The projections reveal that there are two rooms in the frame. One central figure who has the involvement in the work who has the reflections of his mental process appears in work. The figure moves in the two rooms repeatedly with his thought process.

Kaleka conceptually explores the moving images into this work where structure and projections are altogether connected philosophical aspects of an individual's mental experience of visual interaction and also the visual interpretations. In work, the amalgamation of moving images along with sound expresses a psychic dialogue between the artwork and the viewer.

'*Not Anonymous_ Walking to the Obscure Fear of A New Dawn*' (2017-18) Single Channel projection on multiple surfaces, 275 x 122 cms. 9 minutes 18 seconds loop

The study of the research finds that the work is a mixture of dramatic and mysterious narratives by Kaleka (Plate 4.28). In the single-channel projection, there are involvements of a lot of visual interpretations. The work appears with a chaotic ambience where a viewer can observe that there is a child crying . Then the video reflected a deer which is running in forestry, and suddenly a moving image appeared in the video where the head of a deer was found bloody in the ground. The video also reveals a man who suddenly fell on land along with the chaotic sound appearance in the projection.

The image of deer again comes with a smooth situation where an observer can find a human being mother feeding her breast milk to the deer, which creates a philosophical message to the global society. Then the video explored that the deer is going towards forestry, but gradually the forestry also reflected burnt locations into the video. There is a visual language in the video which also carries the aspects of cycling of the globe.

'Bound' (2018)

Single-channel projection on burnt wood. 275 x 122 cm, 5 minutes loop.

In work, the study of the research finds that the artist explored situations of sufferings (Plate 4.29). The video reveals a lying man in the projection which is on burnt wood. The man appears with sorrowful expressions and in depressions and sufferings. In the video, there is an appearance of a dog or fox figurine, which is also mysteriously vanishing with a short impression of gestures. The work by Kaleka has a philosophical presence of symbolic narratives along with conceptual elements in the work . The work has the gesture of frustrations, sorrow, sufferings. This work has a strong appearance in Kaleka's solo exhibition entitled *"Fear of A New Dawn"* which was held in March-April 2019 in New Delhi.

4.3 New Media Artworks of Surekha

Indian contemporary women artists are recognised as among the most stimulating. Provocative and visually inventive of contemporary art creators who instinctively or explicitly are representing through intersectional identifications, creating work that navigates the complexities of identity in the contemporary world (Nochlin, 2003). Surekha is one such artist who surpasses the fixations of most of her male counterparts. She is known as a video artist. But the appropriation is too restrictive. It fails to register the diversity that her work extends to or the critical force that the terms artist and video are subjected to in her work. Surekha is better described as a site-specific multimedia projectionist. Whether video projections or eight films, of just a performative photograph, the significance of Surekha's work is generated through a complex interaction of space, projection, imagery the viewer Surekha's work contents several broad issues; such as myth, item, history and collective memory, identity and human relationships. What distinguishes her practice is that these themes are made present in work through an underlying ambivalence concerning the role of imagery and reality. In an interview she discusses several of her artworks and her working practice. Surekha has exhibited widely in India and internationally and continues to work in Bangalore.

4.3.1 Surekha's Art Practice: The Body Represented to Recurrently Re-emerge as a Polyvalent Site

The research study analyses this has been a continuing thread, Surekha in her early works has used the material of rice paper almost as a kind of skin. Simultaneously the artist was also using it as fabric. And along with this Surekha was also representing fragments of autobiographical narrative– women's stories/narratives from almost more than a century back, where they interact about their experience of wearing a blouse for the debut time under the British colonial time (Surekha, 2019). In a way, the artist was trying to extend our notion of the body, trying to connect different things. Later, Surekha experimented fabric to make costumes which conveyed a sense of the body but which could also have been some strange entity (Hazra, 2011).

When Surekha started making videos, the artist tried to explore a particular issue by constructing different characters. The study analyses that in Surekha's videos, there is often a tension between 'documentary' and 'fiction'. The artist tends to edit her videos very less in a minimal way and then there are jiffies where the observers might acquire insecure of the identity of the onscreen body which is the artist Surekha's or is it that of the fictional presence she seems to be depicting. Sometimes it could even be just a minimal appearance that lobes into relief – like the point in Waves - *"Reaching Myself"* where the artist is seen adjusting her clothes (Hazra, 2011).

In Surekha's works actions that makes the artist relook at the narrative and how it has been constructed which explores and reminds Surekha of another thing. The research study analyses that in most of the Surekha's video art, the body as such doesn't act. Other energies characteristically perform upon it: like the waves that toss and turn the body in *"Reaching Myself"*. And also the act that might be engendered by this non-acting body can be a set of effortless gestures which are barely remarkable in itself but which becomes essential within the overall narrative of video (Hazra, 2011).

In Surekha's art practice, the artist had explored that some of her videos then work almost like a recorded performance. As in *'Moment of Strange Stillness'* – a work that Surekha executed in Sri Lanka – where the artist implemented motionless in a public space for around twenty-five minutes, and the whole length was documented on video. But this video was not just a record of Surekha's performance. In essence, it apprehended certain moments of the spectator's reaction and later in the final piece. These responses became a set of entry opinions that could give a very different reading of the work (Hazra, 2011).

The research study analyses that through her art practice Surekha initially drew to performance and it is, in the second stage of her blouse project, when the artist was working directly with rice paper and stitches then she instigated to feel that the work needs something else, another element as it were. As an entity by itself, it looked incomplete (Hazra, 2011). That's when Surekha started using photography - body with the fabric. And the artist began using it in a way where the body and the material began to merge into each other. Later around 2000, the artist started to think and use the video camera more frequently. Surekha almost used it as a sketching tool – imagine the scenario that an individual is there, he/she has the video camera with himself/herself, an individual gets an idea and to carry forward and shoot it. So there is nobody of that elaborate planning that one typically associated with video production. In fact, in most cases, the artist doesn't even work from a very planned script. All though Surekha does have the idea in her perception. So this kind of process allows the artist to execute a broader range of things with a certain level of flexibility and spontaneity. However, there are also a couple of videos, which are much more deliberate and controlled than the others (Hazra, 2011). A viewer can observe that it is this 'sketching' potential of the medium that has contributed significantly to the practice of video art. However, talking about sketching, the artist is also interested to know more about the way an individual has used stitching in some of Surekha's works.

In the work process frequently with stitching, Surekha created the world of stitching that is intimately connected with women's stories – stories we have grown up with and which circulate through oral traditions (Hazra, 2011). Surekha's thought reflects that it is where the video came in handy. The research study identified Surekha through her New Media Art practises bringing two technologies together – the ancient skill of stitching and the relatively newer technology of the video. So the work that appeared out of this was *'Threading the Threads'*. The work represented a group of women sitting around and stitching a quilt-like work together while sharing stories among themselves. But even in this deceptively harmonious public setting, the artist was trying to build a different narrative as it were. As an individual watches, these women stitch and enjoy their stories; his/her eyes also travel to the coverlet that is being stitched. There an individual identifies that it is not a beautiful decorative shape that is forming there but reveals a clutch of random, chaotic lines and needles. So in a way, the sews tell their own story and then when someone plays the music of the actual oral stories along with the image of these chaotic stitches, altogether a different narrative level emerges. The next part of this work was done mostly with urban women. Many of them were the artist's friends, though not necessarily artists. Surekha installed a private space and invited these six women into that space individually. Once they were inside that space, the artist requested these women to do something that they considered a near movement or share something about themselves that they have never shared before (Hazra, 2011). All these interactions were recorded and then projected onto the same object – that is the private space Surekha had formed for them. So when a spectator came upon the work, he or she could hear the voices of these females actually obviously whereas the image remained unsure and uncertain. Also, what is stimulating is in what way specific domestic spaces become quite evocative. For example in *'Bhagirathi bringing water'* the bathroom space grows a space for contemplation, or in Urban Heroines- the boiling concept the kitchen develops a space for an ironic play on power (Hazra, 2011). Similarly, the stimulating is in what way sure internal spaces develop relatively reminiscent.

In fact a significant part of Surekha's a series of work was shot in her house – because most of the domestic ambience are very intimate spaces and which also often have a strong political subtext. Apart from that sometimes the artist goes out and shoots, in a beach or gym for example (Hazra, 2011). So in a way, if an individual looks at it, most of the interior spaces in Surekha's work are located inside a house whereas exterior spaces are largely within nature.

The research study analyses that through the process like for the work that Surekha did at the Mysore KHOJ workshop where two images stand out from the artist's childhood memories of growing up in Karnataka days and visiting Mysore on holidays – one is that of the Mysore Palace, predominantly when it was lit up in the evenings. The other is of the jasmine garlands, the famous Mysore Mallige. So when it was absolutely necessary to host the KHOJ workshop in Mysore, Surekha had decided to work on jasmine. And during the workshop, Surekha explored working with the local photo studios, which have a tradition of photographing women with their jasmine plaits. It is an exceptional preparation in these studios with the women standing and facing the camera. At the same time, a deliberately positioned mirror at the back shows off the jasmine braid to the viewer. When an individual looks at the jasmine ponytails in these photographs, they almost look like the spinal cord. Now, though these photo studios are still very much there in Mysore, finding one, which had an archive of old photographs, was difficult. But eventually, Surekha did manage to locate one which has meticulously preserved almost every single picture that they have shot over the last sixty years. The studio was set up by the grandfather of the current owner and has been in the operational mood without a break (Surekha, 2019).

The study analyses that in Surekha's art practice, over the years, there has been a lot of engagement with the city of Bangalore may be because Bangalore has been the city of personal space to the artist. Surekha was born and brought up there. She was born into a peasant's family, and the artist's ancestors must have stayed here for at least two hundred years. Actually, over the years Surekha has seen the transformation of Bangalore, particularly its rural areas. She has witnessed the city taking over the village. The artist's parents lost their land and had to adapt to new ways of living and working. Nowadays, of course, Surekha's community has more or less adjusted itself and is part of an overall urban framework. However, the artist's surroundings still have their village fairs, festivals and a variety of rituals and folk performances. Even though Surekha doesn't believe in these rituals, she finds them to be a part of her immediate past, as they give an individual a glimpse into areas of the artist's lives which they are rapidly forgetting. The city is divided roughly into two regions – the Market and Cantonment. Surekha originally belongs to the Market area but has started venturing out into the Shivaji Nagar and Cantonment area. Now, the artist would say that she is in the middle – simultaneously part of both these contexts.

4.3.2 Surekha's Art Practice: Personifying Beauty and Pain

There is always a blend of contradiction and complementary revelation in our, uniquely feminine, relationship with clothes. Women cover themselves for modesty, yet, through tailoring and adornment make their sensuality surface. Feminine conceal their shape and emotions, but the body's structure, movements and condition moulded by daily routine and feelings, emerge from under the fabric and impregnate it.

Surekha's costume-body was made of sumptuous, rough silk, its translucence over gentle, smooth areas and its opacity, when harder and crumpled, allowing for the intuition of other women's presence in the artist's empathic identification, of exceptional qualities, desires and sensations merging with harsh ones. The deep, dark red maroon evokes passion , pleasure, decay and dying. The kurta-robe is embellished with and painfully bound to tight knots and long twines which viscerally recall guts, ligaments, veins and nerves as well as votive threads on sacred trees tied by women yearning or fearing for their children. The related photographic work shows a woman wearing a dress. The plastic impact of the two-dimensional image completes the flatness of its sculptural version. The aura of simultaneous sensuality and anonymity lets the viewer perceive and absorb it in terms of a universal and personal statement-suggestion in which the artist remains embodied.

Surekha's aesthetic methods and concepts are unconventional and contemporary but derive their real character, references and expressive dynamics from the matrix of the immediate environment determined by its patriarchal tradition and imagination which has evolved from the organic world, the materials and objects of labour and everyday experience. The artist responds to the familiar, yet enigmatic and always highly charged circumstances in a passionate manner – spontaneously, intuitively sensing it through her skin. Being an independent participant in that reality, her physical-psychic engrossment yields a distanced reflection while retaining the essential bond. Surekha, then, relies foremost on the raw physicality of things and substances belonging to the traditional woman, on their colour, texture, fibre and carnal smoothness, opacity and luminosity. Here the handicraft, its processes and its makers become central with the employment of its objects, materials and motifs, even actual persons. The artist stimulates it all towards a poetic and metaphoric impact drawing as much from the inherently intrinsic properties of things as from her compassionate and interpretative response. Her images so become embodiments of human frames, feeling minds and stories – subjective as well as archetypal, of an entire landscape and flow of living.

As Surekha's clothes manifest the body and her body accommodates other women and objects, the substance and the motif continually undergo an oscillation between identities that, seemingly different, contribute to the many aspects of one phenomenon. In her earlier works with dress elements and the sculptural and photographic pieces centred on blouses, the surface as the skin contains the volume of its body, the body manifesting what is latent inside it. Drawing lines exchange their properties and associations with hair, tissues, bones, blood veins and nerves, with plant stalks, trails of water and undulations of scenery and soil, with threads, running stitch patterns, embroideries and block prints. The shades of red among the graphic ground appear to be permeated by the sap of plants and menstrual excretions, the blood of desire, child-birth and sustenance, of wounding from violence and suppressed, long-endured pain, of cracking and decaying. The flow of ageless existence and the fluidity of creative imagination transform into wearing out in labour and oppression and into the craft. Ever shifting her attention from a close, limited area or a single object to a broad overview, the artist tends to work in series informed by multiple and pervasive metamorphoses of a primary image. She frequently repeats an image or motif in one art piece as if unfolding its journeys and permutations through the path and matrix of life. Alluding to the spread of unstitched fabric, like in the sari, in screens, curtains or bed covers, she enhances the metaphor. Her favourite object is a flower epitomising the female condition with its organic and craft links, with the beauty of aspiration, adornment and carnal desire, with maturing and withering. She sees her flowers in red and white. The archaic ritualism of the female and male principle, which paints temple compounds in red and white stripes, reverberates in societal and domestic situations, under Surekha's fingers acquiring tones of innocence and pure joy that contrast with as well as permeate passion and suffering. The '*Eye of the Needle*' works were cut and sewn into a merger of plait, jasmine and backbone. The white of the thin, translucent, shimmering silk forms long, enchantingly fragile braids of radiant petals, while the cotton buds underneath conjure softness and sensuality. Crimson threads run through the middle of each twist as though they were hair and blood veins, the shiny, sharp needles in them adding pain. The quaintly sculptural pieces even out on the surface of the fabric contoured by stitch strokes and spill into diffused, elusive fields of painterly colour, thus under scoring the nuanced- firm pervasiveness of the bodily-emotive state, the physical binding of the woman's hopes to her position in the patriarchy. If the braids imply and evoke her figure, the accompanying photographs focus on her corporeally channelled sensations. Rather than documenting a performance, they create densely atmospheric images where a nude's back is displayed wearing a jasmine braid. The accent is on graceful, and pleasurably self-aware sensuality weighed down to submission.

Their '*small homes*', white jasmine buds become a field of germination and blossoming, a curtain of active-matrix and rhythms of human existence, as the literal turns lyrical. Threaded into a large, rectangular quilt during the artist's interaction with a group of Lambani crafts women, it seems to have imbibed their effort, patient energy and stories. Like the set paradigms of these women's lives stirred by their abundance, the soft, compact cotton buds shape a repetitive, multi-course textile that at the same time exudes a sense of comfort, confinement and sensuous joy. It is violently separated but balanced too by the narrow stream cutting it vertically in the middle, where the running stitches of hairs or veins with needles have woven another pattern that alternates a regular, pre-set rhythm with a milder, silky spill of waves and tenderly chaotic eruptions. As if in reciprocation to the latter, the surface of this landscape from its underbelly unearths the emotive bodies of the women and the artist that are embedded within it.

Although inspired by mundane domesticity, it reveals traits of the feminine state akin to those ingrained in the ceremonial umbrella of royal splendour of Rajasthan. Enlarging its shape in semi-transparent, white silk, Surekha emphasises the enchanting opulence of the object that becomes its image. She dots its dome with an abundance of lusciously open red hibiscus flowers. The connection between the real hibiscus blossom which resembles artfully crumpled fabric and the craftwork metamorphosing into aesthetic motifs is mediated by the looser red twines that make their angular paths through the parasol, encircle it and hang from it, also by the delicate outline drawings with ladies' palms that, like in classic miniatures, hold the flowers. It is only through the pitched beauty and mood-intensity of the image yields its sinister implications. Illuminated from behind, or rather, from within, the designs on the dome yield tonalities of blood and of fire that spread onto and into the white of the '*Flaming Feet*' parasol and let one intuit the glorified victim-hood of the *sati*. Its structure and patterns conjuring a sense of dizzy rotation, the object nearly metamorphoses into a landscape of female vitality – one that exults in the imposed restraint and unknowingly finds creative freedom within it. The pervasiveness between this condition and the aesthetic means is achieved again through the filtering of the surface, stroke, colour, volume and space, of opaque and translucent qualities enhanced by light, hesitant super impositions and tremulous cast shadows.

The '*Flaming Feet*' title could have been given to the two-channel video loop '*Between Fire and Sky*' which, in fact, for a split second shows a young girl walking through flames. Both these works, however, start from opposite ends to arrive at a similarly layered lyricism. Whereas in the tactile-elusive umbrella only the hue-fed atmosphere evokes fire, the video opts for recognisable imagery with flames and a girl captured by the camera and leads it to deeper suggestiveness. The aura of movement inherent in the former piece stirs a compulsion to give it flesh. Besides, the performance factor vital to

Surekha's photographic works must have naturally resulted in filming. The artist treats the filmed world quite like the material object that serves as a trigger towards a filtering metamorphosis of the positive image into poetry and metaphor. The video has a burning, flickering silhouette of an adolescent's hopscotch projected on the floor which at times approximates the contour of a body . In contrast, shots of the girl hopscotching amidst clouds are projected above it on the wall. Innocence between the lightness of imagination and the scorching reality comes to encapsulate the predicament of early womanhood.

If moods and associations arise from that place collaged juxtapositions of ordinary sights, '*Three Fragmented Actions of Silence*' uses direct shots with and ones altered by superimposing , blending, fleeting fragments, by adverse and abstract-like effects gained from scratches, blinking and technical refuse that add to a very aesthetic, though film-specific, painterly graphic character. The lyrical finesse that comes with roughness enables a feeling of fundamental existential contradictions as sustaining and complementary. The dual - positive/negative image of the artist eating and recreating a flower echoes in the veiling and unveiling of her face to conclude with two pairs of blue and red lined hands which turn into a confluence of water and blood, called '*blue river, red river*'. The work speaks as much about the processes of living as it does about Surekha's aesthetic and conceptual method. Although her body is shown throughout, it is the substance of film that has appropriated it for the revelation of mysteries latent within it.

The video must be virtually instinctual for Surekha considering its role in popular culture together with the already dominant film and photography which express the grass-roots ethos. As another consequence, she appropriates photographs as found objects and collaborating with them, entirely like she does with crafts women, on emotive and conceptual levels, stimulates them to acquire a revelatory potency. '*The Fragrance of Jasmine*' is a collection of eighty-three photographs from a small-time photo-studio in Mysore posing girls and women in bridal dress and jasmine braid against a mirror which reflects the braid's glory. Such pictures are taken on special occasions in early childhood, at puberty, wedding and pregnancy. The sheer number of the regularly arranged photos creates a rhythmic body-wall of female life stages, its entrenchment in tradition being visible in the dated mode of the decade's old shots. The decor of the small studio recurs with slight variations, its indulgently kitschy clutter loaded with poetry. There is some theatricality to it which passes onto the carefully costumed figures in ornate, opulent finery put on with relish but evidently beyond means. The expressions vary from innocent delight to unassuming or self-admiring pride and sadness. Throughout, under the weight of the brocade silk, jewellery and braid, not only the little girls betray a premature, artificially instilled-internalised adulthood, even a tired passivity set in societal strictures. The spontaneity ingredient in the making of the self-image becomes overwhelmed by the predetermined paradigm. The heavy floral braid over the girls' spines is given centrality and enhanced by its full reflection, so almost transforming them into bright objects of beauty owned by the patriarchal order. A play on the psychology of the subject and the viewer goads them to meet in the act of observation. The girls are aware of their appearance and its mirror reflection while looking straight into the camera which has immortalised both. They are made to look into the eyes of the spectator who is facing his, or especially her, fragmented reflection in the mirror mounting of the pictures. As the artist's guiding eye is intuited too, the viewer becomes the subject, and the issue becomes the viewer, thus incorporating Surekha's bodily sensitive stance.

The artist has internalised individual persons in local environs as much as the female condition, her attuning disposition ready to accept different cultures into her subjectivity and from social or historical perspectives. When in Rajasthan, she discovered the female fate behind the warrior's majesty. Working in Bristol, she reacted sensitively but as a human being to the city's past of maritime trade and colonialism as well as to the unacknowledged memory of Indian soldiers who died in the British army during the World War II. Her materials then are an old sail and paper poppy flowers commonly used in Europe to honour those who died in battle. '*The Inside Out*' photograph has a woman wearing a skin-costume of sail cloth. A mass of poppies line it from within, their long pins piercing the surface so that the body-dress becomes a defensive-aggressive coat of armour and proof of the vulnerability. At the same time, the distinction between the victim and the victimiser blurs. The blood-crimson blossoms exchange and blend properties of fabric design, tokens of homage and evocations of tissues and organs. The pervasive merger owes its impact to the oscillation between the flatness of the surface with graphic elements and shadows against the sensual plasticity of the illuminated torso and the bright glowing poppies.

Gradually this experience calms down and sublimates under Surekha's feminine sensibilities. '*They grow everywhere*' continues the reference to the poppy symbolism but absorbs it into the texture and flow of *sari* fabric. A thick carpet of flowers lies on the ground recalling the sudden abundance of wild poppies on battlefields, believed to spring from the blood of fallen soldiers and serving as an epitome of and an offering to their sacrifice. Four cascades of white silk descend from and rise to the ceiling as though gathering the blossoms into their folds and expense as the flesh of their pattern carries the memory through the surface and the trajectories of living. In tune with the Indian spirit, the sumptuous finesse of the translucent, luminous silk holds sensual tenderness and lushness on par with the pure asceticism of mourning. The fabric is the body of commemoration, and in the accompanying photographs, the artist takes it for her veil and drapes it over her back, lowering her head in a quiet, respectful immersion. The diffused tonalities of red pervaded by light seem to draw the shadow of death into the passionate intensity of existence. The roughly cut prints have been mounted in charmingly bright cheap frames which brings them back to the ambience of the local photo-studio.

The tenderness with which Surekha cherishes the memory of the dead and nurses its mood contains an equal amount of care and effort that go into locating and preserving instances of fatality. The work *'They grow everywhere'* has a sibling of the same title – an altered reflection and a completion-in a long sequence of uniform framed mirrors that stand like a commemorative wall which absorbs the concrete yet the sudden occurrence of life here and now. Over an uneven rhythm and almost embraced by rows of red poppies, each mirror face bears photographic fragments of real wall surfaces wounded by bullets, the artist running her crimson stitch around them to mark the spots as if in a healing gesture of protection. A futile act, it is nevertheless vital to our humanity, offering a possibility of catharsis. Its role underlies all-sustaining labour – that of useful purposes and artistic ones, and the small image a relief with an iron smith shot in the head can be grasped as an alter ego of the artist bonded to her subject matter. The intuition grows on and into the viewer walking along this wall of somewhat blurred mirrors whose surface accepts and merges reflections from the external surroundings inclusive of the viewer's body.

The highly aesthetic language that addresses universal dimensions of violent death may not suffice at a time of actual proximity to warfare. Hence, Surekha during her Sri Lankan Theertha art workshop at Candy returned to the directness of reality captured on the camera. The photographs in *'The Moment of Strange Stillness'* show her seated in the pose of meditation, her eyes closed amid the green sceneries with expansive hills, abundant vegetation as well as busy roads of the nearby town and domestic or mercantile interiors. Shifting between atmospheric, formally nuanced harmony and vivacious, sometimes oppressive chaos, the shots exude a yearning for serenity against the signs of aggression represented by the bullets with cyanide and reliable, long nails that point at the meditating figure as well as by the commerce that has turned LTTE bullet capsules into fashion accessories and Buddha statues into tourist commodities. One image documents a street scene with a military biker and the ancient Buddha monolith towering hazily from the faraway hilltop. In another, Surekha once more appeals to the cathartic power of art-making, when she is sitting in meditation on the road, framed by an empty canvas stretcher. Back home, she placed each of those sixty photographs in a wooden box as though in a shelter, in an art mounting and an architectural niche that could belong to a sacred space. Real objects being present there, the occasional bullet and the nails that join the boxes, form the square base of the earth plane. Through this she erects the fragile skeleton of a stupa- like mound, once again transposing the concrete into the emotively aesthetic.

Since enough time has elapsed to enable both intimacy and a distanced aesthetic resolution, drastic qualities of the real strive for a balance in visual metaphor drawn from sheer sensation, incorporated as well as intuited now on a much more severe plane. Surekha's earlier '*Selving A Body*' series traced the contours of hand and feet bones in the context of sartorial embellishment. Her latest works dealing with the finality of our mortal state focus on the motif, and frequently the physical authenticity, of human bones. Assembling several synthetic casts of the hip bone, Surekha arranges a considerable flower, '*The Bouquet*'. Soft and harsh, it piles up, rises, opens and sinks, simultaneously as though metamorphosing into an archaic sacral mound. '*Bones and Flowers*' is an array of ten casts taken from the back of the human skull, its translucent substance alluding at the once animated bodily fluid, as it emphasises the lines on the cranial surface together with its part resembling a violent suture. The obvious conjures poetry and through its surface lets one see the flowers-objects embodying the spirit. There is more sadness in them presently, and the pale commercial blossoms of plastic come through with a faint lyricism instead of vibrancy, their design is interrupted by the insertion of bullets and their marks amid sporadic pieces of charcoal.

Two casts have already singed a deep, dense black auguring doom, and the residual red blossoms of warmth within reveal themselves only from close on. Fragile and predetermined to cessation, life even in its death holds an imprint of survival struggle and a seed of rebirth. Surekha reinvents the motif of the incorporated costume which brings to the surface the physical and emotional state of the body. The Shield resembles a sleeveless dress following the sensuous volume of the absent female figure. Loosely tied together by white twines from segments of the human spine, its mass creates a nearly ornate floral design which pulsates. It retains a hint of fluid plasticity and mostly flattens out, almost graphic under the ominous blackness. Again, the artist wishes for an intimate, embodied experience with a more positive note of faith in the resurgence of sensual forces from decay. In the accompanying photograph, she wears the same dress on her bare skin. Illuminated frontally, the hard flower bones are like an eerily splendid necklace and like a coat of armour that strives to protect yet reveals inner vulnerability. It also absorbs some of the beauty of the live person, its mild-rugged plasticity almost conjuring the waxed fleshiness of flowers and supple skin. Thus, having progressed through a grave trajectory, Surekha has returned, firmer and subtler, to the foundations of her imagery.

4.3.3 Nature into Surekha's New Media Artworks: Forms/Contents/Processes

Surekha is practising since last three decades nearly and the research study analyses that through her art practice she believes that if she looked back and says what happens since previous twenty-five years almost – it's one is Surekha trying to sees art as sort of knowledge, acquiring knowledge and then pushing the boundaries of imaginations and working in different layers and at the same time trying to create a new language.

After her studies in Santiniketan that was in 1992, Surekha went back to Bangalore, and during that time, she was doing teaching and also trying to explore what she can do with her artworks. So that was the time Surekha was doing a lot of Installations, but at the same time, her art practice also expressed how she could use her modernist teaching like coming from Santiniketan. That was the specific period that Surekha through her art practice started using rice paper as a media which is a very traditional media which explored the last two hundred years in Santiniketan like through water colours. Surekha brought it, used it, but at the same time in the artworks, her background of literature was there. She reads a lot from *Vachana Sahitya*. These stories influence many as most of the concepts are feminist and a lot of gender issues.

That was the time Surekha also came across literature from Kumaran Asan- where there are talks about the body in a sense went about gender, so that is one autobiographical story which is subtle the artist a lot and also which realised Surekha the whole history of women hood, the history of Indian women. So this story is taken from autobiographical writing written over a hundred years back. This is about some of the lower class of community from Kerala. They were not supposed to wear blouses, almost like a hundred years again. So in the story, a woman gets a gift from her cousin, a blouse and when gets it, the woman gets anxious, and she wears it and shows it to her husband. The husband liked the wearing of the blouse, but when the woman wears it and comes out, her mother looks a turned calls her asking her to remove the blouse. But this woman wanted to wear the blouse, so her desires are so dominating, so she started wearing a blouse at night, and when she comes out, she removes the blouse.

The study of the research analyses that this story suddenly made Surekha meant, made her realise what sort of patriarchal system and how women can be governed by too many things like patriarchal issues related to gender. Then for the artist what is essential is the desire where the women wanted to turn to look at the body and twisting-turning those of the things Surekha likes small freedom which was very important. So through the readings by the artist that was the time Surekha started working with using rice paper blouses and started making blouses and working- treating them as almost like skin and also using lot of crafty images in a parts of the body so somehow those things the artist started and incorporated the rice paper that was Surekha's work entitled *'Selving A Body'* (1998-1999) (Plate 4.30). The work has explored the materials of rice paper, pigments and thread.

Immediately after that Surekha was expressing that somehow she had to take that work beyond just an object of craft and that almost like twenty years back people did not know how to react to that work also so then the artist started making photographs in relationship with the body. Surekha's thoughts like to the extent that works into a or something on to the body. Then in the year 2001, Surekha started making photographs about the body, costumes and all and later that photography and others continued with the costume making about the body as an extension of the body for work for like three-four years. The artist had started using poppies and ship sails and then committing the body as a field of violence. Then this is also the time when Surekha was very much interested in video making. So together, the artist started to explore both objects, installations and video art, and that is still the beginning of the learning videos and also like it was VHS that time. So the artist started using a video camera almost as a tool like a sketch because that very period she was not sure whether she would like to make massive projects or whatever. So during that time, Surekha started using the camera as a sketching tool. Then she started a lot of experimental videos altogether like the artist was working on like installations, photography, videos and together but that was the time the artist also started her even forms, even like the contents, the ideas extending that from the artist's studio practice to the public arena. So until then, Surekha's approach was based on literature and creating something inside the story/studio but also taking a lot from history.

Since then the artist also started incorporating the public space and then Surekha's photo actions started photo performances and then by the end of 2010 the artist began working lot of issues related to the city of Bangalore and several video installations and also like these who process of making also like in the beginning Surekha was liking making short videos and the end altogether they used to be shown as the vast body of work like video installations like one of the first project is *'Communing with Urban Heroines'* (2007) the artist's gender issues, her concerns on the gender issues and also like what was happening outside.

Surekha's video art practices concerns for gender issues came about more firmly in her works, such as *'Communing with urban Heroines'*. Regarding the works, Surekha reflected that *'Communing with Urban Heroines'* (2007) is a culture-specific project which was Surekha's first video installation on a larger scale. It comprised fourteen videos, installed together; it positioned gender-specific experiences of the contemporary urban woman, In the face of the almost regularised, sure, yet mysterious death through water and fire. Domestic violence is the most ignored form of gender-specific violence when compared to abuse due to terrorism or war. Based on her set way of unnatural deaths in the city of Bangalore, Surekha created these videos.

Now the study of research goes through an analytical review on Surekha's *'Communing with Urban Heroines'*.

'Communing with Urban Heroines'

The show *'Communing with urban Heroines,'* is a culture-specific video installation by Surekha in March 2007 in Bangalore (Plate 4.31). The show contained a video installation by Surekha, together titled as *'Community with Urban Heroines.'* The viewer had to view each of these videos as individual pieces and as a single chain of installed videos, with mutually built-in relation, within the situation.

A metaphor, used to cross the limits of realism, becomes a realism of its-own-kind in Surekha's diptych video called *'Between Fire and Sky '* (2008) (Plate 4.32). It has a girl playing hop-scotch on the cloud (Projected on the wall) and on fire (Projected as an overview, on the wedded floor). A girl on a cloud and on fire is a double-metaphor of reality. The projection of light- hop-scotch on the wooden texture of the floor gives a sense of immediacy as well as site-specificity. And desire of the audience for physical participation on fire-hopscotch is evoked and rejected for there is this overview of Janaki herself doing it, for the audience. We can see it from the top view; the eye expands its metaphoric self as a physique to participate. It immediately is taken back because of the presence of Janaki almost underneath one's feet.

In other words, the frame of the video and the image within, correlate in all her videos . Just like the above said vide. It was as we the audiences' experience of any of her videos and what occurred /narrated inside were inseparable. A woman's poster, the constructed positioning of a woman-in urban and urban woman, was placed within the premise of deliberate ambiguity. The former is an outsider aspirant, while the latter is a new avatar. This is Surekha's first take on narrates (along with the does). The woman in the videos is desirous of a multiple role, but as the variants of the very same woman. They don't charge, but their situation and hence their roles do. They make tea out of mixed as well as teasing puns 'Boiling concept'. Even as a super woman, she needs to prepare tea and to make tea as a super human act are two contemporary readings which criss-cross each other, beyond other related experiences. The close up of the boiling tea has a geo catastrophic presence, the tea is non-consumable but the evocation of the deletion to man in superman is consuming. Her presence in the gym, burring concept is also a presence located within the instruments of a physical interventionist. She herself as ornamented imagery- due to close up shots of legs, profile and the like, arranges herself within the video in Surekha way as to face the ever assuring photograph of Frida in the video installed opposite, as if there is a routed offering occurring within the kitchen, in the process of merely making tea. The titles including business and boiling are epistemological exigencies engaged both the physician and the morticians, respectively it is at such a strange, restless juncture that a new urban woman and a woman within urban, both try to relocate themselves with an identity. Sociologically, if she occupies a male's space 'Burning concept' it is a public sphere that she negotiates. But without being loud in addressing the space of a cliché, she somehow minimises such set modes of sociological interventions. The whole idea of video installation was engaged to participate in such post-production interactive occurrences, wherein the artist would camouflage herself as the image as an iconic imagery Bhagirathi, as an action film making (as a montage), as an abode (making a home). The meaningful projection of image as a sign with a meaning is what is being contested herein due to the classical symbol plus meaning as an image, wherein the female-image was secondary to the overall frame/format of the video (as in Three Fragmented Actions of silence: Act I, II & III).

Towards this end, the videos '*Making Home*' and '*F-lovers*' are exaggeratedly Ammos and the most prominent projection, Janaki, is a thousand times wider than these two. The defined, domestic space that she minimises into realising the perfect area that she demands, within an urban, semi-elitist, seemingly masculine (though not male) space like a gym, or like the firmness of a peaceful posture amidst the chaos of Sri Lankan Political historicity.

After reversing the process of reality turning into metaphors- Surekha's facilitates mother mode of locating her heroines within the urban. Along with the tax and kitchen photograph series, she comes up with a newer reading of a widely accepted notion of viewership. In flowers for the kitchen, flowers become the silent tokens in an empty kitchen space. Surekha makes her private myths public. It is also an act of replacing reality with metaphases! For instance, the clouds in '*Janaki between fire and sky*' were recorded during the flight journey while the art remains as a person. Still, a permanent part of the artist's memoir so does the Colombo, Buddhism and the polihealunversp in a moment to strange stillness. Anal eristic geography, a religion and a political standpoint together metamorphosed for mobile space. In '*A moment of strange stillness*' the urban media, that is, the video technicalities of reversal shows the movement is resisted from within its reality; she is still unperturbed even when people walk backwards. The frames and the imagery within are indifferent in stretching the urban, to make space for her heroines. The personal/personalising of space is a constant concern that threatens together in her videos. '*making Home*', '*Bhagirathi*' and '*Boiling concept*' are videos that were shot within a domestic space that, yet again, shifts a local, living, real area into immediate metaphoric artistic locations. The protagonist is in a private bathtub '*Bhagirathi*' is facing the trial posed by the lonely and nostalgic camera. Desires to pasteurise that, which was stored in the memories of childhood. Thus there are not only multiple autobiographies . Modes of the depiction of the artist, but they are multi-dimensional as well. The final autobiographical shift, also a/to shift from the real self to image to the actual of the media is in three fragmented actions of silence: Act I, II &III in the horizontally divided frames, the top half contains the artist taking out, petal by petal from the mouth and pasting it to its actual Stan as it creating a flower, act of impossibility set within reality of filmmaking in reverse. In the lower half, it is the same reverse scene of eating petals in negative and upside down.

In act II '*Unveiled images*' the technique of 16mm and super and camera. Less film, the montage of file shots and footage does something ranging to a simple act of a veil, un-covering face, in blue-sepia. Superimposed with montage, the mask unveils various realities. Within a couple of minutes, the image acquires the density of a biogas-mask, a veil, a west-Asian character and the like. In Act III, the blue and the red live on the palm lines, transforming into a pool of blue river and red-river by the end of reacting. Thus it is the characters-supposed to represent be a metaphor, of enacting the artists self, of the desire to exist us heroines in the urban, which also means a lot of appropriation with existing modalities, re-inventing one person, as though to play with the possible play of paradoxes to submerge the real process, montage, image and even the ever-ambiguous interplay of videos in mutual terms! Altogether, the video installation's title desire to *'Communing with Urban Heroines'* is in itself an act of an urban heroine. If one recalls, Surekha's association with the city is a semi-urban, middle class, semi orthodox upbringing within a geo-political location of Bangalore in the 80s. Yet, she maps another kind of personality to several subjects at once. They are the artist as a woman, the metaphorical representation of herself as a woman and artist at the same time someone being like that in geography that was masking itself with the idea of being urban and a desire to stretch her area into activism.

The video installation show opened with an interactive talk *'making violence unthinkable'* by Donna Fernandes. She is an activist who, being part of vino Chana, addresses women's issues predominantly- the domestic violence and unnatural death.

Surekha's research on domestic violence in the city of Bangalore also is a body of concern into her art practice related to gender issues. The artist went and worked with some NGOs and then worked on the archives then she created subtle fictions based on the stories of real documents, the real death cells, the city which was like a document like almost two thousand deaths in a year and most of them are domestic deaths. So In her art practice, what ways did the artist create fictions out of it instead of using the same story and based on myths and folk. They were the thing like *Bhagirathi* – a story which was about a woman who was like a given sacrificed to get water and then later the *Sita*s – the half scotch on fire. The artist created fourteen video installations showing in Bangalore based on those stories. At the same time, Surekha did not limit herself only to art projects. She was also invited by NGOs to speak on the realities around gender issues. The artist explored that was one of the ways of projects which she connected with city, fact and working as through art form.

'Unclaimed Urban Fictions' was another project by Surekha that was also the time she was also doing a lot of performances and photo actions and projects in different places. Through these projects, the artist is also wondering

about the accomplishments which artists do suddenly. What were the actual some of the real-life performances outside. The artist tried to find a few people who are like real heroes . A woman planted four hundred trees at a stretch ten kilometres for not having children and people who started just laughter claps. The artist questions how these elders relate to the city and created all these the laughter claps are women who lived in the carbon part for about thirty years alone and a single woman and then a more significant like living there. So there are many stories and also the resources at the same time when anyone thinks over the bungalow city itself. The artist explores what a city is like when people see from the outside like a city of silicon valley, or it's like a city of info-technology. Still, suddenly when an individual comes he/she can see the stories under the knee which are like unheard biases. The artist brought all those stories and had an installation for all this recycling. Some of the discarded object, discarded computers to keyboards and the entire space it looks like peer entering sort of technological space, but suddenly anyone can see all those un ad voices of the city or an individual don't want to see like unclaimed he/she don't wish to, but they are just as they. So when an individual walk through he/she has some ten to fifteen stories of the city which anyone likes in some of the computers which were like someone somewhere not on but in between an individual walkthrough want to experience the city. Surekha uses the street sound as complementary to the project. The artist had these four short videos of all those extraordinary people, ordinary but exceptional people for voicing their relation to the city.

 Regarding the critical breakthrough of Surekha's art practice, the research study analyses that the artist through her travels has got the breakthroughs . So because of it , any new place helps an artist to look for something new and experience and create something new. In Surekha's life that happened in Trinidad as though she was like her work also had an art and craft and public space and though she was working with different issues related to the society. That was the time the artist suddenly encountered the Trinidad Carnival where the whole city, people, artists altogether and they worked for six months and the street itself became a bigger space for art and craft and performances. This interested Surekha a lot where craft can reach the public community. The artist worked with the designers and a lot of youngsters for one and a half months, and she emphasised that one breakthrough she enjoyed because where the people community start interacting together to create something.

 And the other one is like the Louvre . It's a lab where Surekha learnt sixties and seventies film making, handling Rostrum cameras, Bolex and also

Super Eight cameras, learning telecine and the techniques of editing, so that was also another exciting thing which also admires because in the sixties and seventies even to get a footage of one-minute artists had to work with a Rostrum camera for about one year taking some thousands of images and finally putting it together to create one small moving image. But now an individual has so much access to images and how he /she sees because what happens in now is somebody asks anyone to do something and instead of looking to his/her archives because there is so much. An individual can't even don't to anyone's file he/she went shoot it and give it to them. So that was one of the important things that made Surekha realise the importance of the moving image.

4.3.4 A Case Study of New Media Art of Surekha

a. *'Selving a body'* (2000)
b. *'eyes of a needle'* (2003)
c. *'cooking concepts'* (2008)
d. *'f-lovers'* (2008)
e. *'surveillance'* (2008)
f. *'they had their home here'* (2009)
g. *'line of control'* (2003)

'*Selving a body'* (2000)

Textile and photographs

'Selving a body' is a New Media Artwork by Surekha, which conceptually explores the gender equality of our society. The literature inspires her work from Indian social reformer, philosopher and poet N. Kumaran Asan specifically the writings emphasised the issues of gender. In this work, the photographed image of a female body is revealed with an emphasis of physically cut marks on the specific body. These cut marks are processed in work with the application of threads, pigments, and elements of textiles. The artwork globally conceptualised the different issues that women face in daily life situations.

'*eyes of a needle'* (2003)

Textile and Photographs

Surekha's New Media work entitled *'eyes of a needle'* explores a female body as an aspect of vernacular (Plate 4.33). The work revealed the photographed image of a feminine body with the existence of a spinal cord or backbone. The title of the work itself questions the patriarchal barriers that women regularly face into different aspects of life as a quote of social norms of the society. In practice, a female body is draped with a transparent cover where the image of nude upper parts of the body is conceptually tried to interact a lot of gender issues which is existing in the regions, and patriarchal societal norms started to gaze if any women tried to come out of the situation with her idiom.

The image of the spinal cord of the backbone also has a dialogue between the viewer and the artwork. The application of textile elements showed that the spinal cord of the spine is the main strength of a body, and if a spinal got distorted, then a lot may be damaged. So in this New Media work of Surekha, there are visual interactions which the research study analyses that the women psychologically face a lot of dilemmas by which sometimes loses their identity of freedom which an individual deserves. The title of the work itself has a lot of interpretations of the identity crisis of femininity. Many times, women have to face the eyes of a needle in various dimensions through the norms of patriarchal society where an individual feminine has a lot to express through her doings. Still, by binding many/much she can't reveal her opinion of the thought process to express herself. The artist is trying to show the specific domain through her New Media work entitled '*eyes of a needle*'.

'*cooking concepts*', (2008)

Video Installation

In Surekha's video installation entitled '*cooking concepts*', the artist explores the various issues of gender-related to domestic violence (Plate 4.34). In work, there are projections which continually reveal an indoor activity in the kitchen. In this work of Surekha photographs of various kitchens with flowers and triptych-videos mutually become an integral part of the video installation. The work is the artist's artistic concern regarding her research-survey of domestic violence and unnatural deaths in the kitchens. The appearance of flowers in the installation of the kitchen are symbolic, and they form an 'allegorical homage' to such violence. The video installation reveals an indoor activity that happens in the kitchen space. The mundane act of cooking metamorphoses into an evocative game: it ironically repeats changes yet, within the domestic routine of the feminine, as though it follows a given scheme of meandering.

In work, the simple, casual and mundane act traverses into an over-life size occurrence, throughout video-time. The simple act of mixing and kneading the dough, in the due process, 'reminds' of mountain scapes and various body organs. The work, in the end, processes metamorphoses into appearances that lie between the body organs and flowers. The study of the research analyses that in this work, the food ingredients acquire a more full, deviant and altering meaning, away from the context means in the general sense. Subsequently, it forms a grid of ever-changing forms and purposes. The relation between the way in the work that 'appears' and meaning it 'acquires' is also ambiguous. The inverted reflection of the human images in the video synchronises with what the identities are preparing. It is as if the dough that they are handling is an extended part of the women's own bodies. The interaction between the characters in work is that of alienation (grid) and unification (meta-grid), at the same.

The video installation by Surekha entitled '*cooking concepts*' explored is strategically positioned between three videos. The sportiveness in the video teases the viewer's ambiguous position: as being in an artistic premise and a kitchen, simultaneously. In work, such 'perceptive-shifts' between the imaginary grids in between the same visual as two things – kitchen and a video – is intended. In this work, the study finds that the shifting perception of three formations, beginning every five minutes again, always as a private space of the kitchen and as a public area of artistic projection makes the viewer/observer to cross various metaphoric, empirical and perceptive grids of gender and politics. In work, the existing girls/women themselves appear to continually cross the line between serious cooking agents and mere playful teenagers.

'f-lovers' (2008)

Video-Sculpture

In her New Media Art practice, '*f-lovers*' is one of Surekha's works that explores what is happening between two lovers (Plate 4.35). In employment, there is a kind of revealingness expressed between the two lovers that reflected. The video-sculpture appeared in a way that the two characters exchanged and played with flowers simultaneously. The flowers, along with the lover's gazes of mutual obsession, act as a metaphor to varying modes of expressions and evocations of subtleties of love and desire. In the video, the amalgamation of the pillow as a sculptural form also has the symbolic resemblance. The images of two characters in the video have the involvement of desire which is conceptually voiced through the activities of male-female. The existence of flowers in the video frame has a lot of interpretations between the lovers as they appeared in work.

The study of research analyses that there are fascinations of desire between the two characters, which identifies as lovers in work. In the video frame, both the male-female appearance has acted symbolically through their gestures of love. The different postures with the amalgamation of flowers through various activities by the lovers have conceptual interpretations in the video. The artist very conceptually used the sculptural form of the pillow, and within this pillow, the frames of the video have a lot of visual interpretations between the lovers. The artist tries to conceptualise the intimacy happenings between the '*f-lovers*' through her this video-sculpture.

'*surveillance*' (2008)

Video-Sculpture

The study of the research analyses that the work entitled '*surveillance*' by Surekha has explored the careful observance by an eye through the video which is surrounded by a sculptural form of pot and is revealed in reverse positioned (Plate 4.36). The artist has shown the real image of eyes projecting within a space of a pot. The research study finds that the existence of eyes in work also has a characteristic appearance of resistance. The patriarchal social norms have lots of barriers for the feminine in real-life space as a tremendous psychological arena. The eyes in the pot have a lot to express but being existing under the scope of sculptural form the internal soul has got stuck on expressing the individual's thought process which the situation that women face into their life under the dominance of patriarchy. Surekha, through her work, conveys those conceptual aspects of gender issues. The eyes always have the facts which psychologically there into an individual's mental experience. The work has explored these thought processes and reveals into the video-sculpture of Surekha.

The title '*surveillance*' of the work also has the conceptual dialogue to represent. The eyes actually observe all the dilemmas that women regularly have to face under the quotes of societal norms and also are taken care of all aspects that feminine want to express through her idiom. The body may represent a physical identity in space. Still, the observing eyes are a woman's mental aspect which analyses almost all the crises she has to face in the various elements of norms lying under society.

'*they had their home here*' (2009)

Photo and Video Installation

The work by Surekha entitled '*they had their home here*' has in-depth research-oriented exploration which conveys the issues related to gender (Plate 4.37). The images that are represented in the work have symbolic representations as well as conceptual presence. The presence of flowers in the kitchen space has a lot of symbolic interpretations. The study analyses that in the name of notions of beauty there are lots of domestic violence women have to face in their home spaces. In the work flower as a symbol of beauty which has the involvement in kitchen space has the clear intention of how women have their role in kitchen space. Still, at the same time in the name of that specific space, an individual woman has to compromise a lot which she wanted to emphasise into her life practices. So the artist reveals that in a conceptualised way.

The appearance of palm in work explores how patriarchal norms have psychologically created barriers into a woman's life that a woman has to restrict herself only in the domain of housekeeping gestures and not go out to do their inspiring things. And many times the reason behind has been said that it is written in her *vaghya*. The image of the palm reveals into the work to conceptualise that fact which women have to face in many cases. The work also has the appearance of an image of an indoor room with an open window. These gestures in work raise the gender issues that women, at times, have to face in her life.

'line of control' (2003)

Video

The work entitled '*line of control*' by Surekha has explored the existence of identity within a boundary (Plate 4.38). The work represents that an ant has continuously tried to cross a constructed barrier, but the living being facing genuinely struggled to pass the same. Surekha's work has emphasised on gender issues. In this work, the artist symbolically expresses her thought process. There are many processes for which women have struggled with living with the boundaries of social construction. The work reveals that an ant is continuously moving within a limit with anxiety that when that identity will cross the constructed sphere and can walk through towards its own choice. Surekha is working with a lot of issues related to gender and identity, has explored conceptually the same aspect in this work through the using subject matter, which is a constructed sphere and an ant.

4.4 Conclusion

Through the chapter titled *"The 'Third Object'/ Urban Signs and the Vulnerable Body: New Media Artworks of Ranbir Kaleka and Surekha"*, the research went through with the detailed analysis of the New Media Artworks of Ranbir Kaleka and Surekha in a conceptual dialogue.

The study identified that Ranbir Kaleka's video installations had explored the third object where an individual can observe psychological aspects in Kaleka's protagonists of artworks. The visual interpretation of Kaleka's subject matters has the involvement of conceptual interaction within an image. In his video installations, there are the identifications of third objects where a character has dual approaches, one has the physical presence, and the other has its psychological reflections. There are approaches to a lot of interpretations within an image of Kaleka's art practice. The prime protagonist in Kaleka's artworks has a lot of visual interaction along with conceptual descriptions to reflect. A central vision has identified dual or more aspects and conversations into Kaleka's New Media works. So the third object has a significant presence in Kaleka's video installations. Through his art practice, Ranbir Kaleka reveals a dialogue between the artwork and the observer. They are thoughtful conversations that continuously happen in the images of Kaleka where there is an involvement of the third object which is sometimes the social surroundings, sometimes dilemmas of human existence and sometimes there are a lot of psychological interpretations.

The research study analyses that Surekha's body of New Media works executed with video art, installation and performances and transactions with diverse topics including Indian identity, gender, ecological issues and military history. She has been discovering how artistic practice can engage with public and private spaces. Surekha often uses photography and video to inter connect the domains of archiving, documenting and performing, by reacting on how visuality can engage with society. In her New Media Art practices, there are approaches to the vulnerable body.

Surekha's exploration through New Media works has the conceptual appearance of feminine identity crisis under the societal norms of patriarchy. In Surekha's New Media Art practice, there are involvements of gender equality, domestic violence that women have to face in their homes/houses under the dominance of patriarchal norms of society. The artist's research-based video installation works also highlighted the unnatural deaths of women in the kitchen.

The study of the research tries to establish the findings that both Kaleka and Surekha have their specific expression of thought process. In his work of video installations Kaleka emphasis on the amalgamation of painting with moving images by which the artist explored the involvement of protagonist as layer after layer and in these ways there is a presence of the third object . The research study determined that Surekha through her New Media practice emphasises on the content of gender issues and approaches of the feminine body as a space of vulnerability .

PLATES

Plate 4 . 1 : Ranbir Kaleka . *Sweet Unease* (detail) . 2010-11 .
Oil and Acrylic on Canvas with Video Projection .
Courtesy : Latitude 28 . Web . 22 February . 2019

Plate 4 . 2 : Ranbir Kaleka . *Long sleep of the storyteller* 2012 .
Oil on Canvas . Courtesy : artsy.net . Web . 22 February . 2019

Plate 4.3 : Ranbir Kaleka . *Family Picture II* . 2009 .
Archival Inks and Oil on Canvas .
Courtesy : artsy.net . Web . 22 February . 2019

Plate 4.4 : Ranbir Kaleka . *Urban Utopia, Done Undone, Menaced by dragonflies* .
2014 . Digital Print on Canvas . Courtesy : artsy.net . Web . 22 February . 2019

Plate 4 . 5 : Ranbir Kaleka . *A- Panoramic-Spectrum Ground* . Courtesy : sitanshi talati-parikh . Web . 22 February . 2019

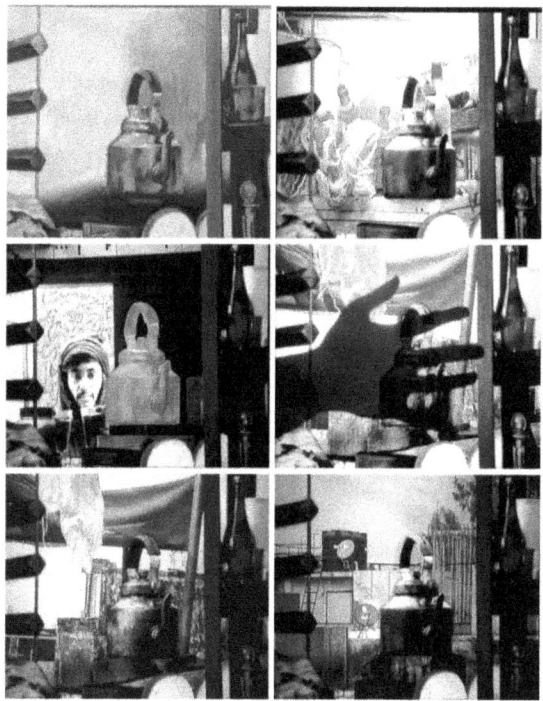

Plate 4 . 6 : Ranbir Kaleka . *Kettle* (detail) . 2010 . Projection on painted canvas . Courtesy : artsy.net . Web . 22 February . 2019

Palet 4 . 7 : Ranbir Kaleka . *Man Threading A Needle* (detail) . 1998-99 .
Single Channel Video Projected on oil painting .
Courtesy : Ranbir Kaleka . Web . 22 February 2019

Plate 4 . 8 : Ranbir Kaleka . *Fables from the House of Ibaan* (detail) . 2007 .
Oil and Acrylic on Canvas with Video Projection and sound .
Courtesy : saffronart . Web . 22 February . 2019

Plate 4.9 : Ranbir Kaleka. *Crossing* (detail). 2005.
Four Channel Video Projection on Painting.
Courtesy : Ranbir Kaleka. Web. 22 February. 2019

Plate 4.10 : Ranbir Kaleka. *Cobbler*. 2003.
Digital photograph on Metallic Paper.
Courtesy : Ranbir Kaleka. Web. 22 February. 2019

Plate 4.11 : Ranbir Kaleka. *Reading Man*. 2009.
Acrylic and oil on canvas with aluminium sculptures and armature and wall clock.
Courtesy : Ranbir Kaleka. Web. 22 February. 2019

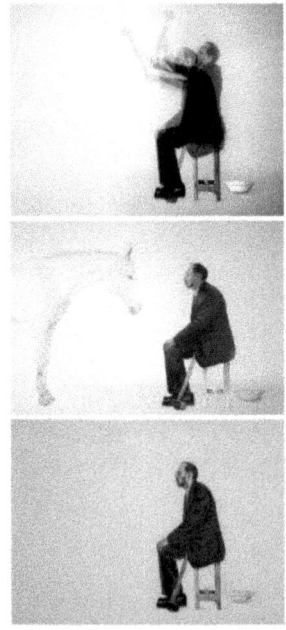

Plate 4.12 : Ranbir Kaleka. *Cul-de-sac in Taxila* (detail).
2010. Single channel HD Video Projection on painted canvas.
Courtesy : Ranbir Kaleka. Web. 22 February. 2019

Plate 4.13 : Ranbir Kaleka. *Conference of Birds and Beasts*. 2010.
Digital Photograph and oil Painting on Canvas.
Courtesy : Ranbir Kaleka. Web. 22 February. 2019

Plate 4.14 : Ranbir Kaleka. *The Great Topairist's Astonishing Dilemma*.
Hand painted on Digital Paint on Canvas.
Courtesy : MutualArt. Web. 22 February. 2019

Plate 4 . 15 : Ranbir Kaleka . *Not from Here* (detail) . 2009 .
Four channel HD Video Projection on Painted Canvases .
Courtesy : Ranbir Kaleka . Web . 22 february . 2019

Plate 4 . 16 : Ranbir Kaleka . *He Was A Good Man* (detail) . 2008 .
Single channel video projection on a painting .
Courtesy : Ranbir Kaleka . Web . 22 february . 2019

Plate 4 .17 : Ranbir Kaleka . *Wall* (detail) . 2009 . Single Channel Video .
Courtesy : Ranbir Kaleka . Web . 22 february . 2019

Plate 4 . 18 : Ranbir Kaleka . *Forest* (detail) . 2009 . Video Projection on painting .
Courtesy : Ranbir Kaleka . Web . 22 february . 2019

Plate 4 . 19 : Ranbir Kaleka . *Consider* (detail) . 2007 .
Two Channel Video Projected on two canvases .
Courtesy : Ranbir Kaleka . Web . 22 february . 2019

Plate 4 . 20 : Ranbir Kaleka . *Man With Cockerel - 2* (detail) .
2004 . Single Channel Video .
Courtesy : Ranbir Kaleka . Web . 22 february . 2019

**Plate 4.21 : Ranbir Kakela. *Man in Water* (detail).
2003. Two Channel Video Projection.
Courtesy : Ranbir Kaleka. Web. 22 february. 2019**

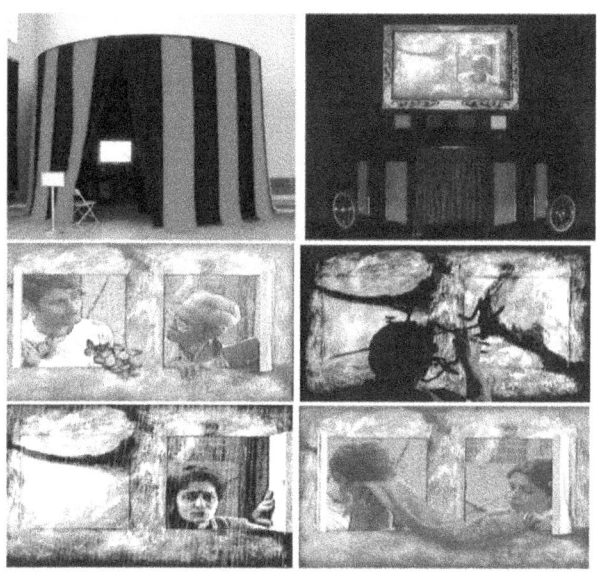

**Plate 4.22 : Ranbir Kaleka. *Windows* (detail).
2002. Single Channel Video-sculpture.
Courtesy : Ranbir Kaleka. Web. 22 february. 2019**

Plate 4.23 : Ranbir Kaleka . *Music Room* (detail) .
2002 . Single Channel Video .
Courtesy : Ranbir Kaleka . Web . 22 february . 2019

Plate 4 . 24 : Ranbir Kaleka . *Video Lounge* (detail)
2002 . Six Channel Video loop with sound .
Courtesy : Ranbir Kaleka . Web . 22 february . 2019

Plate 4 . 25 : Ranbir Kaleka . *Powder Room* (detail) . 1999-2000 .
Single Channel Video -sculpture installation.
Courtesy : Ranbir Kaleka . Web . 22 february . 2019

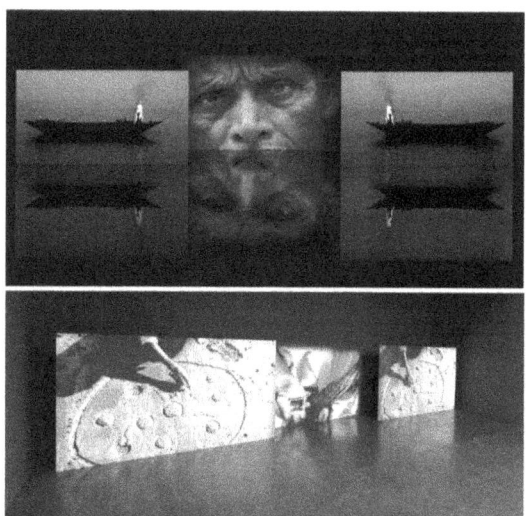

Plate 4 . 26 : Ranbir Kaleka . *House of An Opaque Water* (detail) . 2012 .
Three Channel Projection with sound on three panel .
Courtesy : Ranbir Kaleka . Web . 8 April . 2019

Plate 4.27 : Ranbir Kaleka. *Fearsome Acquiescense of A Monotonous Life* (detail). 2019.
Two channel video installation with sculpture.
Courtesy : Ranbir Kaleka. Web. 8 April. 2019

Plate 4.28 : Ranbir Kaleka.
Not Anonymous_Walking to the Obscure Fear of A New Dawn (detail). 2017-2018.
Single channel projection on multiple screen.
Courtesy : Ranbir Kaleka. Web. 8 April. 2019

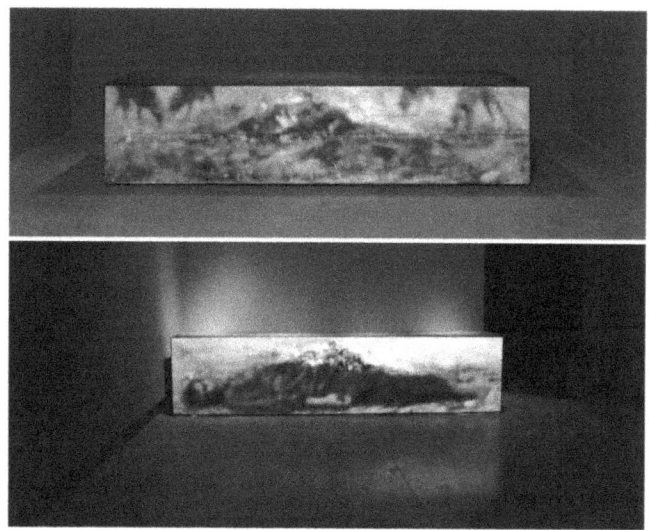

Plate 4.29 : Ranbir Kaleka. *Bound* (detail). 2018.
Single channel projection on burnt wood.
Courtesy : Ranbir Kaleka. Web. 8 April. 2019

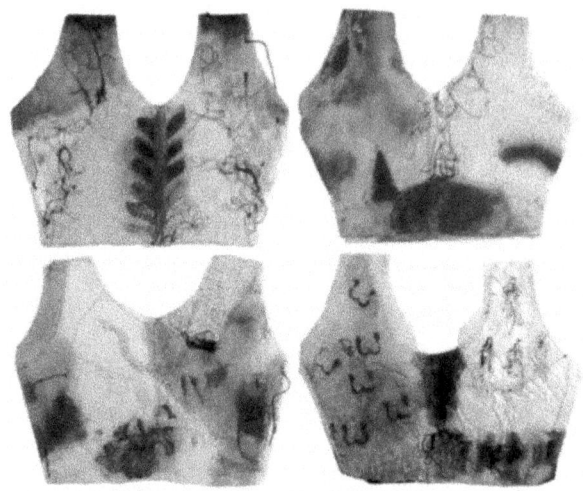

Plae 4 . 30 : Surekha . *Selving A Body* (detail) . 1998-1999 .
Rice paper , pigments and thread .
Courtesy : Surekha . v-ideo.art . Web . 25 May . 2019

Plate 4 . 31 : Surekha . *Communing with Urban Heroins* (detail) .
2007 . Culture Specific Video Installation .
Courtesy : Surekha . v-ideo.art . Web . 25 May . 2019

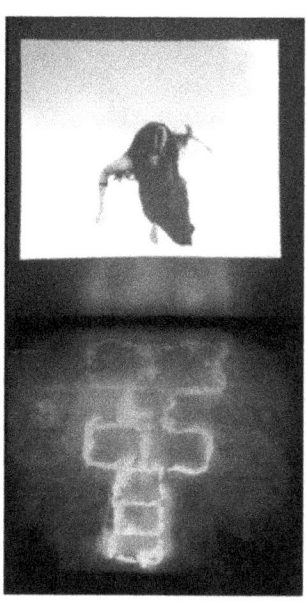

Plate 4 . 32 : Surekha . *Between Fire and Sky* (detail) . 2008 . Diptych Video .
Courtesy : Surekha . v-ideo.art . Web . 25 May . 2019

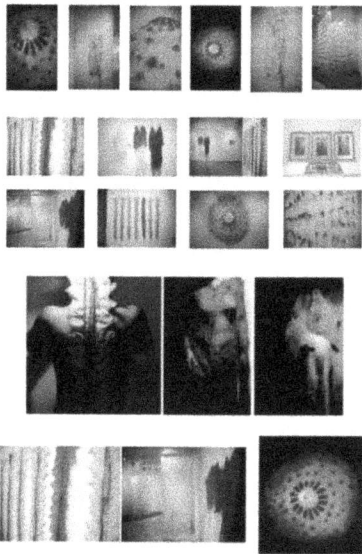

Plate 4 . 33 : Surekha . *eyes of a needle* (detail) . 2003 . Textile and Photographs.
Courtesy : Surekha . v-ideo.art . Web . 25 May . 2019

Plate 4.34 : Surekha . *cooking concepts* (detail) . 2008 . Video Installation .
Courtesy : Surekha . v-ideo.art . Web . 25 May . 2019

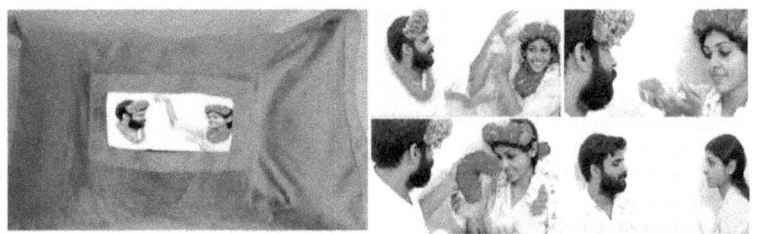

Plate 4.35 : Surekha . *f-lovers* (details) . 2008 . Video sculpture .
Courtesy : Surekha . v-ideo.art . Web . 25 May . 2019

Plate 4.36 : Surekha . *surveillance* (detail) . 2008 . Video sculpture .
Courtesy : Surekha . v-ideo.art . Web . 25 May . 2019

Plate 4.37 : Surekha. *they had their home here* (detail). 2009.
Photo and Video Installation.
Courtesy : Surekha. v-ideo.art. Web. 25 May. 2019

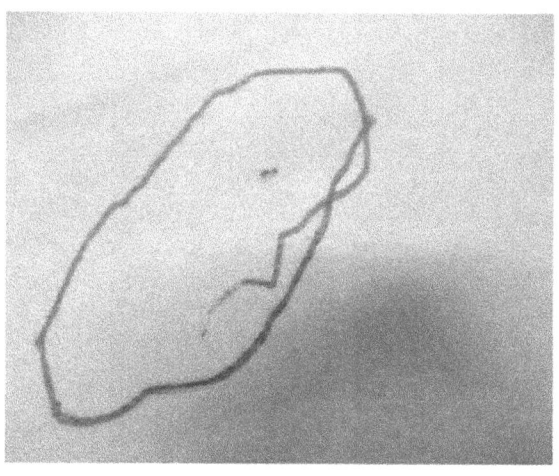

Plate 4.38 : Surekha. *line of control* (detail). 2003. Video.
Courtesy : Surekha. v-ideo.art. Web. 25 May. 2019

References

Bhattacharya, Audita. *The current political situation and events have affected us deeply.* New Delhi, The Indian Express. 2019.

Bornstein, Kate. *Gender Outlaw: On Men, Women and the Rest of Us.* New York City, Vintage Books, a division of Penguin Random House LLC, 2016.

Carter, Angela, and Joan Ross Acocella. *The Bloody Chamber and Other Stories; Wise Children; Fireworks.* New York, Alfred A. Knopf, 2018.

"Fear of a New Dawn |Ranbir Kaleka." *Vadehra Art Gallery*, www.vadehraart.com/fear-of-a-new-dawn-ranbir-kaleka.Accessed 11 September 2019.

Greer, Germaine. *The Female Eunuch.* London, Paladin, 1971.

Hazra, Abhishek. *Three Fragmented Actions of Silence.* Pleasure Dome .2011

Hooks, Bell. *Feminism Is for Everybody: Passionate Politics.* New York, Routledge, 2015.

Jones, Ronald. *Shilpa Gupta.* New York. Frieze, 2012.

Kaleka, Ranbir, and Art Today Gallery. *Ranbir Kaleka.* New Delhi, Art Today, 1996.

Kaleka, Ranbir, and Volte Gallery Mumbai. *Ranbir Kaleka.* Mumbai, Volte Gallery, 2012.

Kaleka, Ranbir, et al. *Ranbir Kaleka: Moving Image Works.* Bielefeld, Kerber Verlag, 2018.

Kalra, Vandana. *Video artist Ranbir Kaleka reflects on the present times, his current exhibition in Delhi and being at ease with one's medium.* New Delhi, The Indian Express, 2019.

Kalra, Vandana. *Video artist Ranbir Kaleka reflects on the present times, his current exhibition in Delhi and being at ease with one's medium.* New Delhi : Indian Express, 2019.

Matlin, Julie. *NFB Pause: Chris Lavis and Maciek Szczerbowski talk Gymnasia.* NFB Blog, 2019

Monfried, Lucia, et al. *Little Women.* New York, Baronet Books, 1989.

Naffine, Ngaire. *Gender, Crime, and Feminism*. Aldershot England; Brookfield, Vt., Dartmouth, 1995.

Overdorf, Jason. *Moving for a living.* blogspot, 2013.

Plath, Sylvia. *The Bell Jar*. New Delhi , Robin Books, 2018.

"Ranbir Kaleka." *Rkaleka.Com*, www.rkaleka.com. Accessed 10 Mar. 2019.

Robbins, Michael. *The Second Sex*. New York, Penguin Books, 2014.

Rush, Michael. *New Media In Late 20th-Century Art.* London, Thames & Hudson, 2005.

Sarkar, Ria. *Ranbir Kaleka: A Visionary and a Storyteller.* artsome, 2014.

Suri, Himanshu. *Eat Pray Thug.* New York, Aicon Gallery, 2015

"V-IDEO Login." *Www.v-Ideo.Art*, v-ideo.art/videos/. Accessed 10 Mar. 2019.

Wollstonecraft, Mary. *Vindication Of The Rights Of Woman*. S.L., Penguin Books, 2020.

Woolf, Virginia. *Room Of One's Own.* 2019.

CHAPTER-V

THROUGH THE WAYS OF MEMORY AND THE TECHNO-IMAGES: RE-INTERPRETATION OF NEW MEDIA WORKS OF SHILPA GUPTA AND BOSE KRISHNAMACHARI

5.1 Introduction

In the 1990s, when fundamental reformations accepted India on the way to a free-market economy, its isolation from the world economy started to decrease, and its global influence rose . In due course, this abetted the country's globalisation over the progression of the succeeding decade. Simple statistics tell the story that while India's annual economic rate of growth since independence has been stable at one per cent. An individual can be identified that between 1999 and 2008 the yearly economic growth percentages were nine-point six per cent and eight-point nine per cent in Gujarat and Delhi, correspondingly and that is signalling the belongings of India's free-market economy. If that degree of success did not hold through the country, it nevertheless created the new India that we think of today. Not unpredictably, these reforms also coincided with the emergence of a new generation of Indian artists and Shilpa Gupta is prominent among them. Observing back crossways her career, Gupta commenced with her first solo exhibition in 2001 in New Zealand, it appears evident that her work established in step with globalisation's significance – and its effects. At the same time, she continued to be very self-aware as an Indian woman crossing the hope for and healthy uncertainty of massive change in India and throughout the world (Jones, 2012).

Gupta's art practice mediums search from shaped discovered objects to video, interactive computer-based installation and performance. Gupta is engrossed in human perception and how information, visible or invisible, gets transmitted and internalised in everyday life. Gupta is continuously executed on how objects get explanation, its placing, and how viewers experience it .

Gupta's work deals with regions where these definitions occupy anyone out, be it borderlines, labels and ideas of censorship and security.

Gupta's work makes visible the aporias and in commensurabilities in the developing national public range in India, which comprise gender and class barriers, religious differences, the continued power of suppressive state devices, and the seductions of social homogeneity and theoretical ideas of public consensus enabled by emerging mediascapes. Shilpa Gupta was born in Mumbai where the artist received a BFA in sculpture in the year 1997 from the Sir J J School of Art. Gupta's art practices have engaged with art in its participatory, interactive and public dimensions for over two and half decades. The artist has persistently mapped the defining power of social and psychological borders on public life.

Gupta's works involve inter-subjectivity and phenomenology, which continuously remind a viewer about the relational and highly mediated surfaces of the act of observing, retrieving and remembering. Remain it brass labels, stamps, objects impounded at airports, motion flap boards, or prohibited material that crisscross physiological and geographical gaps. Gupta's practice pushes the boundaries of how the art object is understood.

Born in Kerala in 1963, Bose Krishnamachari is regarded as one of the contemporary Indian artists who involved his art practices prominently towards the New Media Art. Krishnamachari completed his art leanings from Sir J J School of Art, Mumbai and later did his MFA from the Goldsmiths College, University of London. His work, thus augmented by a 'here and now' belief and experience of contemporary culture, adopts effortlessly from various disciplines such as literature and design, and periods.

Through his explorations interestingly, Krishnamachari emphasises as much attention to form as he does to conceptual and contextual concerns. Startling planes of flat colour juxtaposed against skilful, almost photographic, representations of identifiable persona, imbue the work with an 'international' sensibility. Bose admits to combining western image-making techniques such as the multimedia installation with the vernacular, in a proposition to appear at an expression that is entirely contemporary and stimulating.

5.2 New Media Art Practice of Shilpa Gupta

Shilpa Gupta is one of those artists who has been working on a complicated set of notations, including New Media, robotic works, lights, photographs, motorized mechanisms. The artist's art practices are prime of life, making notations which concern her.

The Indian artist Shilpa Gupta was born and educated in Mumbai, where she also lives and works. Gupta arrived into the global art market very early in her artistic career; she practises a universal language which is related to formal and conceptual vocabulary of Western Conceptual, Minimalist, and Relational art (Kayser, 2017). Yet Gupta's exploration of local hand-made paper, fake Indian administrative forms, hand-woven fabrics, and botanical medicine, as well as the narratives entrenched in her works, ground her practice in a South Asian context. The artist's intention is somewhat to foreground the preconceptions which an individual tends to project on his/her environment rather than engaging liberally with it. Many of Gupta's artworks challenge essentialist and nationalist ideas of identity in the framework of the ferocity that antiques intercommunity and family life in the Sub-continent (Kayser, 2017). The artist's work is mainly concerned with the estrangement between India, Pakistan and Bangladesh, which is cultivated by nationalist governments.

The study of the research analyses that Gupta works against essentialist notions of identity as demarcated by social and political forces with narratives of gendered and religions, and the nation-state's logic of territoriality. The artist proposes a thoughtfulness of character as multi-layered that has to do with the reminiscences, partisanships, and affects that daily activities and human encounters map onto the mind through the roaming movements of the body. Gupta's attention in the complex fabric of Indian regions, which branches from the places of earlier historical days of trade, with Europe but also with the rest of Asia particularly with China, Japan, Afghanistan, Iran et al. is combined with her resolve to expose the imperceptible bodies and motivations that are the living rhythm of these cities (Kayser, 2017).

Gupta's works, which manifest and celebrate the subaltern lives of those cities, can be understood of in next of kin to the work of other Indian artists like Amar Kanwar or Raqs Media Collective, which are permeated with a Gandhian/Swadeshi politics of love and respect for these humble characters, in addition to being modulated with a Marxist agenda. Although Kanwar's works function, in the confrontations of art historian Geeta Kapur such as a form of reparation in that they to celebrate the bravery and tolerance of unidentified Indians who are victims of local destructive practices, Raqs Media Collective's installations have metonymic proximity to global trade to condemn it. Gupta's works roam between these two extremes as she offerings the viewer with the belongings of occupation on a diversity of people from India, Bangladesh,

Pakistan through substances that are the deliverers of effects, dry, apparently neutral material that taken from the realm of infrastructure such as information panels, microphones, luminous signposts.

While both the complexities of Gupta's personal contextual and the political features of her art practices fit with her generation's worries with urban space and religious fundamentalism, the study of the research focuses on artworks which are emphasised with the subjectivity at the fundamental of everyday life. Observing a set of works offering narratives of actual journeys in the city rather than between cities but also between social standards and politics. It will analyse the interplay between language and the materials that convey it. Gupta's works also integrate frames, glass boxes, light boxes, and white walls, inducing in a Western viewer ignorant of the odd situations of the stories, what the research study prerogative to be a meditative deportment which is a reflection on the poetics of the body and mind of dialogue with time and space. Representing Irit Rogoff's concept of "inhabitation," Henri Lefebvre's "rhythmanalysis," and Michel de Certeau's "The Practice of Everyday Life," this research study attempts to express the New Media Artworks of Shilpa Gupta in a different perspective. At the same time, the immateriality of the works embodies a form of invisible resistance to controlling forces. The study concentrates that this process of work opens a viewer's reflection of everyday life with aesthetical approaches beyond the Marxist/anarchic paradigm of the "deterritoralisation of the globe" as a politics of confrontation to global capitalism that underpins Irit Rogoff's philosophy. The study of the chapter significance to link it to an "aesthetic of life" based on the concept of individual activity regarding coercive, political, economic and social forces and a dialogical connotation with the atmosphere, which can be found in some western philosophers as well as in Asian aesthetics.

Shilpa Gupta's work is deep-rooted in the life of Mumbai, a port city on the Arabian Sea that faces Pakistan. This megapolis of twenty-two million inhabitants, minorities of which are Muslims and combines shantytowns with the most progressive Indian corporations' headquarters, traditional family life with the cultural features of post-modernity. It is a revelation for the "glocal" era. Reflecting the city's difficulties, the artist describes herself as being interested in multiple, diverse, and intersectional identities. Gupta focuses on the hazard to this complex fabric posed by the rapid globalisation of India in the 1990s that is hard-pressed for the consistency of tastes and lifestyle. A succession of violent incidents related to the rise of religious fundamentalism marked the artist's young generation, the destruction of the Babri mosque in

Ayodhya, Uttar Pradesh, in December 1992 by Hindu extremists, and the bombings and riots that happened in Mumbai in 1993. In 2001 the pressures between India and Pakistan over the contested area of Kargil in Kashmir focused Gupta to initiate a public art project called '*Aar Paar*' with Lahore based artist Huma Mulji. They invited artists from both regions of the border to exchange art practice between Lahore and Mumbai. Later posters were emailed and printed nearby to build consciousness of the point of view from the "other side." It forefronts the chasm even between artists, showing how entrenched territorial policies can be. Gupta created a poster called '*Blame*' which portrayed a bottle full of red liquid with a label of text. In the year 2002, '*Blame*' converted an object and a performance in which the artist obtainable people travelling on local trains to take home an actual bottle, bearing said label and filled with an ambiguous red liquid. The bottles were received with scepticism, outright rejection, but also understood by some who took a bottle with them. Gupta's activity carries an oral warning in regards to the stoppage of terrorism activities. On other occasions, people sauntered out of a restaurant where '*Aar Paar*' posters had been placed as table mats (Kayser, 2017).

Gupta explores the New Media work '*Blame*' (2002-2004) which is an interactive Installation with '*Blame*' bottles which contains stimulated blood, posters, stickers, video, interactive performance. The work interpreted the duration of 1 min 49 sec loop Installation, 118x51x134 in | 300x130x340 cm. (Plate 5.1).

Gupta toured disputed areas in Kashmir, visiting Srinagar and travelling alongside the border. In 2013, Gupta created '*1278 unmarked, 28 hours by foot via National Highway No 1, East of the Line of Control*' (Plate 5.2). The work contains a set of marble slabs that recall the grave stones used in Kashmir. A number that is reaching between 1 to 1,278 is etched on each slab of the work. 1,278 mentions to the number of unmarked graves that were excavated by the Indian army to obtain the bodies of presumed Kashmiri terrorists who have been abducted in a single district (Kayser, 2017).

Gupta explains in an interview in a way that in 2009 the artist came across a text about unmarked graves in Kashmir which is a report called Buried Evidence: Unknown, Unmarked, and Mass Graves in Indian administered Kashmir made by several activists including (the prominent names) Parvez Imroz, documenting thousands of unmarked graves in Kashmir (Kayser, 2017). The number 1278 refers to the number of the unnamed and unmarked graves found in Kupwara which is the district located farther to the northwest, on the very edge of the country.

With this work, Gupta intends to pitch consideration to the proceedings that happen in this part which is near the Pakistani border, so it is far from the capital city and thus from inspection, where safety is required with means beyond legal rules in a thought process of where land and people's life have been shared.

In the work the use of the iconic green paper on which the viewer may obligate to existence a caretaker, together with the careless placement of the installation art include to the quasi-invisibility to the entire piece which is placed behind a unproductive wall, detached by a corridor from the central alley, and wrinkled up as construction material in to come, an individual could easily blunder the slabs or could dismiss them as being less significant. The green forms, casually located on a neutral shelf, fail to drag much attention. By establishing the chance confrontation of the observer with the alternative neglected graves through their perambulation within the exhibition area, the artist reveals the way these substances and proceedings present themselves in real life , while reading the news dispatched by the media equipment. The title of the installation underpins this symbolic journey, exciting a turn on the National Highway N°1 which connects the capital city of the country with areas "at the edge," where hard actions are performed in the name of security. The darkness of the crimes is underpinned by the lack of expressivity and the effect of the substance. It thus ensures the reliability of the spectator to decipher the signs to perceive the gravity of what is addressed (Kayser, 2017).

The elegant marble enhanced with a black line and its intriguing numbering contradicts with these markers of indifference, insensitivity and forgetfulness, triggering the spectator's curiosity. When viewing the text, they become aware of the facts or are established in their hypothesis that the slabs stand for gravestones. In this way, the crimes appear abruptly, not through the previous alert in a newspaper but as direct encounters in a field. The spectator's contact with the slabs sounds like someone walking in a Kashmiri village and swiftly coming across an unusual bulge of the earth, under a tree, on the side of the road. In particular, the Indian authorities utilise these unmarked graves, which they deliberately established in the middle of villages, contrary to tradition, as obstacles for would-be independents. As a result, no one takes the courage to take care of them for fear of being observed and arrested by the authorities. By building the 'fake' experience, the artist emphasises the viewer's awareness of the real event.

The performative process by which they symbolically perform to become caretakers of the gravestone differs with the aesthetic anomia of the paper. Then by signing the same, they present it with symbolic meaning, that of satisfaction, a moral necessity to fight negligence and demonstrate empathy. Likewise, if the observer does not fill in the form, they are faced with the question of moral responsibility and suggest that the power of civil society rests in individual responsibility. The appearance may appear as complimentary or requiring deep-felt meaning when done by Westerners ignorant of the work's geographic and political context. Nevertheless, when the work was exhibited in Mumbai in 2013, the audience became involved with the work in a much more instant way. The slabs were installed in private homes rather than a gallery. Gupta expressed in a way that when the object lies in an individual's house, maybe a person visits the individual and asks about it. Then the specific individual becomes the storyteller, or he/she might miracle and go back to look where it originated from. The intent of the artwork is related to how the observer spends into the object, which in turn is about one's connection to anything. It concerns the way context, place; memory can operate on whatsoever. It is cracked, it is personal, it is never necessarily true, it is always contested, this is still fragile. A few people observe the stone because it is an artwork so there may be a sense of greed in that gesture, and also some discomfort, because of what it symbolises in a way that can an individual stay with that? Some people returned the part because they possibly will not have it in their house. Their parents declined to live with it. Someone mistakenly broke it and was terrified. Many individuals hid it.

5.2.1 Shilpa Gupta's New Media Art and the Narrativity of the Body in Space and Time

This is an outstanding example of the way that Gupta constructs her works, as involving conceptual narratives, made of consecutive encounters that create layers of texts and touches entrenched over time in the object. Meetings between the artist and observer—artists or lay oneself—result in narratives discussed and transferred, leading to conflicts between the work and its audience, and back to a dialogue between the audience and the artist. '*1278 unmarked*' stalks from the reading of a report but also from Gupta's travelogue to the Martyr Cemetery in Srinagar the place where those who died in the scuffle for an independent Kashmir are buried. Gupta expressed that someone is reading aloud the age of the boys that they were between 16, 21, 22 and their feeling of grief that overcame her. The work reveals further narratives as long as by the spectators who take apart their home, they talk about the relevance with their relatives and friends and report it back to the artist. Gupta reflects these progressive times of storytelling represent the thoughtful and heartfelt journey in space and time that underpins the process of thought structure. The works add a physical and kinaesthetic dimension to this mental process that both imitate the bodily appearances of mental and emotional meandering and reveal the process of becoming conscious metaphorically.

The topoi of perambulation and confrontations as a trigger for a voyage of self-discovery, away from the impact of officially /socially erected narratives, is a recurring purpose in Gupta's works. It alludes to the identity between walking and the meandering of thoughts, the enfolding of affects such as in language. Indian culture in the way of religious, learned, or visual, emphasises a dialogical connection between space and time as a way to obtain truths that are beyond the images of the real. This is at the essence of the *Mahabharata*, the great epic poem about spiritual enlightenment, but it is also observed in folk storytelling cultures such as in *Patua* paintings. It constructs Indian classical music which is based on a circular repetition of motives, or *raga*. Gupta affixes this liberating role to objects of daily life rather than aesthetic artefacts. The artist explores that she is interested in perception and therefore, the creation of knowledge and aspirations in everyday life. It could be an object an individual desires in a shop window, the way a person looks or makes an assumption regarding a particular group or community. Gupta is interested in the multiple meanings which an object can embody, and the shift that can take place from different positions.

Gupta's interest in daily life as a subversive narrative is also central to her contribution to the 2015 exhibition '*My East is your West*'. Among her several installations, the 'Enclave project' (*Untitled*, 2013-14) executed drawings, videos, photographs correlated to regions along the frontier between India and Bangladesh, which for complicated historical reasons, are enclaves of Indian territories within Bangladesh and vice versa. The result is an administrative limbo of Kafkaesque proportions. The works are the result of a continuous survey by the artist of people's lives in some of these locations. The artist traces the flow of people and goods such as cows, SIM cards, DVDs, and gold . These are sometimes either smuggled or sometimes lost in the no man's land between borders. According to Gupta, this flow of goods works as proof of an unstoppable will to endure. A series of drawings are done with a transparent codeine-based syrup which is a medicine. The syrup is legal in India but illegal in Bangladesh. A small text in work resembles at the bottom of each drawing. The font utilised for this text is the same administrative font used in the '*1278 unmarked*' installation. The texts are incredibly witty, yet a concentration of actual regulatory orders. They underpin the laughable efforts by local authorisations to govern the flow between the enclaves and the borderland more frequently. One drawing represents fenced outskirts, with a plane line marking the area, and a vertical pole suggestive of the pillars that support spiked wire. The text below says that India is building a fence which is 150 yards inside the zero line. Often cattle taken for grazing here, crossing the Border Security Force post, is reported missing at the local police station.

Underneath a representation executed with dots of various diameters adjusted in several rows, the text reads that the guard at the border post at the Tin Bigha Corridor firmly states that only 30 cows are formally allowed to pass over at this single entry and exit location particularly on Mondays and Thursdays of a week. Hundreds and numbers of cows stand grazing in the territories at the border (Kayser, 2017). In yet another drawing, a soccer game necessitates a situation connecting border protectors and the people of the enclave. The involvement of text below in the drawing in which the players and the ball that was made with codeine, are almost hidden. Beyond the absurdity of unnecessary administrative regulations that the artist's purpose is to emphasise that life goes on in these zones of administrative oblivion, that daily life in the borderland belies state intentions and the owe of people and goods continue, prompted by historical and social affinities, geographical continuity and economic imperative. In other works of Gupta, she endeavours to symbolically re-establish a territorial connection between Bangladesh and India into installations that narrate the exchange of things between cities on each side of the frontier, such as Dhaka and Calcutta or even Mumbai (Kayser, 2017).

'*Untitled*' (2015), the work relates to the acceptance of famous hand-woven sarees from *Dhakai Jamdani* in Bangladesh, which are carried crossed the border by foot and then by train to Kolkata (then Calcutta), where demand continues over generations, not with standing partition. The creation consists of a striped fabric turned up on a stick and represented in a transparent museum pedestal. A text transcribed in a dry, Courier New font, is placed in the case, in the manner of old-fashion Arts and Crafts museums. Yet the text has no explanatory legality. The font resembles that of manufacturing typewriters, besides in practise in India's rural regions. The imitation includes erasing the name of the village by typing the letter 'x' over the central letters.

The artist expresses that the fabric has been stripped and covered around a stick, specifically a walking stick, a fight stick or a stick off the loom . Protected on to it, above and over again, it morphed so that its primary reference to a saree shift in a state of doubt. The text is carried out of a dialogue between Gupta and an emissary who bears the sarees crossed the border. There is a new contradiction among the unified treatment, which remains the spectator's mind and the narrative of a quest. The mysterious and conceptual composition evokes Joseph Kosuth's assemblages, which Gupta has been interested in since her student's years, where a text along with similarly parched and sophisticated, is a container towards an invisible field, that of the mind, beyond the material and the practical. '*One and Three Chairs*' (1965) (Plate 5.3), which Shilpa Gupta has seen, similar to a commercial or museum tag. The text concerning the chair underpins the authority ascribed to explanatory texts and their capacity to condition the mental representation of an object. The photograph, with its brightness , moderately separates the viewer from this required opinion and guides him/her back to the concept of the existence of the article. This process shares an inclination with Husserl's method of "reduction" whereby the ego, according to Nathalie Depraz, releases itself from the object to take note of the act of consciousness directed towards the object, allowing another dimension to emerge from it, which precisely frees the ego from the ordinary pre- givenness of the world. To do this, there is a need to practise an epoche, that is a gesture of suspension with regards to the chronic course of one's thoughts, brought about by an interruption of their continuous flow.

Like Kosuth's composition, Gupta's work construction also facilitates this epoch. Contrary to Kosuth's work, the text in '*Untitled*' (2015) is the cause of freedom of the spectator's vision while the thing is the component of conceptual confrontation. The complexity of the object and its apparent need of connection with the text form a ravine between the spectator's expectation of an artwork in a glass pedestal, and what they understand and learn. This prevents any definite knowledge of the object and from perceiving the text as an interpretation. Stripped of their expectations of cognitive content, the observer is revealed to the narrative carried by the text, a journey in a train between a village in Bangladesh and Kolkata. By describing the story of this journey, with a font that influences a mechanical typewriter, to the continuous gestures of typing unique letters to construct an order, the text produces a virtual kinaesthetic sense. The font mimics the swing of the dry clapping generated by the metal pad penetrating the paper and, by metonymy, of the steady rhythm of the train wheels on the rail tracks. At the same time, a viewer imagines the gentle consciousness of the man walking, and then sleeping during this overnight train journey. The device reinforces the sense of time implied by a journey across a territory, but also unites a private, "secret" rhythm (that of the breathing) with a public rhythm (the train tracks), through the typing of the story. The text thus transforms space travelled into time. It associates the journey with a uniquely individual experience—that of a man sleeping through the night in a train and reconvening with himself. The train figures prominently in the Indian imagination, both as charting the map of the Sub-continent, as linking remote territories, and finally as a marker of partition.

Gupta avidly read Khushwant Singh's 1956 novel '*A Train to Pakistan*' in which the train crossed the frontier functions as a sign of hatred and crime between former neighbours and economic partners. Gupta's work seems to be healing this chasm by transforming hate into a trading partnership again. The text resonates with the shredded sarees hidden between Bangladesh and Kolkata. While tending to an exclusive bureau in performing this healing. This mysterious metaphorical mode intimates that some representations cannot be gripped through the thing, just as the course of life cannot be morphed into things. Language, on the other hand , can reproduce the union between body and mind that is the transporter of our unique knowledge of the receiver in space and time. Here the text, gratitude to its writing, is enclosed with the fabric of life, with the probability of mind/body association.

Gupta's art practice explores that the artist observes the senses as a medium to transmit to human surroundings what human beings recognise. Still, they also transfer to an individual what remains unrecognisable—Gupta interested in emotions, or lack of it, and memory and its residue. Just as business is both an amendment of political resistance – against boundaries– and of psychological flexibility, the work is an act of deliverance of the viewer's mind from the conditioning of the museum occurrence. It creates a gap between the case, the object, and the text. In this way, the research study can also relate its formal and semiotic setting. The two works receive a related purpose that indicates the new parts of the paper—a minimal, severe font that underpins the void versus the black line—suspended sentences and grammatical discontinuity that influence the silence between concepts, all to the effect of carrying a feeling of incommunicability. There are no similarities . Gupta is understanding of Ono's art and was offered a copy of 'Grapefruit' by a friend who saw similarities between their work. The two artists experience a collective consciousness to an "inward view of the self," that is acquainted with Zen Buddhism. Yet, hostile to Ono's haiku-like texts that evoke a private confrontation, Gupta's text carries the experience of a vernacular crossing over the border, involving walking, paying a middleman and spending the night in a train. The journey of the trade man is moulded through her text into an inner journey in as much as a displacement on a boundary. It conveys, through its form, the sense of freedom that being in-between performs, particularly during extended hours on a train, which the viewer can compare to the psychoanalytical process.

Shilpa Gupta's works are indeed a representation of the narratives created by people appropriating the location they live in, in contempt of official borders, through their real and conscious life. The work suggests that dealers, merchants, exporters or smugglers build neighbourhoods and convey experience through their displacements across towns and frontiers, which they reverse (Kayser, 2017). The travellers seem presented with the capability to roam freely through physical, economic, and by extension, imagined province. Gupta has accumulated these stories while sojourning on the territory. The work later carries this insubstantial territory to the spectator's imagination, where it can trigger their own experiences of travelling. Gupta expressed that she engaged in walking. It seems that we converted humans when we were able to reach and walk and had the energy to study into a stone and see a vehicle. Movement is one of the essential actions that we do. Birds move, people move. The border is often only at the check post. And people drive, and it's especially hard to contain this, over an uneven terrain that is punctured with rivers and more so, with human need and often desperation. The informal, illegal trade is part of daily life in the borderlands, where the border both constructs and subverts the state (Kayser, 2017).

5.2.2 Shilpa Gupta and Irit Rogoff's "inhabitation"

Gupta observes migrations of people and commodities as intelligent of engaging the unnatural confines of nation-states and global capitalism. Her projects emphasise trade as cultivating a trans-national community. The research study understands the artist's works and reports in a capitalist sense, as declaring that work organisations build cultural symbols, a concept fundamental to Marxist theory. For Louis Althusser, this resembles a slow-moving process organised by the dominant class through the state apparatus. For Marxist anthropologists it is an unconscious manner, arising from daily life. Leslie White asserts in *"The Evolution of Culture"* (1959), that a socio-cultural system is a substance and consequently thermodynamic system. It is subordinated to rules of conservation and expansion of strength, which also command the progress of trade and industry, the origin and wealth and poverty. In *"Terra Infirma"* (2000), Irit Rogoff also extracts transnational but strongly connected neighbourhoods of traders, as remaining able to counter the homogenising model of globalisation. Gupta provides the example of Indian communities photographed by Indian artist Gauri Gill in Kabul in a way that those have been living in Afghanistan for hundreds of years such as traders who address Dari Afghan language but have moved to India and still dream of Jalalabad (Kayser,2017). Connecting to the curatorial projects of Bengali Anshuman Dasgupta, Rogoff also argues that the zones of disidentification or no man's land, like Kashmir or West Bengal, are such transnational space such as people spend less attention to being on this side or that side of the boundary because it has earnings, because they're acceptable, because of mysterious little things that float in and out of both parties. Rogoff analyses the process of the gliding through border lines to smuggling such as they both operate as a postulate of evolution of fluidity and of propagation that overlooks boundaries by creating a performative disturbance that does not present itself as conflict. For Rogoff, smuggling is a form of incorporated resistance to prevailing economic systems. It produces the bottom-up intelligence, partly experimental, partly theorised, that allows us to rethink maps of what we think we know. It is more effective than a Marxist top-down analysis of neo-capitalism and moves exceeding the ideas of hybridity which is based on the centrality of the subject matter. She names "inhabitation" this combined agency based on trading, of foods and textiles, sounds and literature on stuff circulating. The chapter of the research study understands Gupta comes from the Agrawal community, as tending towards this understanding of trade of foods, textiles and artworks as producing bottom-up knowledge. She is well informed of the politics of business and smuggling, as it has been discussed in several texts and exhibition catalogues written specifically by Geeta Kapur. By emphasising on particular physical locations and action, Gupta brackets to withstand the forces of global economics, its dematerialisation of life, and its destruction of local inhabitants. She says that physical position is one of the many things that circumscribe the functioning of the human intellect. We have begun an excellent watershed time today, where the hearts of all situations are floating freely in a deep global sea whose borders encounter the East as they reach the west and individuals approach to their shelters as per their purposes, their diplomas and as perchance too. The East is distressed concerning this more severely today, as social space is remarkably closely intermingled in this region, with several generations still living together under the same roof (Kayser, 2017).

5.2.3 Shilpa Gupta and Henri Lefebvre: Rhythmanalysis

While she experiences Rogoff's valorisation of activity as performative, Gupta's concept of the latter appears somewhat different. The muted, frequently reflective temperament of her works correlates to individual campaigns and unparalleled confrontations, suggesting a complicated relationship between the singular and the plural. The study of the research analyses to establish her uncertain situation firstly in connection to Henri Lefebvre's uncertainties. In *"The Production of Space"* (1974) Lefebvre, in context to Marxist orthodoxy, was significant of the thoughts of mental, subjective and philosophical locations. There is but one kind of area, he asserted, that of the effectiveness of increasing which defines the social relations of production and their cultural representations that are concerned with logico-epistemological space, the area of social practice, space occupied by sensory appearances, including products of imagination such as projects and projections, symbols and utopias. For Lefebvre everyday life is necessary to the generation of capitalism in so far as it is saturated by the routineised, repetitive, familiar daily practices, that produces indifference, obedience to practices and social practices and therefore are the best guarantee of non-revolution. This effective method can be inverted to create the revolution of the minds. Culture—especially poetry and Visual Arts— and an appreciation of our regular appearances can modify the cycle of separation and reveal not our internal consciousness but the consciousness of our actions that are directed towards specific goals and which he calls the *"thought-actions"*.

In Rhythmanalysis, his last book of 1992, Lefebvre, who by then had instantiated himself from Marxist Doxa, examines the perceptible the individual private awareness and the body—all of which are anathema to materialism and metaphysics—for what he deems to be their commonality of rhythm. The "rhythm analyst ," he contends, is like a psychoanalyst—he accepts to the *sonances of the experience* as well as murmurs, and finally to censorships and studies at the dominating-dominated relationship between the two. He grows aware of the inequalities in rhythms between people and things to release the sensible noticed through the tangible existence of the moment. Gupta also explains that sensations and their representations are related to action. Still, somewhat than indicating *"conscious thoughts"* or *"thought-action"* organised at a goal, she emphasises on the hidden thoughts that happen in the vagabondage of smuggling, on the *"murmurs"* created by people of an enclave playing soccer with the guards at the border, on the rhythms of the slabs of Kupwara, staked against one another that oppose their affective charge to the rationale of the administration. Shilpa's objects are bearers of the emotional memories of both the individual and the collective, that lie hidden in the *"in-between"* of events, of borders. Gupta expresses that she wants to function of the human consciousness, the individual vis-à-vis the group, and the nation-state, beyond and in between, and how it changes when the zones shift.

Gupta's works allude not only to replacements leading position in the cultural context but also to activities—frequently inattentive and unacknowledged—that happens within the outside world and the inner self. She expressed through her practice that what we see and how we see is very subjective, very context-based. Gupta is interested in the conscious and unconscious space that lies in between the object and the formation of meaning. Therefore, a secondary story is attached to the idea of the frontier, which is primary to her work. At the same time, the first is the frontier which divides neighbourhoods supported by widespread and spiritual narratives; the second involves the internalised descriptions and mental maps they create. This concern is non-unique in India, and also resembles central to Anshuman Dasgupta's curatorial projects and to the works of Amar Kanwar, an artist who Gupta profoundly appreciates. Although her unique contribution consists of dispatching this knowledge of the area and creating maps from local associations in India to an international public through the vocabulary of conceptual art, helping bridge the two distinct social contexts. In '*Speaking Wall*' (2010), the viewer is tempted to step on a small line of bricks–strikingly related to Carl Andre's "*Equivalent VIII*" (1966)–to climb towards the wall and to put on headphones. The barrier has an enclosed yard sensor that detects how far or how close the observer is from it. The sensor begins the artist's documented voice which provides the observer directions, within the headphones, to move towards the wall or apart from it. Between two sets of forms, the voice alludes to the appearance of an invisible fence, of a succumbed house during an eight-minute loop. The interchange of preparations to move with the information of an unseen scenery accentuates the gap between the here the figure and the over there the created space. A difference is established between "thought-actions" and inner mindfulness, between immediacy and lapsed time. The inconsistent nature of the condition of consciousness triggered by those consecutive minutes is liberating, perhaps because of the body above/mind coordination.

While the authoritative voice-over and the digital panel invoke state control, the smooth, feminine view of the artist remains the rational paradigm on which this control is based, as chance, poetry and embodied sensation come to mark the border that moves with the wind and is erased by the rain. The question of who takes care of a grave that lies beyond the edge, who has the keys to a house, is also part of this narrative.

The inspiration for '*Speaking Wall*' stalks from a discussion with Pakistani filmmaker Farzad Nabi through an automobile trip in the year 2005, back to

Lahore from Wagah, a frontier town where highly ritualised celebrations of opportunity and closing of the border gate take place daily. Nabi considered a house on the Indian side of Punjab, a home his family owned before partition and of which his ancestor has the keys till that day. The house, the keys, and the grave assemble a conceived space that interrupts the official beliefs of leave-taking. The boundary converts a perfect space connected with the cult of ancestors, an actual "Patria", a region attached to family genealogy. The idea of swing here is required that of the tracks with the sound, of the body with the wall, and the free beat of the rain that leaves frames. The installation foregrounds the separated rhythms that pulse in every single detail. It establishes their encounter and produces a eurythmic harmony in place of arrhythmia, and thus healing. This again suggests proximity with Henri Lefebvre's "rhythmanalyst." The thought of the displacement along the border, in a house and corporate space of residence, is sustained by the swing of natural movement inspired by the installation. It is itself the consequence of the interplay between the rhythm of the voice, the observer's listening, and their bodily reaction.

5.2.4 Shilpa Gupta and Michel de Certeau's "anthropological space"

Because Shilpa Gupta's work distributes with displacement in a social sphere, it is prolific to read her works beside Michel de Certeau's concept of "anthropological space," a "space as practice." Certeau, a former Jesuit, ascribes refined dimension to occupying a place. It is a procedure of defence by the unknown, the neglected somebody. Using the parable of a physique looking on the main square, Certeau recommends that each perambulation is unparalleled and triggered not only by substance restraints but also effective and sentimental needs such as intersecting the street after shopping at the butcher to say hello to the florist. It produces a bizarre, performative psychic image that indicates personal bureau on the time the subject occupies. This meandering identifies the relationship to the world of each individual, and as such, there are as many spaces as particular spatial experiences. Those idiosyncratic areas are composed evidently by first-person anecdotes which he calls the walker speech clause, as when people express their efficiency from their everyday happenings of walking, from the corridor to a room, to another. The chapter of the research find this same pattern in Gupta's '*Speaking Wall*' (Plate 5.4), and it is striking that this installation creates from a discussion with Farzad Nabi, in which he conveyed his personal and familial memories of inhabitations, during a trip in a secluded space, a car.

In '*Speaking Wall*', an installation from 2009-2010, the visitor wears a headset, walking up onto a row of blocks that dead-end into the wall. Then something unanticipated takes place. A sound in the headset represents the visitor wherever and when to move along the bricks; the audience member's identification is arbitrarily moved to the performer. To make this all work, Gupta has installed a sensor in the wall so that it knows where the 'performer' is when issuing its regulations. This displays a moving performance as the voice starts talking about changing boundaries that represent the individualities of both human and object enigmatic. The view of the wall shows a story regarding a frontier that was expressed in the earth and presented to the wind, thereby shifting a few centimetres. Such arbitrary borders are meaningless, of course, which makes the performer's identity pointless, too. 'So it's fine,' the wall says, "*so I no longer need your ID, no longer need to know your name, your religion, your sex and the place you came from*" (Gupta, 2009). There is no need to know anyone's identity when borders across landscapes are constantly being re- drawn by nature or, more likely, by humankind. Gupta asks once again: how much has changed?

Gupta explores the work '*Speaking Wall*' with interactive Sensor Based Sound Installation. LCD screen, Bricks, Headphone, 8min interaction loop 118x118x118 in | 300x300x300 cm.

Shilpa's installation serves as a transmitter of those memories to the viewer's sensitivity through a body-mind practice. In that feeling, the citation of Carl Andre's Minimalist brick pathway—though ignored by the artist—becomes essential, given Andre's concern with walking and reflection. To Andre's stress on inner thoughts, Gupta combines the purpose of interacting with an undisclosed identity. Connecting to commandments, Certeau states that a narrative is the beginning of all a support to initiate a movement that gives it a "foundation". It is pure as it ensures that action will be beneficial, auspicious. As a sacred act that provides a favourable consequence, "a narrative activity proceeds to develop where frontiers" and "the sense out of boundaries" are concerned. '*Speaking Wall*' is unquestionably a narrative about a frontier, about partition. It appears to influence to the lack of a favourable framework in the creation of the boundary between India and Pakistan, and to the genocide and perpetual war that is required. It may be proposed that Gupta's narratives, which obscure and shift the boundary, convert history by late restructuring a space in which graves are reunited with their caretakers, people with their houses, family members with their estranged land (Kayser, 2017).

A text by Gupta termed '*A Drawing made in the dark-1*'(2015-2016), further underpins this essential role of body-mind relationship in her works. It reads: "*Go continuously then turn right at the tea stall and carry on to the main road. Later after the church, you will notice a Border Post pillar on your left side. Walk over the field, cross another pillar which belongs to the other side and you will observe a shop trading wood. It is the third house from the junction there*" (Kayser, 2017).

The text is like guidance covering delivered by an individual tradesman to guide differently . It also indicates the artistic representation of the track, which is created by walking. Gupta expressed that it's like an individual comprehends the trip so well that he or she does it so often, that an individual can move it while closing their eyes. In both this work and '*Speaking Wall*', the narrative performs as a bridge between two subjectivities, that of an actual traveller and that of the spectator, through the means of the latter's body. In '*Speaking Wall*', the bodily viewer drives according to the preparations and is suddenly compelled to formulate a proper place and extent, a house below the rain, a wall, a grave, a set of keys, in the narration of the sound. The artist foregrounds the separate swings that pulse in each unique element. In '*Drawing*', the information reprinted on the paper document as a bridge between a substantial journey and the thought of the spectator who moves vicariously, following the departure of their eyes as they are reading the text. The feeling of movement is supplied by the swing of reading that is itself the outcome of the communication between the spectator's reading rhythm, the organisation of the text on the paper and the semiotic meaning. They all combine to carry the recognition of a walk. This second work scatters light on the difference between reading a map—a cognitive and abstract action—and walking a region. In the following case, affective components, such as drinking a hot tea cup, talking with the storekeeper, walking across a field and considering the scrapes of the grass, become surrounded in the memory and re-energised by the reading. It suggests that the accurate representation of this kinaesthetic process would be a map, which is a unit of measure that reflects the speed and direction of the displacement of the body through space. The plans made by Le Corbusier for the Capital of Chandigarh in 1964 have such a unit of measure (they are based on steps of 80 cm). By changing the group from an abstract concept (the metre) to one based on actions, Le Corbusier wanted to make visible people's lived experience of walking through space, between buildings to which he ascribed a sacred symbolism. He was thus reverting to a pre-modern way of mapping. Portolan charts, the mediaeval maritime maps made by Mediterranean pilots (portolani) and used between the 13th and the 18th century, are examples of such pre-modern maps. They are not based on a system of abstract coordinates and astronomical observations, as later one, but on distances, estimated according to the duration of the navigation, and a direction given by the compass, in a bottom-up process. Their scale is provided by a unit of measure that is only visual (a segment) but not explicit. Hence the distance between two locations can only be calculated by comparison with the gap between other places, within each map.

It can be required that specific procedures of analysis based on the actual displacement of bodies (or vessels) disturb the modern interpretation of maps, created by geographers continuously from the ground, into astronomical predictions and today with satellite views. This is what Shilpa Gupta endeavours to do in '*1703 km of Flood Lighting— Department of Border Management Home Ministry of India*' (2015- 16) which is a work placed next to '*Drawing in the Dark*' (2017) (Plate 5.5). The previous is made by building a (fake) map of fulmination offices along the frontier with country Bangladesh. The artist practised carbon paper and a crayon to execute this map, puncturing the paper to create the lightning posts. Regarding the work, she has always been interested in light—what we know and what we don't know. Carbon paper is used to make a copy, often for maintaining recordings, and has been cleaned again and again on the paper which is then penetrated through. The result is a mesmerising work that appears made with a blue crayon. It irradiates a diffuse light as if one was walking on this well-lighted road, under the rain or in the fog. The tiny puncture holes reveal the white paper underneath and glide like stars. It carries a sense of uncertainty mixed with clarity, but also of threat, as when one approaches a border inundated with lights of control at night.

The installation '*1:998.9*' (2015) (Plate 5.6), concludes Gupta's endeavours to revise borders representationally. After entering the room, one understands a performer at a table drawing lines on a portion of hand-woven cloth, by persisting a stick on a carbon paper. On his, lies a massive, coiled white mass of fabric. The fabric comes from Phulia, which is a border town well-known for its beautiful textiles. The man, who appears to be of South Asian origin, observes the tissue and draws something on to it, making a succession of marks. He then shifts the fabric to the right by a few centimetres. It takes many weeks for the vast heap of white fabric to be processed. The cloth is three thousand three hundred and ninety-four metres long, which is a precise 1:998.9 of the length of the actual fence being built at the border between India and Bangladesh. Gupta claims it is the most extended security barrier in the world between the two nation-states. This barrier aims to protect India against terrorism and smuggling, but also creates a potentially lethal barrier for the population of the wetlands in the Bengal Delta who live in a volatile environment that is subject to the effects of climate change.

'*1:998.9*' looks as an allegorical contestation of the barrier that, when it ends in 2017, will limit the flow of people. It can also be perceived as the replay of the drawing of the border between the two countries, made quickly in July 1947 by the Radcliffe Commission under the stewardship of British officials. To a panoptic view of the terrain, it opposes a repetitive, slow gesture made by a (fake) local, who draws lines according to his inner rhythm. The work is not related to the Radcliffe Line, nor to a particular range, though they could be lines in one's hands, borders on the ground, mountains, rivers, it could be map lines, lines of people walking routes, as in '*Drawing in the Dark*'; but always criss crossing each other. It is related to a map, but mental as well as physical. It is quite indefinite, and it has many meanings. It is a map line but not a map line, the things which are not on maps – which are also maps. Gupta explains in a way that the bizarre choice of scale is a little off from a rounded 1:1000, and also deals with a sense of inherent doubt with the large scale mapping exercises that are undertaken. The work is a narrative of individual freedom and the right of any living being to disrupt officially sanctioned territory.

Her proposal strongly echoes Certeau's assertion that : Reviews of routes fail what was the performance itself of passing by. The operation of walking, then wandering or 'window shopping,' that is the activity of passers-by, is transformed into points that draw a totalising and reversible line on the map. The suggestion left behind is relieved for the practice. It shows the (greedy) stuff that the geographical structure has of being talented at transforming action into legibility. Still, in doing so, it causes a way of being in the world to be forgotten. To the ideal of the modern city and its rectangular grid of great avenues, Certeau opposes spaces that are haunted by many different spirits hidden there in silence, spirits one can 'invoke' or not, the only places where people can live.

Similarly, Gupta's preparation of the exhibition space for '*My East is Your West*' in the region of Venice is a journey in the dark. Shutters and fabric have obliterated windows . There is but a dim light projected on singular works, forcing visitors to discover one artwork at a time, through a slow walk, and to internalise somehow the invisible journeys of the anonymous traders, smugglers and enclave settlers that are presented to their view (Kayser, 2017).

Inside the exhibition in Venice, there was a sign here in one room, then another indication in another piece so that one can put composed things slowly, and something is held back and not carefully revealed. It is like being in the dark, an individual slowly makes his/her way, and one never really knows everything. The artist wanted to create a kind of silence around the pieces. The artist often treats her works in a similar way, where Gupta leaves the room dark and sheds light only on the part (Kayser, 2017).

Certeau ascribes a refined dimension to these anonymous journeys, the drive to mark the world with one's imprint, however minimal and invisible. There is an implied Christian mysticism in this celebration of each mark on the modern urban territory, as the symbol of the unique importance of each soul, however ordinary. It somewhat differs from Gupta's philosophy of life—her perspective as the persistence informs an Indian of robust collective experience. Yet the common point is the celebration of subaltern, ordinary, vernacular imagination and subjectivity, emerging from actions and interactions with objects. Like Gupta, Certeau posits that every day, physical displacements are a form of resistance of an "I," as humble as it may be, against "technocratic" rules : As unrecognised raisers, poets of their actions, quiet discoverers of their paths in the jungle of functionalist rationality, consumers produce through their signifying practices something that might be considered similar to the "wandering lines" drawn by the autistic children studied by F. Deligny. In the technocratically constructed, written, and functionalised space in which the consumers move about, their trajectories form unforeseeable sentences, partly unreadable paths across a space, the trajectories trace out the ruses of other interests and desires that are neither determined nor captured by the systems in which they develop (Kayser, 2017).

In this sense, Certeau's text helps the research study analyse Shilpa's works beyond the eventualities of the limited, the past and the political. At the essence of this take on displacement is the celebration of individual agency.

5.2.5 In conclusion: Shilpa Gupta, Michel de Certeau and Henri Lefebvre

It is in appearance that Gupta's works comprise a transcontinental narrative, in which borders and boundaries are presented as subjective restrictions that create hatred, preconception, and fierceness. They recommend that these preconceptions can be overwhelmed by a party of community-based individuality, represented and functional through the exchange of people and goods, ranging from primary medicine to expensive sarees, a process that Irit

Rogoff has intellectualised as "inhabitation." So far, as traces of a subject-based dislodgment through space and time and of the inner echo, which they harvest in the traveller's mind, her works can be well understood through the idea of the "pedestrian speech act" coined by Michel de Certeau (Kayser, 2017).

Certeau and Lefebvre both agree with the body-mind connection as the development of proclaiming the "ordinary gestures" of the ordinary individual against social constructions. While Certeau contends on an anthropological and metropolitan situation as well as on a bond between the mind and space, Lefebvre expands the frame to all "sensible" realms "everywhere where there is the interaction between a place, time and expenditure of energy." While Certeau appearances for the pattern of one's touch on the terrain, suggesting a gap between the subject and the space, Lefebvre believes a quest of "eurhythmy" amongst the individual body and its location of environment, which is not only an urban and social but also natural and animal, which is at the main of Gupta's art practice. In re-forming these inside spaces, dialogue performs and tempos in her installations also permitting the visitor to inspect them in a lonely way, through their observation, Gupta executes an aesthetic understanding in which invisible reminiscences and effects created by "being in the world" are re-energised, presented to one's perception, and replicated upon in a phenomenological means. Instantaneously, the bonds between a particular world and the community built up by society are revealed as a condition of being. Here lies her thorough dismantling of invisible borders.

If this work is well received in a fully international context, both Western and pan-Asian, it might be because a common perspective on the body-mind relationship and of the aesthetic of everyday life has emerged since the twentieth century, that reunites Western and Eastern views. This chapter discusses Shilpa Gupta's work with the help of Western thinkers but could have also considered Indian, Japanese and Chinese perspectives on "everyday life" and their understanding of the relationships between the individual and the environment. This shared curiosity in "becoming aware" of the tempo of the body and its connection to space will deliver further shade and augment the thoughtfulness of Gupta's works (Kayser, 2017).

5.2.6 A Case Study of the New Media Artworks of Shilpa Gupta

Some of the references of Shilpa Gupta's New Media Artworks can be taken for detailed analysis. Such as,

    a. *'For, in your tongue, I cannot fit'* (2017-18)

b. *'Words Come From Ears'* (2018)
c. *'We change each other'* (2017)
d. *'24:00:01'* (2010, 2012)
e. *'Untitled'* (2012)
f. *'Untitled'* (2004-05)
g. *'Untitled'* (2005-06)
h. *'WheredoIendandyoubegin'* (2012)
i. *'Singing Cloud'* (2009)
j. *'Threat'* (2009)

'*For, In Your Tongue, I Cannot Fit*' (2017-18)

Site-Specific Sound Installation, 100 speakers, microphones, printed text and metal stands

Shilpa Gupta's New Media work entitled *'For, In Your Tongue, I Cannot Fit'* (2017-2018) (Plate 5.7) explores the artist's year-long research into jailed poets from everywhere the world. The connection between the poet and the state has been a troubling one, across time and geographies. As New Media practices in global art practices, Gupta's this work has been the part of recently held Venice Biennale 2019 and also in Kochi- Muziris Biennale 2018.

The work *'For, In Your Tongue, I Cannot Fit'* revealed multi-channel sound installation– featuring 100 microphones suspended above 100 metal rods, each piercing a page inscribed with a verse of poetry – tells stories of deep conflict, exploring the political and societal restrictions that seek to control both the imagination and physical mobility of poets. The artist about the work expresses that the action takes an emotional journey through 100 stories, 100 poems and 100 small gestures of resistance that celebrate the freedom of thought.

'*Words Come From Ears*' (2018)

Motion Flap board, 17x96x5 in | 43x244x13 cm, 15 mins loop

In her work *'Words Come From Ears'* (Plate 5.8) is a motion flap board, evocative of those found in transportation regions and conveyance centres to connect timings and agendas. As it dangles from the ceiling, it undermines its intended purpose, Gupta substituting its informational text with poetry and textual snaps about the intricate measure of persons and ideas. As the split-flap display interchanges, new words and prose look as if present poignant and timely discussions which in turn rapid queries about the structure and deconstruction of identity through time and place.

'*We Change each other*' (2017)

Animated Outdoor Light Installation, Site Specific

Gupta's '*We Change each other*' (Plate 5.9) is an outdoor animated light installation which signifies the inevitable mutation and dispersion that follows when two beings or cultures come into contact with each other. Gupta explores the flux within inter-personal spaces, be it between two people, intergenerational , or those shaped by religious, political or gender divides with her poetic use of language, translating the phrase 'We change each other' into Hindi, Urdu, and English – the writings of the three largest represented religions in Bandra, where the artist lives and works. In an increasingly polarising world, witnessing mass migrations, only one of the interwoven languages lights up at a time, reminding the viewer to look at the 'Other'.

'*24:00:01*' (2010, 2012)

Motion Flap board, 30 min loop, 70x10x11 in | 177x25x28 cm

Gupta's work entitled '*24:00:01*' (Plate 5.10) concentrates and explores a mechanised split-flap board – technology once common to railway stations and airports around the world – in which words and phrases gradually emerge, and letters continually change. In work, misspelt disjointed words unsettle the viewer as the text transitions from one word or phrase to another, rapidly transforming meaning. The work expresses that without a distinct subject or context, a fragmented story evolves beginning with a subjective expression. The story then lasts through ideas of being in the right place and nationhood, as well as elicitations of personal associations, fear and terrorism. The work plays with the impartial role of public signage – rather than transporting evidence and instructions approximately , it lyrically and progressively physiques coatings of vague connotation.

'*Untitled* ' (2012)

Single-channel video projection, 3min 42sec video loop, 18.3×10 in | 47×26 cm

Gupta's '*Untitled* ' (Plate 5.11) executed white threads projected in the video with the amalgamation of mud represented in a sophisticated manner. Sometimes a hand's grip is trying to explore the shape of threads in the video.

This projection reveals a psychic interpretation of visual interaction to an individual viewer.

'*Untitled*' (2004-05)

Interactive video projection and sound with projector and Computer, 8 minutes Interaction loop, 236.2×315 in | 600×800 cm wide

Gupta's interactive video projection entitled '*Untitled*' (Plate 5.12) explored the feminine figures who are in dancing gestures moves along with the vocal text revealed in the screening. Along with these reflections in the video, some written texts also show in work with conceptual aspects. The moving figures' sign - gestured position also has a lot of psychological interpretations in work.

'*Untitled*' (2005-06)

Interactive Installation with touchscreens

The study of the research analyses that Gupta's Interactive Installation with touchscreens entitled '*Untitled*' (Plate 5.13) reveal dented onto the walls is the panoramic view of the Dal Lake, established in the heart of the capital city of Srinagar, where no road nor homegrown has escaped ferocity and anxiety for decades present day.

Kashmir overlaps a cultural, political and religious culpability line. The valley has observed much fear, pain and doubt, uncertain separately by its history and the constant struggle between the two nations that untruth at its borders – India and Pakistan, which had already fought three wars subsequently, was disconnected in 1947.

The patterns on the walls are of *Shikaras* – floating houseboats which tolerate rare designations such as 'Manhattan', 'Bombay Dreams', 'Paris' 'White House' and even 'New Sydney' as if ideal here continuously story elsewhere. Paradoxically some of these are also names of key metropolises of the world, nodes of concentrated power, where terror too has struck as if in revenge.

The work explores punctures into these walls of a room, which are inverted, in places where there would have been windows to look outside, are instead objects of fractured reality transmitting unsure data.

The visual interactions in the works have dimensions where an individual can identify a lot of conceptual interpretations. The visuals have conversations between the viewer and between the specific geographical setting.

'Wheredolendandyoubegin' (2012)

Led Based Light Installation, 346.5×27 in |880×68 cm

Gupta's work *'Wheredolendandyoubegin'* (Plate 5.14) has the text content of 'Where do I end, and you begin' which is a led based light installation that has conceptual aspects related to mental elements. The visuals of the works interacted with a led based light which is displayed outdoors. The upper space of the lighted texts has the appearance of a cloudy sky in the evening time. The night view has different dimensions in the works. The opposite portion of the work has the presence of a railway track.

'Wheredolendandyoubegin' has the content to pinch an individual viewer with its texts which at a glance didn't clear what is wanted to say. Still, the content-text of the work allows the audience to concentrate his/her to consolidate what is actually written and equally bound to think what the artist wanted to interpret through her New Media work of art.

'Singing Cloud' (2008- 2009)

Most of Gupta's display sustained a sombre mood or a poetic register, as in *'Singing Cloud'* (Plate 5.15), explores her amorphous throng of 4,000 microphones – turned into speakers – suspended from the ceiling. With deftly lyrical language, she touches on fear and prejudice, greed and power.

'Threat' (2008-2009)

Soaps, Interactive Installation, dimensions of 5, 9 x 2, 5 x 1, 6 in each soap.

The work *'Threat'* (Plate 5.16) encompasses a wall accumulated of brick-sized blocks of brown soap. Each soap is inscribed with the term 'THREAT'. Gupta, inviting her viewer to take a brick home, by which Gupta converts the spectator into interactive performers once again, with the result that this wall – her 'border' – is always in a state of global dispersal. On the one hand, borders in and of themselves foster benevolent national and cultural identities; but closed borders or defended borders are threats to the ideals of the free exchange of ideas and values, individuality, dissidence and upward mobility. Gupta turns each brick of soap into a symbol that places the onus on each of us returning home across our borders, to wash away the threats to a genuinely globalised society, culture and economy.

5.3 New Media Artworks of Bose Krishnamachari

Krishnamachari's work includes a different treatment of photographic elements as well as vibrant, colourful abstraction. The artist's art practices embrace a spectacular combination of colour, texture and distinct designs, with a strong intellectual base. Born in Kerala, Bose Krishnamachari studied at Sir J J School of Art, Mumbai. Krishnamachari's artistic voyage from his village in Kerala to Mumbai has been an exciting, cultural and learning experience. The artist's contribution to the art started with his concentration in paintings and theatre. He represented in theatres in the translated versions of Samuel Becket's play in Malayalam. He relished film, music, poetry and reading.

Regarding Krishnamachari's art learnings, the artist first joined Kerala Kalapeetom, which is a small art institute in Kerala. However, after Bose stimulated to Mumbai, his perception of art wholly transformed as he initiated himself adequately conveyed towards abstract art. The visual language of the form of non- representational art was exceedingly fascinating to him.

Bose Krishnamachari's work comprises vivid abstract paintings, figurative drawings, sculpture, photography, multimedia installations. Krishnamachari's masterly application of colours, his techniques and his procedure of various mediums are a source of inspiration and conjecture. In his art practises the lyrical mix of colour and strong geometrical patterning on paper and canvas is a unique visual experience, conveying a sense of magical realism.

The conceptual approach of modern British art enthralled him most of the time during his tenure at Goldsmith College, London. During his early days of art practice in Mumbai, Krishnamachari used to interact with artists like Akbar Padamsee, Laxman Shreshtha, Barve, Gieve Patel, Deepak, Navjot Altaf, Sabavala, Tyeb Mehta, Riyas Komu, Prabhakar Kolte, Mehli Gobhai, Atul Dodiya and Sudarshan Shetty. Bose was excited by their abstract works and inspired by their confidence in experimenting with different mediums.

In his installations, the artist enquiries the implication of the remaining powers that influence the art world and discourses the undeserved discernment in different layers of society. Krishnamachari encounters the single understanding of an image as he searches for abundant meanings. Even in his abstract works, he persuades the viewer to look for several explanations. In the artist's first solo show in the year 1990, Krishnamachari exhibited a minimalist style by creating an abstract black on black with white perforated paper, reminiscent of Braille. The subtle work echoed a satirical observation of the unfriendly and unapproachable gallery environment.

Additional famous rejoinder in contradiction of authority was vibrant in *AmUseuM* in the year 1992. This introduced a series of open spiral bound books decorated with poetry. It is interesting to observe how some of the pages were glued together. Krishnamachari painted over them, placed them in glass cases giving them a museum-like appearance. Here the artist had shaped a fusion of various castigations, including literature and design. With the bright blend of "muse", "use" "amuse" and the sacred "AUM" in the artist's title the sarcastic artist uttered '*No museum*'. The artist energies further by generating his artistic preserve with found objects.

Krishnamachari carried this idea further in the year 1995 when he rehabilitated objects like tiffin carriers which are an integral part of the life of a Mumbaikar; band handles, *diyas*, and a workman's gloves into museum fragments by adding gold and placing them in small voids covered with glass like a display case.

Bose Krishnamachari understands the actual artistic practice is more notable than any theories, concepts, ideas. He trusts in Karl Marx's philosophy that Man is a maker. This kinship with the artist's community led to a groundbreaking work called "*De Curating- Indian Contemporary Artists*" in 2003 consisting of 94 paintings and sketches of living Indian artists. This tribute to the art world, composed of established and promising artists, was compiled after research of three years. Being himself an artist Krishnamachari empathised with their trials and tribulations.

5.3.1 The Artistic Journey of Bose Krishnamachari : Transformation from Abstract Painting to Multimedia Interactive Installation

Krishnamachari was not interested in categorising his art practice in a particular domain. Even though the artist believed in the notion that yes, of course, categorisation is an art historical tool that can help to understand the oeuvre of an artist, in that sense, Krishnamachari's post-J J School and post-Goldsmiths works, up until the early years of the last decade, was principally abstract and conceptual in style. But there is a phase in the artist's formative years in Kerala and in Mumbai in which Krishnamachari used to do highly figurative (life painting) works. The artist was interested in portraiture and developed his skills doing a lot of portrait painting, which the artist still makes use of in his art practices.

The abstract style in Krishnamachari's art is more theoretical and philosophical than a visual technique. The artist used to remember Mondrian once said that by overdrawing on a line one could stretch a line to infinity, so Krishnamachari's abstractions are the postponement of a line, a stroke and a thought process. Development of this idea into the notion of artistic freedom resulted in the making of the 'Stretched Bodies' series, which is currently known as one of the artist's hallmark styles. Each time Krishnamachari approaches a canvas intending to make a 'stretched body' the artist is extending the possibilities of artistic freedom and the freedom of creative skills.

Krishnamachari has always been interested in design and construction. The study identified that in his childhood, the artist saw his father creating designs for interiors and architecture. Krishnamachari used to help him in his work, and it gave the artist a sense of, and hands-on experience in, design. When Bose travelled to Europe and the US during his education in London, the artist looked at this aspect of design in post-modern and contemporary art.

Krishnamachari believed that form and design is the stuff that gives internal strength to a work of art. The artist identified that Cezanne, Matisse, Picasso and the like realised this 'reality' of design in their work and, when we get to the post- seventies' conceptual art, design (the Memphis group and Ettore Sottsass) becomes significant. The artist observed the impermanence in everything; Bose was also interested in books, not only as knowledge repositories but also as 'objects' with different forms lying on the streets of Mumbai, and its absurdity. An artist's early solo shows he made conscious attempts to bring other Visual Art experiences and practices as seen in the exhibition 'Amuseum'. Through his art practice, Krishnamachari explores that for a bright artist, any new medium unlocks many challenges and possibilities. Treating them straight, using one's aesthetic intelligence is very important. The artist's practice would reveal that he is intelligent enough to handle these new mediums and spaces. Today, Bose presents his identity more like a fluid one – as an artist, a designer, a curator, an organiser, a fashion adherent, a gallerist, and so on. His practice doesn't want to be categorised.

5.3.2 Reading and Travel: The Significant Fragment of Bose Krishnamachari's Art Practice

The research study identifies that Krishnamachari through his art practice, explores that an individual understands art through two different channels; firstly through sources and secondly through the direct encounter. During Bose's student days in Kerala, the artist's understanding of world art was gained through books and journals. In this Krishnamachari would say there is always a sense of distorted understanding if anyone observed a Picasso or Van

Gogh and thought about them in terms of the history developed around them. So, in an individual's imagination, a 2'x2' painting would look as gigantic as a mural. When an audience or observer encounters the real work of art, he/she gets a sense of size and medium, which is unromantic, as opposed to the understanding that he/she gains from the mediated history.

The research study identified that the artist has benefited from both readings and travel. Krishnamachari developed his romantic notion of art history through mediated history, and the artist developed his sense of reality through direct encounters with world artists such as museums, studios, galleries and art fairs et al. which was facilitated by Bose's never-ending journeys. Observing a work of art in a particular setting is very important. For instance, following a practice of Jeff Koons or Andy Warhol in the US is as high a feeling as observing a Ravi Varma painting in Trivandrum. The location gives an individual a different understanding. At the same time, the museums are the spaces where the practicality of works of art are shaved off and positioned in separation, although further artworks enclose them. We recognise these artworks over a written history in the side panes.

In contemporary gallery exhibitions, one can identify that there is an urgency, imminence, a reduction of time. At the same time, an individual knows that there is a time gap between the origin and presentation of a work of art. An individual also realises there is a location difference between its display in one space and another.

When Krishnamachari travels within his own country, the artist's aim is always to spot new talent, to see what he or she is doing and to understand why he or she is doing so. Some critics say that Krishnamachari is a 'talent scout'. The research study identified that yes, Bose is a talent scout, the artist is a military drill-master and a scheming commander because what Bose is looking for is a result.

5.3.3 *The Artist and the Mumbai: Bose Krishnamachari's Art Exploration*

This chapter of the study analyses that the artist did not choose Mumbai. There are always changes in life. Bose was undergoing a sort of art training in Kerala and was very active in literary and theatre circles – the artist used to act in experimental plays. Then an older friend suggested to the artist that Krishnamachari should migrate to Bombay and study at the Sir J J School of Art. It was in the early 1980s. The artist then applied, but the authorities rejected his first application form. It was a kind of challenge thrown at him. Bose stayed in a place called Sakinka (a rundown neighbourhood in North Mumbai), worked in an exotic restaurant called "Mela" as a portrait artist, learned languages and then re-applied the following year again. This time Bose was accepted and went on to graduate successfully. Bose was top of the class throughout his education. The artist had a beautiful portfolio, which he lost from the college locker – he attaches a sense of loss with that missing portfolio.

According to Krishnamachari's conception, Bombay was a reservoir of energy. After the artist's graduation, he continued to go to the college every day, meeting the young students of Applied Art, Architecture and Fine Art in the canteen; they used to call it 'canteen activism'. Bose expanded his circle of friends; Ranjit Hoskote, then a budding poet and art critic, became the artist's friend. Bose used to assist several senior artists in the setting up of their shows. Financially he was struggling then, but the city of Bombay gave him new experiences every day, and it was impossible to leave.

Renowned artist, Akbar Padamsee, suggested that Krishnamachari should curate a show with young artists. He took action, but somehow the project did not take off; maybe the artists did not believe in Bose then. These experiences gave the artist the confidence to live in Bombay – it is a city of people not of 'djinns'; it is a city of life, not of tombs; it is a city of 'chawls', not of historic ruins. Life here always inspires Bose. Even if he had the opportunity to live in any other city, he didn't think that he would give up Mumbai.

Bose Krishnamachari believes that a work of art by any artist, whether the artwork/artist is successful or not, cannot be observed as separate from the main body of its setting. Even when it does not define itself as a part of the socio-political body of its origin, it carries the traits of the body, the thoughts of its existence. In that sense, whatever happens to Mumbai finds repercussions in Bose's work, although this is not a deliberate attempt on the artist's part.

Krishnamachari's works are directly connected to the people of Mumbai because Bose core heartedly believes that he is a Mumbaikar. The Mumbai city, historical, prosperous, cosmopolitan et al. has different layers of socio-cultural and political dynamics that make Mumbai what it is. Every layer is not a visible layer. The obvious cannot be called the essential or core and, at the same time, the hidden is not always necessary or indispensable. What Krishnamachari is trying to understand through his art is this gaseous exchange.

In '*Ghost/transmemoir*' and the *dabba* installation, Bose tried to receive the vocal and images of the persons who express their city; there is a sort of selected discord in this artwork. Together with the image of a successful film star, an individual can identify the vision and voice of a dealer at the Church Gate railway station. The common thing they have is the city of Mumbai. In the '*Mumbaikar*' series, which has iconic portraits of the artist's household attendants (without whom the artist believes that he wouldn't survive in this city), and also 108 photographic portraits of Bose's friends in Mumbai, he portrays a Mumbai which is of people. These people are both political and cultural; they are the results of the political makeup of this city; their portraits summarise Mumbai in their miniature worlds, and they are the small copy of the city Mumbai.

5.3.4 Bose Krishnamachari's Artworks and the Interactive Audience Participation: Beyond the Artist's Taste

Audience participation is essential in Krishnamachari's works. When the artist presents his works for a local audience, for example in Mumbai, Delhi or Kolkata, in a way the artist presumptuous an acquaintance with their rejoinders, this might central to a kind of complacency. Krishnamachari wants to be challenged and questioned; he likes the friendly debates that surround a work of art, and the artist likes helpful criticism that looks beyond personal taste.

When Krishnamachari presents his works to a foreign audience, the artist expects the same challenge. While the home audience is familiar with his background, the international audience looks for clues so that they can connect with Bose's artwork. There was a period when the external spectators wanted 'Indian' clues in an Indian artwork. Today, they don't wish to appearance for the 'ethnic' Indian-ness in the artworks. They observe how stimulating, how inspiring, and how contemporary the works are. In an overseas location exhibition curators, critics, museum personalities and gallerists talk with an individual more than the regular art lover. In the artist's hometown, any visitor likes to speak with anyone. Perhaps the artist wanted it when a viewer with no professional arts connection questions the artist about what the artist has done.

Krishnamachari's works explore thanks to the allowed global conversation of ideas, commodities, culture, politics, concerns, ideologies, war, and so on, art to have become visible crossways boundaries. It is not impartial that Indian contemporary art is touching all the world; world art is also approaching India . And it is not because the globe has unexpectedly fallen in love with Indian art and culture that around is this global attention. No, it is because of economics and worldwide political contribution. Art is one method of considerate the creation and cumulative excellence of comprehensive co-operation. In accumulation, art has investment value, and with investment in art, individuals across borders trust each other on a commercial level too. So we have a stimulating situation wherever global players come to India and look at our art, buy our art and exhibit our art elsewhere. We respond to this temperateness by doing the same. BMB Gallery, Mumbai, where Bose Krishnamachari is one of the founding directors, works towards building up this global exchange of human understanding through art.

5.3.5 Questioning 'the Idea of the Formation of the Canon in Art': Krishnamachari as a Curator

The study of the research analyses that formation of any canon is the result of an attempt to thwart an existing rule. It is an irony but a reality. Hence, whenever Bose takes on a curatorial project, he attempts to stop a current curatorial position. Krishnamachari has different strategies for employing curatorial ideas; for example, some of his solo shows are attempts at self-curation. Still, he didn't follow a set pattern in his solo curatorial projects. Also, he likes starting with fundamental ideas and expanding them, using works by different artists. This gives Bose an added freedom to move away from canons.

Curatorial efforts were already present in his study days. Akbar Padamsee recognised this and encouraged Krishnamachari to put on shows, but 'De-curating' happened as a response to a canonical curatorial project which refused to include several works, including Krishnamachari's. Bose found it somewhat offensive and going against the ounce of history and actualities. The impression behind 'De-curating' was a sort of deconstruction of a curatorial monolith in India. Later he developed this concept in various forms and always took care that it shouldn't become another canon. Now, if a principle exists in Bose's curatorial practice at all, it is a sort of 'Bose Brand'. A musician friend of Bose, Randolf Correa (Shair n' Funk) mentioned at his openings and parties that Bose connects elite with Dalit. Subsequently all, in Mumbai hedonism co-exists with law-life.

5.3.6 Bose's 3C Theory: Cricket, Cinema, and Curry

Bose's 3C theory is essential to him as an artist as well as a person. As an artist Bose interested in contemporary culture, he is intensely interested in the progress going on in the field of sports/cricket, cinema and curry/culture. The famous 'C's – Cinema (Bollywood), Cricket and Curry (food) – comprise the breath of and everything that is Mumbai. The artist is absorbed in the enthusiasm these belongings create in our daily lives. The three Cs must be understood more as a metaphor than a convincing statement.

5.3.7 Bose Krishnamachari as an Art Directorial: The Visionary Approaches

The study of the research analyses that during the past few years, Bose has been collecting the works of his contemporaries that recognised modernists and historically prominent artists from all groups. It has engaged a lot of energy to develop his art practice, at times exchanging firm received money and at times with the aid of massive loans. But art collecting has continuously been a passion for Bose and the idea of a museum is a natural outcome for this collection. When an individual has a collection of artworks, there is a need to authenticate it by viewing it to people. The personal nature of a group should, at times, be confirmed by sharing it with the spectator. Also, there is a need to carry in new museum involvement for the people from one place to another. The idea of a museum in Kerala acquired form throughout the area market boom, and Bose acquired land in Kerala for this purpose.

Bose imagined it as an international residency containing books, DVD's et al. It must be a space for New Media Art, where it should be involved for documentation and propagation of information about art. At the similar time it will have a devoted section for Krishnamachari's collection of works; a museum of contemporary culture. The study analyses that Bose's next project is to curate a show by Indian contemporary women artists – there are so many women artists working in India now. Bose's idea is not to see through the feminist canon; instead, he wants to do a sort of survey of their art. Bose wants to see how they function within and without a system. It is a multi- pronged project and Bose's approaches are looking forward to it.

Bose Krishnamachari is also well known for identifying the young talent from the Visual Arts arena. His contributions as art director is also prominent along with his artistic journey. He prominently contributes as the Artistic Director and Co-Curator of India's first Biennale – The Kochi-Muziris Biennale 2012, Director of Kochi-Muziris Biennale 2014 and President of the Kochi Biennale Foundation. He has been committing most of his time in making Kochi-Muziris Biennale the cynosure of the art world by dividing his artistic practices time between Mumbai and Kerala.

The Kochi-Muziris Biennale has turned a new page in the history of Indian Visual Arts and culture. When a city converts a cultural hub, it brings about ripple effects in other sectors in society. Krishnamachri's contributions shaped the Kochi-Muziris Biennale into a new high, the collective responsibilities of other members associated with the Biennale developed to sustain the Biennale in proper dimension.

Krishnamachari's art directorial explorations dimensioned the vibrant identity of the Indian Visual Art scene with his vision that culture in all its diverse forms is central to what makes a city appealing to educated people and hence to the businesses which seek to employ them. In the age of globalisation, artistic ability and economic success are more interlinked than at any other point in history. Global cities compete with each other to host international events – both sporting and cultural. It points to the fact that soft power is key to taking a city or a country to economic and social heights. In the global knowledge economy, having a well-educated workforce is the key to success, and such workers demand stimulating, creative environments. It is clear from partner cities' responses that they are well aware of culture's role in making their cities attractive to 'talent'. A vibrant and lively culture consequently also becomes an indirect source of economic success.

Along with the contributions of Krishnamachari, the organisers of the Kochi- Muziris Biennale have uplifted Biennale in a new class. Understanding the predicament and the importance of their support, leading artists have taken up the cause to keep the Biennale going. They have appealed to the government to provide financial support for the event as an art biennale is a powerful cultural tool.

Through the contributions of Bose Krishnamachari, the Kochi-Muziris Biennale has made an impact on the Visual Art world in terms of curatorial selection and artistic quality. Global media has waxed eloquent on the venues and works on display – giving global tourists another reason to visit India and Kerala. In these ways, Kochi-Muziris Biennale has taken off and promises a great future of the Indian Visual Art scene.

With making these contributions, Krishnamachari not only dimensioned the Indian art scene into a new high in the global art arena but also a puff of fresh air to breathe, helping the country take another step towards global recognition.

5.3.8 A Case Study of New Media Art Practices of Bose Krishnamachari

Some of the references of Bose Krishnamachari's New Media Artworks can be taken for discussion. Such as,

    a. *'LaVA'* (2006)
    b. *'Ghost/Transmemoir'* (2008)
    c. *'White Builders and Red Carpets'* (2008)

'LaVA' (Laboratory of visual art), 2006

The installation displaying Krishnamachari's appetite for experimentation is evident in an installation 'LaVA' (laboratory of visual art) in 2006 (Plate 5.17). The artist emphasised on the five decades in design, photography, art and architecture to deliver a situation point for various Visual Art practices. LaVA was a vehicle that sincerely enquired the ineffectiveness of existing institutions and the importance of archives. This achieves this by displaying a contemporary temporary laboratory consisting of records on Visual Arts obtained from museums, institutions, galleries, shops and street.

Krishnamachari's show at the Museum Art Gallery titled LaVA (laboratory of visual art), assembles vital resources and references on various Visual Art practices. It's the exhaustive collection of the maverick artist who continues to challenge conventional concepts of Visual Art practices. Through LaVA, the artist shares a decade of the personal collection with art aficionados. For Krishnamachari, the installation is an artistic intervention with a focus on the last fifty years in design, photography, art and architecture. The artist describes the work as his pet project. It's part of his long-term plan of setting up a permanent library that will house his private collection including works by younger and new artists.

'Ghost/Transmemoir' (2008)

150 x 90/in, 108 used tiffins with LCD monitors, amplifiers, DVD players, headphones, cables, jute ropes, scaffo

One of Krishnamachari's large scale multimedia installations titled *'Ghost/Transmemoir'* takes a different approach to mapping Mumbai (Plate 5.18). The artwork comprises 108 tiffin boxes suspended from a frame and wired with headphones and small screens. Tiffin boxes play a central role in

Indian life, with millions being filled daily by housewives, collected exchange, re-exchange and stored until the home-cooked lunch reaches the office workers. Overall the video installation captured some of the hustle and chaos treats in Mumbai. The small screens present interviews with people from Mumbai, and this portrays their thoughts, celebrations, frustrations, emotions which are equally the individual voices of 20.8 million Mumbaikars.

'*Ghost / Transmemoir*' is a dizzy installation of 108 used tiffin's (or 'dabba'), executed to set video loops viewing interviews with a gathering of Mumbai peoples from all levels of society. It mirrors a significant feature of Mumbai, a city where the 'dabba' plays a vital role in the everyday ritual of delivering home-cooked food. The installation pulses the disharmony and chaos of the city, while the small screen echoes the thoughts, frustrations, religions and emotions of the many people who add energy to Mumbai.

Bose Krishnamachari's works are socio-politically determined, reflecting satires and insurrections. From his art practices of abstraction to installations, the prime focus of his work has always been the surroundings, his encounters with persons, the authority changing aspects within, and how he observes them altogether. The role of the establishment is either upfront or subtly in the background. By incorporating New Media, his intention and impact become more significant in terms of network and interactivity.

Abstract art helped Krishnamachari to follow his thoughts by redeeming his style of expression, sometimes directing at eternity. This is reflected in his '*Stretched Bodies*' series. Here the artist's talent for colour is obvious as he contrasts astonishing planes of flat colour against skilful, virtually photographic, representations of his unique style imparted with an 'international' responsiveness. Through the synthesis of Western image-making techniques such as the installations with the indigenous, the artist creates a visual language that boasts of aesthetic qualities and a magical efficacy.

Krishnamachari's recent body of work juxtaposes icons from different cultures. The works include Mexican artist Frida Kahlo and her husband Diego Rivera, the Russian filmmaker Andrei Tarkovsky, and Rabindranath Tagore. Krishnamachari aims to create a holistic vision by amalgamating spirituality, epic style and (in Kahlo's case) a focus on the self as means to explore more significant issues.

'*White Builders and the Red Carpets*', (2008)

In the installation entitled '*White Builders and Red Carpets*' *(Plate 5.19)*, the artist executes a press conference tableau complete with imposing chairs, which are evocative of modern architectural forms in a city's skyline, and the table fitted with microphones belonging to the frenetic multitude of news channels. This becomes a take on dominant players 'manufacturing consent' using the media as the narrator. The general populace is left with narratives, clearly spoken and edited to fit what the influential leaders would want the common man to hear, giving impetus to their desires in the name of collective welfare.

In the installation, '*Builders and the Red Carpets*' Krishnamachari selects a political viewpoint. He generates a press meeting with 108 microphones on a long red table. The satire is revealed by the 13 impressive white chairs which signify the kind of influential individuals who speak to the press to continue wars for economic gain. The 13 chairs are a symbolic representation of '*The Last Supper*' (Plate 5.20) and the disparaging role religion plays in our conflicts. The installation is also an observation on the necessity of information in the New Media to combat the numerous 24 hour news channels. This work can be measured in many ways. When the artist is coming from a Kerala background and consciously doing abstract work, it's certainly a kind of a shift from what he carried to debate. It's a political awareness which made the artist an abstract painter.

The study of the research analyses that Krishnamachari acknowledges that he is an artist and curator has its share of responsibility. It is a kind of education. For the artist, he believed that every project that he took up was educational . The artist's solo shows are conceived and executed as educational projects. All of Krishnamachari's art practices, personal and curatorial, are very much related to history, historical figures, methods and events. If audiences are not familiar with the history of art, it isn't straightforward to read for her/him. Even the shows that Bose curates have historical references. An individual must show contemporary art practice, and every time she/he does that it must be a memorable moment in history.

Bose Krishnamachari believes in the concept that when an individual creates art he/she creates his/her own philosophy. Bose adds that the aforementioned destiny isn't something that is God-given, but rather the culmination of one's interests, actions and undertakings. Krishnamachari keeps working across different projects because the artist believes that actions are more important than mere thoughts. Krishnamachari believes that art is like itself. The artist in his many interviews mentioned that he never copied the works of others because he doesn't think it is an excessive way of learning . Enthusiasts of his work would be fairly familiar with the representation of the average Mumbaikar in his paintings. Since this is an intriguing concept, an explanation was sought from the artist himself. Krishnamachari has the perception that Mumbai itself, as a city, functions as a great university and has taught him so much. Extremities coexist in the artist's lifetime and the same is replicated in the everyday life of a Mumbaikar as sound. The chaos that an individual experiences in Mumbai is very energetic. The artist didn't convey the meaning of chaos in a negative approach – whenever the city has faced difficult times due to any situations, it has resurrected itself the very next day. It is because everybody is here to live, the artists believe in that optimistic approach.

Krishnamachari explains that in today's world, the components of art and design are an integral, indispensable part of 'existence' itself – vital cogs in the machinery of visual representation. The artist expresses that an individual artist makes art for a better world, for better thinking and better living. Understanding minimalism is very difficult because editing from chaos and channelising anyone's viewpoint into something is not easy. When quizzed about the amount of vivid and bright colours, shades, textures and tones carried by Krishnamachari's paintings, he reveals that boundaries coincide in life. There is one side that is very colourful and the other minimalistic has its different approach. On one side, the viewer has art forms like Kathakali, which is very vibrant and visually attractive, and on the other hand, the viewer has the Gandhi ideology.

Krishnamachari also contributes to the idea that budding artists must explain themselves with developments along with the art form by regularly reading primary sources. Bose has confidence that every artist is aware of our contemporary social structure. Artists should understand how the economy works, read newspapers and get into the habit of reading and not depend entirely upon the temporary aspects of technology. As a reflection, Bose also expresses that he always tells upcoming artists to keep working and not to think exclusively about their career. An individual will get to visit places.

Krishnamachari doesn't have any specific drawing that he cherishes in particular - he is fond of all of his artwork and styles. Another component that Bose visually represents though his artworks relate to the 'here and now' approach as well as concept. Krishnamachari sensed that there is an acute shortage of museums in the country and that has negatively affected the artistic notions of the average artist. With the global thought process Bose believes that there isn't much opportunity here in India to understand contemporary artwork. For example, Holland has close to 140 museums. India has an incredible wealth of art in its diverse regions. Still, the elitism attached to it is wrong. Bose believes everyone should experience art through infrastructure and it's important to allocate space for art infrastructure. Krishnamachari also has the opinion that the nation requires the vision to get up who understands the values of art and culture and help circulate the same.

Most people are aware of the fact that Bose Krishnamachari is also the founder of the Kochi Biennale Foundation (KBF), an acclaimed art platform that was initiated, created and run by artists with the help of the Kerala State Government. Bose expresses that artistic autonomy should be given top priority when it comes to the biennale, and it should not be dominated by bureaucracy. There is doubt about the fact that in a short period, each edition to be exact, Kochi has become the pride of India. Speaking with that great perception the recipient of Lifetime Fellowship Award Kerala Lalit Kala Akademi describes that curators, collectors, museum heads, artists, the common man and it is fantastic to see museum directors observe the biennale and say that it is one of the most beautiful things that has materialised after independence of the country in the cultural world. The biennale supports every aspect of the creative world where there is an educational programme, art by children, and students' biennale.

Of all the artistic concepts that he operates, art is life; it gives individual freedom. It's like a healing balm. It makes an individual aware of who he/she is. Nobody needs to go anywhere to find peace when anyone gets involved in art and culture.

In recent times in the year 2020, Bose Krishnamachari appeared with his solo exhibition almost after a decade. The exhibition entitled *"The Mirror Sees Best in the Dark"* at the Emami Art Gallery of Kolkata (Plate 5.21). The exhibition works reveal Braille artworks which are embossed on the surface and reflected negative and positive space. The ten words were written are like ten commandments which reflecting what is happening in society, including religion, capitalism, God, casteism, regionalism, narcissism, nationalism et al. (Krishnamachari, 2020).

Regarding the conceptual aspects of the exhibition, Krishmanachari explored that of an individual observing the Indian Philosophy -

TamasoMaajyotir-gamaya – *tamaso* means darkness. According to Krishnamachari in Mumbai, he would see reflections on dark waters in the evenings and those rippled lights were music to the artist (2020). The artist feels that extremities coexist. The ambivalence sometimes comes as conflict – in the language of art, an individual can term maximalism and minimalism. The artist's life he has observed those extremes in Kerala and Mumbai also. In recent times/years, to the artist, there have emerged new heights such as nationalism, racism and technology. These have dramatically reshaped our lives. The trap that an obsession can wield in similar to that of a mirror. To Krishnamachari, a mirror is not just a reflector; it is also a receiver that draws an individual in and captures (2020). The artist conceptualised his recent exhibition in these thought processes.

5.4 Conclusion

Through the chapter titled *"Through the Ways of Memory and the Techno-Images: Re-Interpretation of New Media Works of Shilpa Gupta and Bose Krishnamachari"* the research study went through with the detailed analysis of the New Media Artworks of Shilpa Gupta and Bose Krishnamachari with conceptual aspects of visual interaction.

This chapter of the research study identified that Shilpa Gupta's New Media works explore against essentialist notions of identity as demarcated by social and political forces: gendered and religious narratives, and the nation-state's logic of territoriality. The artist proposes an understanding of identity as multi-layered, having to do with the memories, subjectivities, and affects that daily activities and human encounters map onto the mind through the peripatetic movements of the body. Many of Gupta's works confront essentialist and nationalist notions of identity in the context of the violence that predates intercommunity and family life in the Sub-continent.

Bose Krishnamachari explores his art practices pitched in an attitude with a specific geographical setting. The research study finds that through Krishnamachari's multimedia installations the artist many times questions in a conceptual way the significance of the existing powers that influence the art world and tries to address the unjust discrimination in different strata of society. Krishnamachari encounters the mono interpretation of an image as he explores for abundant implications.

The study of this chapter of research tries to establish with the findings that both Shilpa Gupta and Bose Krishnamachari have their specific expression of the thought process through their reveal of New Media Artworks. Shilpa Gupta explores her works through the ways of memory with dimensions of New Media Artworks. Bose Krishnamachari through his New Media practice emphasises on the content of individual's conscious actions with a specific region's expression such as Krishnamachari's working concepts on Mumbai is a visual interaction of that conceptual aspect where techno images also have resemblances.

Plate 5.1 : Shilpa Gupta . *Blame* (detail) . 2002-2004 . Interactive Installation with contains stimulated blood , poster , stickers , video , interactive performance .
Courtesy : Shilpa Gupta . Web 22 February . 2019

Plate 5.2 : Shilpa Gupta .
1278 unmarked , 28 hours by foot via National Highway No 1 , East of the Line of Control (detail) . 2013 .
Interactive Installation . Courtesy : Shilpa Gupta . Web 22 February . 2019

Plate 5 . 3 : Joseph Kosuth . *One and Three Chairs* (detail) . 1965 .
Wood folding chair , mounted photograph of a chair, and
mounted photographic enlargement of the dictionary definition of "chair" .
Courtesy : moma.org . Web . 22 February . 2019

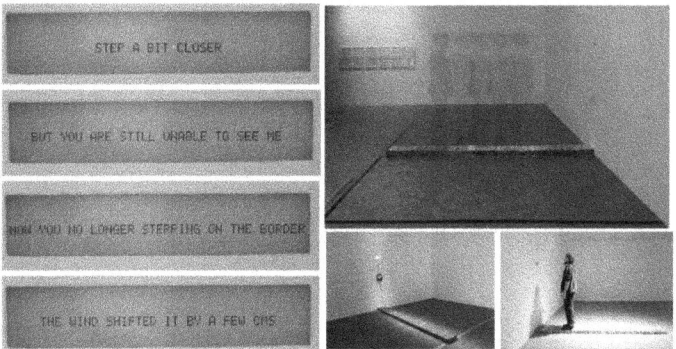

Plate 5 . 4 : Shilpa Gupta . *Speaking Wall* (detail) . 2009-2010
Interactive Sensor Based Sound Installation , LCD screen , Bricks , Headphone .
Courtesy : Shilpa Gupta . Web 22 February . 2019

Plate 5.5 : Shilpa Gupta. *Drawing in the Dark* (detail). 2017.
Installation. Copper pipe. Courtesy : Shilpa Gupta. Web 22 February. 2019

Plate 5.6 : Shilpa Gupta. *1: 998. 9* (detail) . 2015 . Installation .
Courtesy : Shilpa Gupta . Web 22 February . 2019

Plate 5.7 : Shilpa Gupta. *For, In Your Tongue, I Cannot Fit* (detail). 2017-2018.
Site Specific Sound Installation with 100 speakers, michrophones, printed text and metal stands.
Courtesy : Shilpa Gupta. Web. 22 February. 2019

Plate 5.8 : Shilpa Gupta. *Words Come From Ears*. 2018. Motion flapboard.
Courtesy : Shilpa Gupta. Web . 22 February. 2019

Plate 5 . 9 : Shilpa Gupta. *We Change each other* (detail) . 2017 . Animated light Installation .
Courtesy : Shilpa Gupta . Web . 22 February . 2019

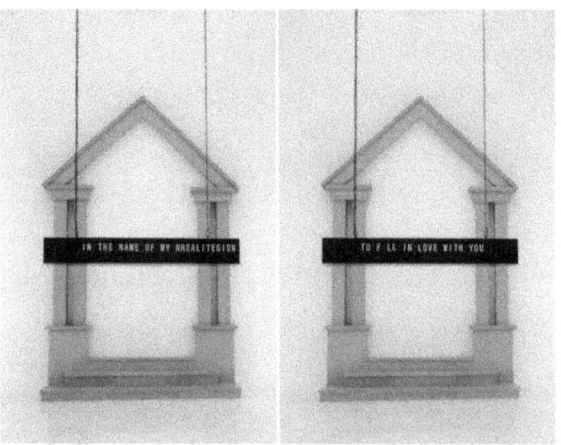

Plate 5 . 10 : Shilpa Gupta . *24 : 00 : 01* (detail) . 2010 , 2012 . Motion flapboard .
Courtesy : Shilpa Gupta . Web . 22 February . 2019

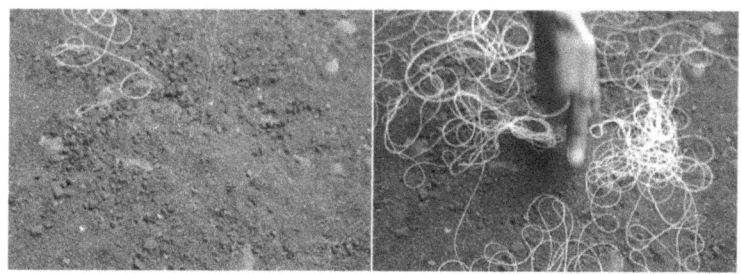

Plate 5 . 11 : Shilpa Gupta . *Untitled* (detail) . 2012 . Single Channel Video Projection .
Courtesy : Shilpa Gupta . Web . 22 February . 2019

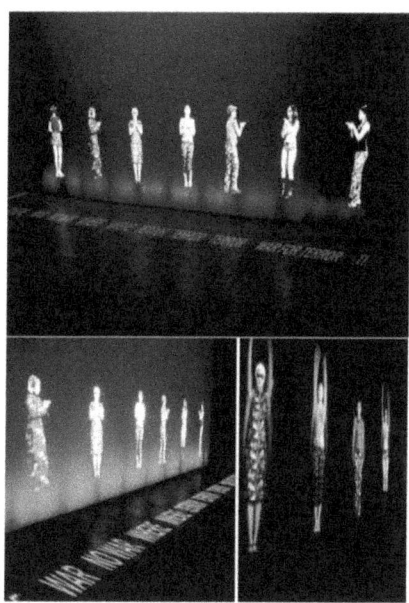

Plate 5 . 12 : Shilpa Gupta . *Untitled* (detail) . 2004-2005 .
Interactive Video Projection and sound , projector and computer .
Courtesy : Shilpa Gupta . Web . 22 February . 2019

Plate 5 . 13 : Shilpa Gupta . *Untitled* (detail) . 2005-2006 . Interactive Installation with touchscreens .
Courtesy : Shilpa Gupta . Web . 22 February . 2019

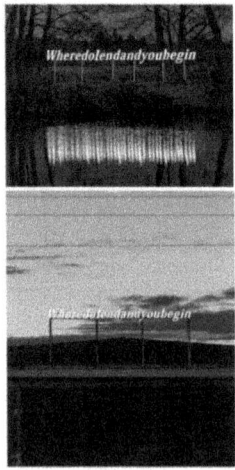

Plate 5 . 14 : Shilpa Gupta . *WheredoIendandyoubegin* (detail) . 2012 . Led Based Light Installation .
Courtesy : Shilpa Gupta . Web . 22 February . 2019

Plate 5 . 15 : Shilpa Gupta . *Singing Cloud* (detail) . 2008-09 .
Objects build with thousands of microphones with 48 multichannel audio .
Courtesy : Shilpa Gupta . Web 22 February . 2019

Plate 5 . 16 : Shilpa Gupta . *Threat* (detail) . 2008-2009 . Interactive Installation , Bathing Soaps .
Courtesy : Shilpa Gupta . Web 22 February . 2019

Plate 5.17 : Bose Krishnamachari . *LaVA (labroratory of visual art)* (detail) . 2006 .
Courtesy : Kochi Biennale Foundation . Web . 22 February . 2019

Plate 5.18 : Bose Krishnamachari . *Ghost / Transmemoir* . 2008 .
108 used tiffins with LCD monitors , amplifiers , DVD players, headphones , cables , jute ropes , scaffo .
Courtesy : projectartworm.com . Web . 22 February . 2019

Plate 5.19 : Bose Krishnamachari. *White Builders and the Red Carpets* (detail). 2008.
One table with red corean on wood, chairs,, red carpet, 108 conference mikes with cables and stands.
Courtesy : Art News & Views. Web. 22 February. 2019

Plate 5.20 : Leonardo da Vinci. *The Last Supper* (detail). 15th century. Tempera, gesso.
Courtesy : Britannica. Web. 22 February. 2019

Plate 5.21 : Bose Krishnamachari. *9 Rasas and One Soft Cut* (detail). 2020.

Courtesy : Emani Art, Kolkata. Web. 22 February. 2020.

References

Adajania, Nancy. *Shilpa Gupta.* New York ,Prestel, 2009 .

Archive, Asia Art. "Interview with Bose Krishnamachari." *Aaa.Org.Hk*, aaa.org.hk/en/ideas/ideas/interview-with-bose-krishnamachari/type/conversations. Accessed 10 Mar. 2019.

Bose Krishnamachari – Art & Soul. www.galleryartnsoul.com/portfolio_page/bose-krishnamachari. Accessed 11 Mar. 2020.

"Bose Krishnamachari." *Art Musings,* artmusings.net/artists/bose-krishnamachari/. Accessed 10 Mar. 2019.

Chomsky, Noam, et al. *While I Sleep.* Cambridge , Le laboratoire, 2009

Christine,V Kayser. *Shilpa Gupta: Art Beyond Borders. Invisible Culture: An Electronic Journal For Visual Culture, 2017*

Dadi, Iftikhar. *Frayed Geographies and Fractured Selves: Shilpa Gupta's Untitled (2014-15)* My East is Your West, Catalog Essay, 2016

De Certeau, Michel, and Steven Rendall. *The Practice of Everyday Life.* Berkeley University Of California Press, 2011.

De Certeau, Michel. *The Practice of Everyday Life. Vol. 1, The Practice of Everyday Life.* Berkeley, University Of California Press, 1984.

De Certeau. *The Practice of Everyday Life. Vol. 2.* Minneapolis; London, University Of Minnesota Press, 1998.

Dickson, Andrew. *Shilpa Gupta: the artist bringing silenced poets back to life.* London ,The Guardian Newspaper, 2018

D'Mello, Rosalyn. "The Art of Not Forgetting." *Live Mint,* 11 Aug. 2017.

Encountering Shilpa Gupta | Artnow. www.artnowpakistan.com/encountering-shilpa- gupta/. Accessed 11 Mar. 2019.

Gupta, Shilpa. "Shilpa Gupta: 'I Am Always Playing with the Idea of the Location in Work.'" *Studio International,* 13 Sept. 2017.

Jayaraman, Gayatri. "Bose Krishnamachari | Why Do Museums Become Mausoleums?" *Live Mint,* 19 Aug. 2011.

Jones, Ronald. *Shilpa Gupta .* New York ,Frieze, 2012 .

Kalidas, S. "Art Laboratory LaVa Showing at Bodhi Art It Is a Contemporary but a Temporary Laboratory for the People." *India Today*, 12 Mar. 2007.

Kalra, Vandana, *I'm interested in perception and with how definitions get stretched or trespassed: Shilpa Gupta* Indian Express, 17 January 2016

Kochhar, Ritika. "Bose Krishnamachari Wants to Take Contemporary Art Places." *Business Standard India*, 13 Aug.2016, www.business-standard.com/article/specials/bose-krishnamachari-wants-to-take-contemporary-art-places-116081201814_1.html. Accessed 10 Mar. 2019.

"Krishnamachari Bose: Latest News & Videos, Photos about Krishnamachari Bose | The Economic Times." *The Economic Times*, economictimes.indiatimes.com/topic/Krishnamachari-Bose. Accessed 10 Mar. 2019.

Lefebvre, Henri. *Rhythmanalysis: Space, Time, and Everyday Life*. London; New York, Bloomsbury Academic, An Imprint Of Bloomsbury Publishing Pic, 2017.

Mehta, Anupa. "Bose Krishnamachari's Project LaVA Anupa Mehta Deconstructs Bose Krishnamachari's Revisit to His Project, LaVA.Read More at: Https://Economictimes.Indiatimes.Com/Bose-Krishnamacharis-Project-Lava/Articleshow/5367979.Cms?Utm_source=contentofinterest&utm_mediu m=text&utm_campaign=cppst." *The Economic Times*, 23 Dec. 2009.

Prakash, Uma. *Bose Krishnamachari* . Art Etc News & Views, *2011.*

Prasanth, Aniket And Rajpal, Seema. *The Bose Krishnamachari Interview: When You Create Art, You Create Your Own Philosophy*. The New Indian Express,2019

"Shilpa Gupta." *Shilpagupta.Com*, 2019, shilpagupta.com. Accessed 10 Mar. 2019.

Wadhwani, Sita. "What's Cooking at the Bose Krishnamachari Laboratory of Visual Arts." *CNN Travel*, 18 Dec. 2009.

Westen, Mirjam. *Shilpa Gupta - Will We Ever be Able to Mark Enough?*. Montréal, Qc: Montreal., Fonderie Darling Foundry, 2012

CHAPTER-VI

CONCLUSION

6.1 Summary

In this research work, a detailed study of New Media Art of contemporary India from the 1990s to till date with emphasis upon evocation and early developments of New Media Art, the emerging practices of New Media Art of India was conducted. The study is further combined with analysis of the six artists' New Media Artworks as a referral to support the textual context in the New Media Art practices of contemporary Visual Art of India. The artists are - Nalini Malani, Jitish Kallat, Ranbir Kaleka, Surekha, Bose Krishnamachari, Shilpa Gupta.

6.1.1 Summary of Chapter-I

Chapter I introduces the topic of the research discusses the background of New Media Art of West and India. The New Media Art had radically transformed the traditional landscape genre in the 1960s Western art when many artists stopped merely representing the land and made their mark directly in the environment. Symptomatic of the countercultural impulses of that decade, artists rejected the gallery as a frame and economic system. They were drawn instead to entropic post- industrial wastelands or the vast, uncultivated spaces. Some artists moved the earth to create colossal primal symbols while others punctuated the horizon with the human- made signposts. In this chapter, it is mentioned that contextually the new development of contemporary Indian art has been started from the sixties—this new trend which reflects a genre of non-conventional practices of Visual Art. The image became more conceptual from this era. With the relation of this new genre, the visual came to a point of zenith at the nineties when artists of India became involved with the broader area of art through the New Media works of art. The title mentioned in the research work has been taken from a catalogue cover entitled *"Image-Beyond Image"* of a group exhibition of 1963. This chapter discusses the evocation of New Media Art in the late twentieth century. During that phase, contemporary artists utilise a whole range of media and methods to explore the world around them. The chapter of research also discusses the artists such as Nam June Paik and Bill Viola, who were the significant contributors in the early development of New Media Art. The study of this chapter mentioned on the emerging practices of New Media Art in India which originates explicitly in the transitional period of the early 1990s, when Western curators began to parachute into India, looking for idioms that they could recognise as "cutting-edge", such as the installation, the performance and video art. The chapter also contains statements of the problem, objectives of the study, scope of the study, limitation, operational definition of essential terms, data and methodology, review of literature and organisation of chapters.

6.1.2 Summary of Chapter-II

Chapter II provides a view of the New Media Art Practices in 1990s India. The chapter deals with the mainstream Visual Arts activities in India; since the 1990s can be categorised its position as an implicated imagery. The art before or till the nineties was considered as a purer or purist imagery and the discourse and institutional processes that occurred an irony between 'around it' and 'in the making of it' gave us an image of 'a visible space within a frame as an art image', by and large. Everything that happened 'around it' such as criticism, appreciation, sale, auction, hegemonic placing of 'one' work as superior to the other; hierarchy, awards, gallery-artist-work nexus and the like served as an appendix 'to' it, in the popular imagination of 'Art', even among about the specialists who wrote and spoke about it. The perfect glorification of mere static image minus its politics for art lingered by and large, till the nineties. On a different perspective, this is how the aftermath of the nineties art circumstances might be imagining its immediate past. Further, did such a pronounced 'imagination' of its immediate past become an 'inevitable necessity' for the art after the nineties, or the art between nineties -2010, for its 'own' existence. Consequently; to imagine what happened to the concept of 'image-as-artwork' before that, in due course. In other dimensions, image-making was metamorphosed into image-circuit, as an optimist might wish to position it in a positivist mode. In this way, the art community closer to the ideal blend currently imagines the hierarchy between paintings and the New Media Artworks. This chapter further discusses the inception of interdisciplinary art practices in India. Besides, this chapter deals about the role of art organisation in the exploration of New Media Art of India in the nineties. The research of this chapter includes the discussion on the part of art directorial in New Media Art of India through the 2000s onwards which is a connection to the discourses of New Media Art practices of India since the nineties.

6.1.3 Summary of Chapter-III

Chapter III discusses the analytical study of artists Nalini Malani and Jitish Kallat with a chapter entitled *"The Legitimised Narratives and the Web of Traffic: Artworks of Nalini Malani and Jitish Kallat"*. The chapter discusses the video art of Nalini Malani. Malani's work is constructed as a narrative that interweaves Eastern and Western mythologies and aesthetics forms to address interreligious violence in India, especially on women. Since the 1970s, Malani has displayed her emphatically feminine stance there, in a country torn between the effects of colonialism and the idealism of a Third World social democracy, as well as being seized by the political and economic changes brought about by rapid globalisation. Employing figures from myths, fairy tales, and the religions of diverse cultures, and reflecting on war, orthodox fanaticism, the effects of capitalism, and the destruction of the environment, Nalini Malani depicts the female position in scenes past and future. The artist's emphasis on the feminine figure as a topos of violence, both received and produced. As an ambivalent figure, both caring and destroying locates her art within feminist discourses. Yet she privileges to be beyond this linkage and to be using mythical images of *Medea*, *Cassandra* or *Sita* as images of conflicts and violence within the human psyche, both feminine and masculine. In the early 1990s, Malani was one of the first artists in India to break from a painting by making ephemeral wall drawings, theatrical works, and video and shadow play. The research study purports to analyse her work and the mechanisms of its reception to evaluate its potential cathartic role on collective consciousness regarding communal violence in India and elsewhere, both for an Indian and international audience, a function which Malani prerogates for her art practice. The chapter includes the New Media Artworks of Jitish Kallat. The artist's works explore the prominent historical stories and episodes that have some dialogues with this planet. The artist's works also reveal a cascade of images, which begin to appear like self-similar images. Kallat very philosophically perceives his thought process which shows the artist's body of where there is a conceptual connection to work with an object. The executed works by Kallat also have the reveal of art practices shift of identity through choosing an image to open to the public.

The working aspect of Kallat also explores the spaces of a progressive society, hidden historical stories where research find a web of traffic in the artist's video installations. The chapter discusses that Kallat's New Media works that have been based on his encounters with the multi-sensory environment of Bombay/Mumbai, as well as the economic, political and historical events that have contributed to its making.

6.1.4 Summary of Chapter-IV

Chapter IV discusses the analytical study of New Media Artworks by the artists Ranbir Kaleka and Surekha. The chapter entitled *"The 'Third Object'/ Urban Signs and the Vulnerable Body: New Media Artworks of Ranbir Kaleka and Surekha"*. The chapter includes the discussion that in the rich and complex history of video art, Indian artists who work with video as a medium, use their works as influential/essential tools to establish their politico-cultural visions and critique. Ranbir Kaleka is one of those Indian artists who has used video as a medium not only to extend the ideas that the artist deals within his paintings and video installations but also create a new visual interaction that could cut across the boundaries. The study of research analyses that through his body of video installations works, Ranbir Kaleka developed a unique technique in the 1990s and has been experimenting with the same for over three decades. Besides, the chapter discusses Indian contemporary women artists who are recognised as among the most stimulating. Provocative and visually inventive of contemporary art creators who instinctively or explicitly are working through intersectional identifications, producing work that navigates the complexities of identity in the contemporary world. Surekha is one such artist who surpasses the fixations of most of her male counterparts. Surekha's art practice includes video, photography, sculpture, documentary, digital and performance-based works centred mainly on the body within its gendered, political and historical context.

6.1.5 Summary of Chapter-V

Chapter V discusses the analytical study of New Media Artworks by Shilpa Gupta and Bose Krishnamachari. The chapter entitled *"Through the Ways of Memory and the Techno-Images: Re-Interpretation of New Media Works of Shilpa Gupta and Bose Krishnamachari "*. The chapter discusses Gupta's art practice mediums variety from deployed found objects to video, interactive computer-based installation and performance. Gupta's New Media practice emphasises in human perception and how information, visible or invisible, gets transmitted and internalised in everyday life. Gupta is continuously drawn to how objects get well-defined, be it places, people, experiences and her work engages with zones where these definitions get played out, be it borderlines, labels and ideas of censorship and security.

Besides, this chapter analyses Krishnamachari's work that is reinforced by a 'here and now' understanding and awareness of contemporary culture borrowed effortlessly from various disciplines, including literature and design, and periods.

6.1.6 Summary of Chapter-VI

Chapter VI analyses the research findings, conclusions and suggests further studies.

6.2 Conclusion

The discussion concludes with the analysis

The most significant change in the world after industrialisation is digitisation, a paradigm shift in technology which has transformed the life of every human on the earth and revolutionised the art of expression, communication and presentation of human thoughts in an entirely new manner.

In the scenario of human society, technological changes have always influenced the evolution of human culture and development. An individual should, therefore, not ignore the role of computers in nurturing contemporary art scenarios. From 1960 onwards the new technological advancement has shifted the art concepts from manual to electronic equipment. By the use of digital equipment through New Media Art, we can think, explore and execute different kinds of worlds and transform human societies in a gigantic manner.

Although some people perceive that New Media Art is a threat to traditional art, the research study analyses with practical observations to show that New Media Art is a branch of Visual Art forms and not the rival of conventional art forms, with time the definition of art has been developing and art is not only restricted to paintings, drawings or sculptures; the gamut of art has been increased due to computer-generated applications with the involvements of conceptual aspects.

New Media Art has provided an exceptional strength to Visual Art in the new millennium, and the outcome is visible in the growth of the practices of various explorations included in New Media Art. Technology has revived art and presented a new concept to the art world. This unique expression of art comprises New Media technologies, computer graphics, animations, virtual art, computer robotics and interactive art that are being executed because of the invention of digital technology.

6.3 Research Findings

Research Finding i) : Contextually the new development of contemporary Indian art has been started from the sixties—this new trend which reflects a genre of non-conventional practices of Visual Art. The image became more conceptual from this era and with the relation of this new genre the Visual Art came at the point of peak in the nineties when artists of India became involved with the broader area of art through the New Media Art practices.

Research Finding ii) : Earlier avant-garde art movements use non-conventional materials and non-traditional media to attack the privileged status of art and the unique, precious character of the art object. With the institutional establishment of contemporary art, boundaries could be crossed without this being a negation of art as such. In Western art from the nineteen sixties, it has been witnessed a far-reaching reappraisal of what art could be. Pioneers utilised the new video technology, while an interest in the physical space in which art was placed lead to artists making installations, performances, videos for specific areas and occasions. New Media artists have moved away from abstraction and towards an engagement with the world around them and by using New Media elements that read impressions of actual, physical reality and the lives of ordinary people can be relayed in marked images.

Research Finding iii) : New Media Art carries awareness to the artifice of its construction and to the spatial cultural and historical context in which it exists. Allusions to past works of art and movements are frequent, and techniques of framing, editing and digital manipulation are not hidden but revealed. It is this reminder of the artificiality of all images that allows contemporary art to engage with mass visual culture while maintaining a critical attitude towards it.

Research Finding iv) : The media, the visual dialogue and its language are evocative of the way we live. India and its art have gone through a sea change in the last to last decade. This is as stimulating as it is scary. The artists behind the lens compel us to see ourselves as we are. The discourse on New Media Art practices in India, such as it is, originates in the transitional period of the early 1990s, when Western curators began to parachute into India, looking for idioms that they could recognise as "cutting-edge", such as the installation, the performance and video art. This narrative of the shift from an art situation dominated by painting, to one in which New Media practices set the tone, is adequate as the snapshot of a decade. Significantly, in new-context media art is peopled by artists whose education and interests are not restricted to a Visual Arts milieu, but enriched by diverse subcultures. The nineties showed the beginning of innovative gallery practices, with more substantial cultural forces that brought photography, installation and video art into the conversation of the Indian art world, imparting to them both intellectual legitimacy and economic currency. In most explorers of New Media Art, in much of postmodern art, the self and self-attachment are imaged through a class of signifiers. In India, more effective technological progress was achieved in video art when digital editing equipment became available after 1990. Once again, it was a TV and non-fiction film that prompted development. Nevertheless, it came as a boon to the New Media artists. In India, artists are also exploring the creative matrix of tradition, spirituality, history, urbanisation and Western preferences to create a distinct India in New Media practices where East is blended with the West.

Research Finding v) : Visual Arts are ever-changing and unstable in character, which philosophically emerged and developed from the mid-sixties of the twentieth century. From that time, new art forms were confronted with different phenomenological problems of modern art theories. The gap between self-concern purity of contemporary art and pluralistic and transcendental post-modern art created a blank and figured space in the second half of the twentieth century. The different art movement started as the seventies carried out some new questions and critiques against the previous art practices. New Media Art was one of them through ensuring important issues against the modernism of art.

Research Finding vi) : Since the nineties, the three most important characteristics of art are – implicated imagery, image-making and image circuit. The nineties art practice in India has been a turning point for the Indian art practice for the reason that most prominent artists of the country; whom we refer today in the context of curatorial projects, Biennales and Triennials were emerging out of the institutional training in the early nineties. There could be a lot of anomalies as well such as the open economy system that occurred within the politics of Indian History, the artist-in- residency opportunities that took artists to unknown geo-political zones outside India, the hypertext and the world wide web that availed a bypass to the artists throughout the country deconstructed a clear cut hegemony implicated by the Academies and then by the white cube system, of gallery monopoly that earlier played a significant role in regulating – the visuals, the opportunities, and the choices of one artwork, artist, art groups over the others. Even International funding agencies spread the feeling that contesting the pre-nineties context of image-making to stress on image- circuit split the image-maker into two parts. For this reason; some artists traverse between the simple painterly grammar and the New Media, owing to the cajoling nature of the funding system.

Research Finding vii) : Malani's work is constructed as a narrative that interweaves Eastern and Western mythologies and aesthetics forms to address interreligious violence in India, especially on women. Since the 1970s, Malani has shown her categorically feminine stance there, in a country torn between the effects of colonialism and the idealism of a Third World social democracy, as well as being seized by the political and economic changes brought about by rapid globalisation. Engaging figures from myths, fairy tales, and the religions of various cultures, and reflecting on war, orthodox fanaticism, the effects of capitalism, and the destruction of the environment, Nalini Malani depicts the female position in scenes past and future. The artist's emphasis on the feminine figure as a topos of violence, both received and produced. As an ambivalent figure, both caring and destroying locates her art within feminist discourses. Yet she privileges to be beyond this linkage and to be using mythical images of *Medea*, *Cassandra* or *Sita* as images of conflicts and violence within the human psyche, both feminine and masculine. In the early phase of 1990s, Malani was one of the foremost artists in India to interrupt painting by construction of ephemeral wall drawings, theatrical works, and video and shadow play. Malani's practice is an art of excess, going beyond the boundaries of legitimised narrative, exceeding the conventional and initiating dialogue.

Research Finding viii) : Jitish Kallat's New Media Artworks continuously explore his working process in a multimedia approach to the subject matter, the works range from esoteric nature capes to political critiques of the socio-economic divine in his home country. Kallat often utilises popular Indian advertising aesthetics that he incorporates throughout his practice. His '*Dawn Chorus*' (2007) series, for instance, depicts street urchins with hair that forms a 'web of traffic' and pedestrians.

Research Finding ix) : In the rich and complex history of video art, Indian artists who work with video as a medium, use their works as influential/essential tools to establish their politico-cultural visions and critique. Ranbir Kaleka's video installations developed a unique technique in the 1990s and has been experimenting with the same for over the last three decades. The artist projects a video on painted canvas such that the painting moves, allowing for a narrative to develop, rendering the work a layered meaning. The physical attributes of painting, like weight and texture, and the accumulation of rendering of colour pigment to give work stability and permanence. On the other hand, video—which has a spatial element as an image made of light—has opposite characteristics of being intangible, fleeting, and temporary. By mixing the two different mediums, the artist amplifies the inherent nature of each medium, at times layering or overlapping them, and forging a new image. By overlaying two different notions of time—the 'still' time in painting and 'transforming' time in the video—the artist devises ways of knowing and meaning-making. The essential focus in Kaleka's work is not just his unique methodology in working with video and painting, but the narrative of the work, which usually focuses on daily issues that arise across India.

Research Finding x) : Surekha's works centre primarily on the body within its gendered, political and historical context. Surekha's *'The Boiling Concept'* and *'The Burning Concept'* (2006) feature characters performed by the artist herself, abstracted from stories uncovered in her research on unnatural deaths and domestic violence inflicted upon women throughout history in the city of Bangalore. In Surekha's New Media Art practice restriction, veiling and silencing are taken up in more direct ways in *'Line of Control'* (2003), *'Between Fire and Sky'* (2006) and *'Three Fragmented Actions of Silence'* (2007), which plays on the concept of veiling through positive/negative video images and overlays of colour and external footage. Surekha's documentary works *'Un-Claimed'* (2010) and *'Romeos & Juliets'* (2010) explore the liminal space between artistic and everyday performance, sketching out an aesthetic reading of the rituals of burial and community gatherings through speedups and slowdowns, muting and repetition while maintaining a heightened sense of their social significance.

Research Finding xi) : Shilpa Gupta's work makes visible the aporias and in commensurabilities in the emerging national public sphere in India, which include gender and class barriers, religious differences, the continued power of repressive state apparatuses, and the seductions of social homogeneity and deceptive ideas of public consensus enabled by emerging mediascapes. Gupta's works which deal with inter- subjectivity and phenomenology, always evoke the viewers concerning the relational and highly interfered aspects of the act of observing, recovering and recognising. Involvement of brass labels, stamps, objects confiscated at airports, motion flap boards, or illegal material that traverse physiological and geographical chasms; her practice pushes the boundaries of how the art object is understood.

Research Finding xii) : Through his installations, Bose Krishnamachari questions the significance of the existing powers that influence the art world and addresses the unjust discrimination in different strata of society.

Krishnamachari encounters the single interpretation of an image as the artist researches numerous connotations. Krishnamachari's art practice explores that an individual understands art through two different channels; firstly through sources and secondly through the direct encounter.

6.4 Scope for Further Research

After having studied the New Media Art of Contemporary India since 1990 focusing upon almost all the aspects as per the research objectives and needs. The further research can be done on the comparative study between the New Media Art of India and with that of other parts of the globe. Also, impact of New Media upon Visual Arts of India can be taken up for further studies. New Media Art of the present time of this century also can be taken up for further studies.

6.4.1 New Media Art Practices of Contemporary India in the 2000s of Twenty- First Century

New Media has ushered in a new era for the acquisition and integration of widely different source material, whether visual, aural or text. What is the nature of New Media Art? Further mystifying this elusive notion is the chameleon – likeability of New Media Art to simulate the appearance of many traditional genres and media. Furthermore, some commonly held beliefs, some of which are contrary to one another, add to the obscurity, hiding the actual scope of current New Media Art practices. For example, one idea, based on New Media imagery made nearly a generation ago, holds that it is careless with sharp and jagged lines, that the colours are uncontrolled and supersaturated and that the predominant forms hinge on infinite swirling repetitions. Strangely enough, this idea continues to thrive even today despite a contrary belief that New Media Art serves mainly to create seamless realistic environments and chapters that are indistinguishable from photographic realism. These imperfect and limiting views blind the viewer to the fluidity and expressive potential of the New Media medium. The tools used to create digital/video art serve many masters both within and outside the Visual Arts. To nail down a specific aesthetic for New Media Art which holds common ground for all its expressive potential would appear to be a daunting, indeed, extra, task. New Media Art has been around now for over twenty-five years. A majority of the images we see each day several different media are created digitally. These new art-making tools have revolutionised commercial art, photography, television, music and film/video and, as such the New Media Art is spread so thinly across so many artistic endeavours, it is, as an art movement, virtually transparent. As artists, who employ digital tools; however, make inroads into the world of Visual Arts, it is essential to consider what precisely this art has to offer. What separates it from what has happened and what are the characteristics that will determine what New Media Art contributes to the unfolding contemporary art scene and the ongoing history of artistic expression?

A critical factor in artwork employing digital technology involves the digitisation of a whole of inputs into the standard material of binary information. Digital technology epitomises not only an implement for mixing the art of various forms, but it is also a new form of mass communication. In this regard, the tool itself is an integral part of a global mediated environment from which artists can draw both inspiration and substantial. The variability of a visual image in this technological or social environment is quite unprecedented. The post-modern concept of appropriation, which meshes with the improved ability for digital tools to acquire and reshape all kinds of experience into a common material, carries over into an attitude toward the established genre of artistic styles.

Using New Media/digital imaging software, designed in many cases to mimic the marks of numerous types of traditional media, many artists now explore expressing an image, as it would appear in several media and styles. This merging of different media and forms of expression is greatly enhanced by numerous digital processes involving saving multiple versions of an image during its production and the ability to draw upon these versions to create a master image that is an amalgamation of each reading. An imaginative exploration of style, media, and composition takes hold when a digital artist understands the freedom resulting from being released from the accumulated preciousness of the effort. This valuableness is required by the cost of expended material and, as the work approaches completion, the built-up anxiety toward ruining many hours of work by following an artistic experiment.

Whereas there is no general appearance to the art being created, every New Media artist has to share two essential modes of display: that is the work can be on a screen or as a digital print. Since the innovative work transpires and resides in the digital matrix of computer memory and storage systems, this 'original' work is essentially immaterial and virtually non- existent until articulated in moreover of these two procedures. Outstanding to its substantially reproducible binary nature and the fact that some form of reproduction or expression is required to materialise the original into any obvious way, New Media Art is, simultaneously, a unique and a copy. The expressive nature of the artist's imagery opposes the fact that either of the two primary modes display offers a flat mechanised image mostly unaffected by changes in ambient conditions and lacking tangible texture. The line between disconnected mechanical production and expressive, handcrafted artistry is blurred to the extreme in New Media, because it is, in fact, both. New Media represents a return to artistic passions in a culture where expressive appearance is valued over material truth.

However, through New Media Art, the growth of internet technology is increasing the global art movement. It also explores the socio-economic and cultural values of society. For both well established and up-growing New Media artists, the internet is an instantaneous art institution where they can explore with their imaginations and feelings to embark upon sensitive issues through the application of various digital tools.

All aspects of further research can not be incorporated here within the purview of the present study. However, whatever has been contented here within its central scope suggests the research mentioned above questions and the possibilities of ongoing research. It is expected that the scope for the further research study of this aspect would generally contribute to the New Media Art as such.

GLOSSARY

Articulation	:	Connection.
Avant-garde	:	New and experimental in the practices of Visual Art.
Banal	:	Common.
Bewilderment	:	Confusion.
Bizarre	:	Very unusual.
Cassandra	:	A mythological character in Greek Mythology.
Catharsis	:	Process of expressing strong feeling through artistic activities.
Chay	:	Tea.
Conjectural	:	Imaginary.
Contemplate	:	Plan for execution.
Defy	:	Openly resistant to obey.
Dhakai Jamdani	:	Famous hand weaving wearing from Bangladesh.
Diya	:	Traditional oil lamp made of baked clay.
Gamut	:	The range or scope of human thoughts.
Genre	:	A particular style of Visual Art.
Haiku	:	Japanese poem with seventeen syllables.
Haveli	:	A traditional village house or mansion in the Indian subcontinent.
Imagery	:	Representation.
Karma	:	Way action in human life.
Kikar	:	A kind of medicinal tree.
Kitsch	:	Objects considered to be tasteless.

Kumaran Asan	:	An Indian social reformer, Philosopher and poet of Malayalam literature.
Loop	:	An endless strip of film allowing sounds or images to be continuously repeated.
Medea	:	A mythological character in Greek Mythology.
Mohallas	:	Neighbourhoods.
New Media Art	:	Branches of Visual Art making activity.
Opulence	:	Richness.
Patachitra	:	Painting based in cloth-surfaces can find in the eastern Indian states of Odisha and West Bengal regions.
Phantasmagoria	:	A sequence of real as well as imaginary images.
Radha	:	A mythological character in Indian Hindu Mythology.
Shikara	:	Floating house boat.
Silhouette	:	Dark shadow seen against a lighter background.
Sita	:	A mythological character in Indian Hindu Mythology.
Sophistication	:	The experience in matters of cultural practices in a work of art.
Sufi	:	A form of devotional music.
Superimpose	:	Kept one impression over another.
Vachana Sahitya	:	A form of rhythmic writing in Kannada.
Visual interaction	:	Communication through visuals from everyday life.

BIBLIOGRAPHY

Abrams, M.H. and Harpham, Galt Geoffrey. *A Handbook of Literary Terms*. New Delhi, Cengage Learning, 2009.

Altshuler. Bruce. "Ed". *Collecting the New*, Princeton University Press, Princeton & Oxford 2005.

Allen, J., "From Media to New Media", in *Mousse*, Issue 26, December 2010, pp. 196 – 200.

Andraos, A. *Eco-visionaries: Art, Architecture, and New Media After the Anthropocene*. Berlin, Hatje Cantz Verlag, 2018.

Anagol, P. *From the Symbolic To the Open: Women's Resistance in Colonial Maharashtra*. Behind the Veil "Ed". Anindita Ghosh. Ranikhet. Permanent Black, 2007.

Aparajita, U. *Culture and Development*. New Delhi, Inter-India Publications, 1994.

Arnason, H.H. and Prather, M.F. *A History of Modern Art – Painting, Sculpture, Architecture, Photography* (4th Edition).London, Thames & Hudson Ltd., 1998.

Ashcroft, B. *Post-Colonial Studies: Key Concepts*. London and New York, Routledge, 1988

Ashcroft, B. Gareth, G. and Helen, T. "Ed". *The Post-Colonial Studies Reader*.

London and New York, Routledge, 1995.

Atkins R. "State of the Art – On-line – art on the World Wide Web", in *Art in America*, April 1999.

Ayers R. "Code in a Box", in *Artinfo*, 3 August 2007, online at www.artinfo.com/news/story/25445/code-in-a-box/.

Balzola, A., Monteverdi A. M. "Ed". *Le artimultimedialidigitali.Storia, tecniche, linguaggi, eticheedestetichedellearti del nuovomillennio*, Garzanti, Milano 2004.

Barbeni, L. *Webcinema. L'imminecibernetica*, Costa & Nolan, Milano 2006.

Barragan, P. *The Art Fair Age*, Charta, Milano 2008.

Basham, A.L. *A Cultural History of India*. Delhi, Oxford University Press. 1975.

Baudrillard, J. *Selected Writings*. Oxford, Polity Press, 2001.

Baudrillard, J. Qublier Foucault Paris Galibe (trans) Nicola Deference1987, Forget Foucault. New York, Seniotext.1977.

Baumgaertel, T. *net.art.Materialienzur Netzkunst*, Verlagfür modern Kunst Nürberg, 2000.

Bazzichelli, T. *Networking. The Net as Artwork*, Digital Aesthetics Research Center, Aarhus University 2008.

Becker, H. S. *Art Worlds*, University of California Press, Berkeley – Los Angeles – London 1982.

Benjamin, W. 'The Work of Art in the Age of Mechanical Reproduction'. Illuminations. London. Fontana Press. 1992.

Berry, J. "The Unbearable Connectedness of Everything", in *Telepolis*, 28 September 1999, online at www.heise.de/tp/artikel/3/3433/1.html.

Berwick, C. "New Media Moguls", in *Art & Auction*, June 2006.

Bhabha, H.K. 'Signs Taken for Wonders: Question of Ambivalence and Authority Under a Tree Outside Delhi'. Critical inquiry 12 (1) Autumn1817. 1985.

Binyon, L. *Asiatic Arts Sculpture and Paintings*. New Delhi, Cosmo Publications.1981.

Birdwood, G.C.M. *The Arts of India*. New Delhi.Rupa& Co, 1988.

Bishop, C. "Digital Divide. Claire Bishop on Contemporary Art and New Media", in *Artforum*, September 2012, online at http://artforum.com/inprint/ issue=201207&id=31944&pagenum=0.

Bittanti, M. Quaranta, D. "Ed." *Game Scenes. Art in the Age of Videogames*, Milano : Johan & Levi, 2006.

Blais, J. Ippolito, J. *At the Edge of Art*, London, Thames and Hudson, 2006.

Blistène, B. "Les Immatériaux: A Conversation with Jean-François Lyotard", in *Flash Art*, Issue 121, March 1985, online at www.kether.com/words/lyotard/index.html.

Bolognini, M. *Machines. Conversations on Art and Technology*, Postmediabooks, Milano 2012.

Bolter, J. D. Grusin, R. *Remediation. Understanding New Media*, 1999.

Bonami, F. *Lo potevo fare anch'io. Perché l'artecontemporanea è davvero arte*, Mondadori, Milano 2007.

Bordini, S. *Arte Elettronica*, Giunti, Firenze – Milano 2004.

Bourriaud, N. *Relational Aesthetics*, Les presses du réel, Paris 1998.

Bowditch, L. "Driven to distraction – multimedia art exhibition by the Guggenheim Museum Soho", in *Afterimage*, January – February 1997.

Brea, J. L. *La era postmedia .Acciónc omunicativa, prácticas (post)artísticas y dispositivosneomediales*, Consorcio Salamanca, Salamanca 2002.

Brockman, J. *Digerati. Encounters with the Cyber Elite*, Hardwired, New York 1996.

Buehrer, V. K. "Dearest progressive scan loading, on victims of Broadband", in *Neural*, n° 23, 2006, p. 48.

Buxmann A., Depraetere F. "Eds". *Argos Festival*, argoseditions, Brussels 2005.

Calhoun, C. 'Cultural Difference and Historical Specificity'. Critical Social Theory: Culture, history, and Challenge of Difference. Oxford, UK & Cambridge USA, Blackwell. 1995.

Campanelli, V. *Web Aesthetics*, Institute of Network Cultures / NAI Publishers, Rotterdam 2010.

Castells, M ,*Internet Galaxy*, Oxford University Press 2001.

Castells, M. *The Information Age*, Blackwell, Cambridge, MA – Oxford, UK, 1996 – 1998.

Celant, G. *Artmix. Flussitra arte, architettura, cinema, design, moda, musica e televisione*, Feltrinelli, Milano 2008.

Chadwick, W. *Women, Art and Society*. London: Thames & Hudson. 1996.

Chaitanya, K. *Ravi Varma, Contemporary Indian Art series*. New Delhi. Lalit Kala Akademi. 1984.

Chancer, S. L. 'The Beauty Context (Looks, Social Theory, and Feminism'.
Reconcilable Differences (Confronting Beauty, Pornography, and the Future of Feminism). Berkeley : Los Angeles, London : University of California Press. 1998.

Chandler A., Neumark N. "Eds."*At a Distance. Precursors to Art and Activism on the Internet*, The MIT Press, Cambridge and London 2005 [2006].

Chandra, B. *Essays on Colonialism*. Hyderabad : Orient Longman Ltd. 1999.

Chan, J. "From Browser to Gallery (and Back): The Commodification of Net Art 1990-2011", in *Pool*, December 28, 2011, online at http://pooool.info/from- browser-to-gallery-and-back-the-commodification-of-net-art-1990-2011/.

Chan, P. "The Unthinkable Community", in *Eflux Journal*, Issue 16, May 2010, online at www.e-flux.com/journal/view/144.

Christov-Bakargiev C. *I Moderni / The Moderns*, exh. cat., Castello di Rivoli Museod'Arte Contemporanea, Rivoli – Torino. Skira, Milano 2003.

Clarke A., Mitchell G. "Eds" .*Videogames and Art*, Intellect Books, Bristol – Chicago 2007.

Connor, S. *Postmodernist Culture, An Introduction to Theories of Contemporary*. USA. UK. Blackwell, Oxford and Cambridge.1994.

Cont3xt.Net "Eds".*Circulating Contexts. Curating Media / Net / Art*, Books on demand GmbH, Norderstedt 2007.

Cook, S. "An interview with Christiane Paul", in *Crumbweb*, 28 March 2001,online at http://crumbweb.org/getInterviewDetail.php?id=10&ts=1241707558&op=3&s ublink=9

Cook, S. Graham, B. Gfader V. Lapp A. "Eds". *A Brief History of Curating New Media Art: Conversations with Curators*, The Green Box, Berlin 2010.

Cook S., Graham B., Martin S. "Eds". *Curating New Media*, B.READ / SIX, Baltic, Gateshead ,2002.

Corby, T. "Ed".*Network Art: Practices and Positions*, London, Swets&Zeitlinger / Routledge 2005.

Critical Art Ensemble, *Electronic Civil Disobedience*, Autonomedia, New York 1995

Crow, T. Lukacher, B. Nochlin, L. Phillips, D.L. Pohl, F.K. *Nineteenth Century Art. A Critical History*. London : Thames & Hudson Ltd. 2002.

Curti, L. 'What is Real and What is Not: Female Fabulation in Cultural Analysis'.

Postmodernism and Popular Culture. "Ed" Angela McRobbie. New York and London , Routlledge. 1994.

Dal Lago A., Giordano S. *Mercantid'aura. Logichedell' artecontemporanea*, Il Mulino, Bologna 2006.

Danto, A.C. *The Abuse of Beauty – Aesthetics and the Concept of Art*. Chicago: Open Court, 2003.

Danto, A. *The Abuse of Beauty. Aesthetics and the Concept of Art,* Open Court Publishing 2003.

Datta, V.N. *Sati*. London ,Sangam Books. 1988.

Davenport, T. H. Beck, J. C., *The Attention Economy: Understanding the New Currency of Business*, Harvard Business School Press, 2001.

David, C. "dx and new media", 20 June 1997, online at www.documenta12.de / archiv/dx/lists/debate/0001.htm l.

Desai, D. *Erotic Sculpture of India a socio-cultural Study*. New Delhi, Munshiram Manoharlal Publishers Pvt.Ltd. 1985.

Duby, G. Altet, X.B. Suduiraut, S. Guillot, D. *Sculpture. The Great Art of The Middle Ages From The Fifth Century To The Fifteenth Century*. Germany, Taschen. 1989.

Duncan, C. *The Aesthetics Of Power. Essays In Critical Art History*. New York , Cambridge University Press. 1993.

Domenico, Q. *Post Production. La culture commescénario: comment l'artreprogramme lemondecontemporain*, 2002. *Postproduction*, Lukas & Sternberg, New York 2007.

Domenico, Q. "Altermodern Manifesto", 2009, online at www.tate.org.uk/ whats-on/tatebritain/exhibition/altermodern/explainaltermodern/altermodernexplaine dmanifesto.

Domenico, Q. *The Radicant*, Lukas & Sternberg, New York 2009.

Debatty, R. "Book review – Media, New Media, Postmedia", in *We Make Money Not Art*, August 27, 2011, online at http://we-make-money-notart.com/archives/2011/08/media-new-media-postmedia.php.

Debatty, R. "Holy Fire, art of the digital age", in *We Make Money Not Art*, 22 April 2008, online at www.we-make-money-not-art.com/archives/2008/04/holy- fire.php.

Deitch, J. "Ed". *Post Human*, exh. cat., Cantz / Deste Foundation for Contemporary Art, 1992.

Delson, S. "If Picasso Were A Programmer", In *Forbes*, Best Of The Web, 25 June 2001.

Depocas, A. Ippolito, J. Jones, C. "Eds". *Permanence Through Change: The Variable Media Approach*, The Solomon R. Guggenheim Foundation, NewYork, and The Daniel Langlois Foundation for Art, Science, and Technology,Montreal, 2003.

Deseriis, M. Marano, G. *net.art. L'artedell aconnessione*, Shake, Milano 2003

Deseriis, M. Lampo, L. Quaranta, D. *Connessioni Leggendarie. Net.art 1995 – 2005*, cat., Ready Made, Milano 2005.

Dietz, S. "Curating New Media", August 2000, in *Yproductions*, online at www.yproductions.com/writing/archives/curating_new_media.html.

Dietz, S. "Just Art': Contemporary Art After the Art Formerly Known As New Media", October 27, 2006, in *Yproductions*, online at www.yproductions.com/writing/archives/just_art_contemporary_art_afte.html.

Doula, S L. "Within Post-Internet, Part One", in *Pool*, April 6, 2011, online at http://pooool.info/within-post-internet-part-i/.

Draves, I. "Interview with Ken Johnson", in *Leaders in Software and Art*, September 4, 2011, online at http://softwareandart.com/?p=747.

Edward, A. S. *Art and Electronic Media*. London , Phaidon Press,2014.

Elders, J.L. 'The Progressive of Being I, A History of the Transcendental Concept of Aquinas'. The Metaphysics of being of St. Thomas Aquinas in Historical Perspective. (trans) Dr.J Dudlley.Natherlands.Library of Congress. 1993.

Elwes, C. *Video Art – A Guided Tour*. London et al.: I.B.Tauris, 2005.

Everett, A. Caldwell, J. T. "Eds". *New Media. Theories and Practice of Digitextuality*, Routledge, New York 2003.

Foster, H. et al. *I Techniapo to 1900 – Monternismos, Antimonternismos, Metamonternismos*. Thessaloniki: Epikentro Publishers, 2007.

Foster, H. Krauss R. Bois Y. Buchloh B. H. D., *Art since 1900. Modernism, Antimodernism, Postmodernism*, Thames & Hudson, London 2004.

Frascina, F. And Harris, Jonathan.Eds. *Art in Modern Culture.An Anthology of Critical texts*. New York : Open University. Phaidon Press. 1992.

Frascina, F. Harrison, C. "Eds". *Modern Art and Modernism: A Critical Anthology*, Sage Publications 1982.

Friedberg, A. *The Virtual Window – From Alberti to Microsoft*. Cambridge(MA) et al.: The MIT Press, 2006.

Fuchs, S. *The Origin of Man and His Culture*. New Delhi ,Munshiram Manoharlal Publishers Pvt. Ltd. 1983.

Frohne, U. Schieren, M. Guiton, J.F. "Eds". *Present Continuous Past(s): Media Art. Strategies of Presentation, Mediation and Dissemination*, Springer-Verlag, Vienna 2005.

Gallo, F. *Les immateriaux. Unpercorso di Jean-Francois Lyotardnell' artecontemporanea*, Aracne 2008.

Galloway, A. R., *Protocol. How Control Exists After Decentralization*, The MIT Press, Cambridge – London 2004.

Galloway, A. R. Thacker, R. *The Exploit. A Theory of Networks*, University of Minnesota Press, Minneapolis – London 2007.

Gere, C. *Digital Culture*, Reaktion Books, London 2002 (2008).

Ghosh, M. *Ai SamayerChhabi*, Kolkata ,Pratikshan Publication Pvt.Ltd. 1992.

Ghosh, M. *Samakalin Bhaskarja*, Kolkata , Pratikshan Publication Pvt. Ltd. 1995.

Goodyear, A. C. "From Technophilia to Technophobia: The Impact of the Vietnam War on the Reception of "Art and Technology", in *Leonardo*, April 2008, Vol. 41, No. 2, pp. 169-173.

Grau, O. *Virtual Art – From Illusion to Immersion*. Cambridge(MA) et al.: The MIT Press, 2003.

Graham, B. *Curating New Media Art: Samoa and 010101*, University of Sunderland 2001.

Graham, B. Cook, S. *Rethinking Curating: Art After New Media*, MIT Press 2010.

Grant, T. "How Anti-Computer Sentiment Shaped Early Computer Art", in *Refresh!*, September 2008.

Grau, O. "Ed". *Media Art Histories*, MIT Press (Leonardo Books), Cambridge and London, England, 2007.

Greene, R. *Internet Art*, Thames & Hudson, London – New York, 2004.

Gronlund, Melissa. Contemporary Art and Digital Culture. Abingdon: Routledge, 2016.

Groys, B. *Art Power*, The MIT Press, Cambridge – London 2008.

Guhathakurta, T. Lineages of Modern In Indian Art: The Making Of A National History. Culture And The Making Of Identity In Contemporary India (Ed) Kamala Ganesh and Usha Thakkar. New Delhi, Sage Publication. London, Thousand Oaks. 2005.

Guhathakurata, T. Monuments, *Objects, History, institution of Art in Colonial and Postcolonial India*. Ranikhet and New Delhi : Permanent Black. 2004.

Guhathakurta, T. 'Orientalism and The New Claims for Indian Art' . The Making Of New Indian Art Artists Aesthetics And Nationalism In Bengal C. 1850-1920. New York. Cambridge University Press. 1995.

Gurewich, J.F. 'A Lacanian Approach to the Logic of Perversion' .The Cambridge, Companion, To Lacan "Ed" Jeam-Michal Rabate. Cambridge : Cambridge University Press. 2003.

Guattari, F. *Soft Subversions*. Edited by Sylvère Lotringer. Semiotext(e) 1996.

Hall, S. *New Ethnicities.ThePost Colonial Studies Reader*. "Ed" Bill Ashcroft, Gareth Griffiths, Helen Tiffin. London and New York, Routledge. 1995.

Harrison, A. 'A Minimal Syntax for the Pictorial: The Pictorial and the Linguistic Analogies and Disanalogies'. The Language of Art

History, Selim Kamal & Ivan Gaskel " Ed" New York and Australia. Cambridge University Press. 1991.

Havell, E.B. *Indian Sculpture and Painting*. New delhi , Cosmo Publication.1980.

Havell, E.B. (reprinted 1928, 1980). *Indian Sculpture and Painting with an Explanation of Their Motives and Ideals*. New Delhi , Cosmo Publications. 1908.

Havel, E.B. (Reprinted 1928/1980).*The Future of Indian Art: Chapter IV. Indian Sculpture and Painting, with an Explanation of Their Motives and Ideals*. New Delhi : Cosmo Publication. 1908.

Hall, D. Fifer, S.J. "Eds". *Illuminating Video. An Essential Guide to Video Art*, Aperture / BAVC, New York 1990.

Haber, J. "Medium Rare", 1996, online at www.haberarts.com/tvscape.htm.

Hansen, M. *New Philosophy for New Media*, The MIT Press, Cambridge 2006.

Heywood, L. L. *Introduction: A Fifteen- years History of Third Wave Feminism. The Women's Movement Today* "Ed." Leslie L. Heywood. Rawat Publications. Jaipur (Original Publishers: USA. Greenwood Press). 2005.

Heartney, E. *Art & Today*, Phaidon Press, London 2008.

Higgins, D. "Statement on Intermedia", 1966. Published in: Vostell, W. "Ed".*Dé- coll/age (décollage) * 6*, Typos Verlag, Frankfurt - Something Else Press, New York, July 1967. Online at http://artpool.hu/Fluxus/Higgins/ intermedia2.html.

Himane, P. *The Hacker Ethic and the Spirit of the Information Age*, Random House 2001.

Hope, C. and Ryan, J. C. Digital Arts presents an introduction to new media. London: Bloomsbury Publishing USA, 2014.

Hughes, P. K., *Breaking and Entering: A User's Guide*, Pace Wildenstein, New York 2005.

Ippolito, J. and Rinehart, R. Re-collection: Art, New Media, and Social Memory.Cambridge: MIT Press, 2014.

Issak, J. A. '*Mapping The Imaginary' .Feminism and Contemporary Art'*.

London and New York. Rout ledge. 1996.

Ioselit, D. *After Art*, Cloth 2012.

Jodi, "dx webprojects", 9 July 1997, online at www.documenta12.de/archiv/dx/lists/debate/0010.html.

Joseph, B.W. "Engineering Marvel: Branden W. Joseph on Billy Klüver", in *Artforum*, March 2004.

Johnson, P. "Is New Media Accepted in the Art World? Domenico Quaranta's Media, New Media, Post Media", in *Art Fag City*, August 30, 2011, online at www.artfagcity.com/2011/08/30/is-new-media-accepted-in-the-artworld- domenico-quarantas-media-new-media-postmedia/.

Jones, C. "The Function of the Studio (when the studio is a laptop)", in *Art Lies*, Issue 67, 2010, online at www.artlies.org/article.php?id=1996&issue=67&s=0.

Jahan, B. *Abstraction In Indian Painting. Post Independence Era*. New Delhi :Kaveri Books. 2008.

James, J. "Eds." *Cholamandal.An Artists' Village*. New Delhi. Oxford University Press. 2004.

Jameson, F. *Oi Archaeologies touMellontos – I Epithymiapoulegetai Outopia* (Vol.1).

Athens: Topos Publishers, 2008.

Jarzombek, M. *The Psychologizing of Modernity*. USA. Cambridge University Press. 2000.

Jayaram, S. 'The naked truth'. Art India, vol-6, Issue2, Quarter 2 (Ed) Nancy Adajania. Mumbai.Art India Publishing Co. Pvt Ltd. 2001.

Jung, C.G. *Dreams*.London , Routledge Publication. 2002.

Kafetsi, A. *ShirinNeshat – Women Without Men,* exh. Cat., Athens: National Museum of Contemporary Art, 2009.

Kapur, G. *A Brief Review of current Cultural Nationalism. Art and Life In India: The Four Decades* "Ed." Josef James. Simla. Delhi. Indian Institute Of Advance Studies with B. R. Publishing Corporation. 1989.

Kapur, G. *When Was Modernism*, Essays on Contemporary Cultural Practice in India. New Delhi. Tulika. 2000.

Kapur, G. 'Place of Modern Indian Cultural Practice'. *Creative Arts of India*, (Ed) Ratan Parimoo & Indramohan Sharma. New Delhi. Books & Books. 1995.

Klüver, B. Martin, J. Rose, B. " Eds". *Pavilion: Experiments in Art and Technology*, New York, E. P. Dutton 1972.

Klüver, B. "E.A.T. – Archive of published documents", 2000, online at www.fondation-langlois.org/html/e/page.php?NumPage=306.

Krauss, R. *A Voyage in the North Sea. Art in the Age of the Post-Medium Condition*, Thames & Hudson, London 1999.

Krysa, J. "Ed".*Curating Immateriality. The work of the curator in the age of network systems*, Data Browser 03, Autonomedia, New York 2006.

Kuo, M. "Art's New Media", in *Artforum*, September 2012, online at http://artforum.com/inprint/id=31950 (last visit March 2013).

Kurzweil, R. *The Singularity is Near*. New York: Viking, 2005.

Kuspit, D. *The Rebirth of Painting in The Late Twentieth Century*. USA : Cambridge University Press. 2000.

Kuspit, D. *The End of Art*. New York. Cambridge University Press. 2004.

Lacerte, S. "Experiments in Art and Technology: a Gap to Fill in Art History's Recent Chronicles", in *Refresh!*, September 2008. Online at www.fondationlanglois. org/html/e/page.php?NumPage=1716.

Lash, S. *Sociology of Postmodernism* .London and New York ,Routledge. 1996.

Laera, M."ArteDigitale: Collezionisti, fateviavanti!", in *Wired.it*, 22 April 2009, online at http://daily.wired.it/news/cultura/arte-digitale-collezionistifatevi- avanti.html.

Lamunière, S. "dxwebprojects", 10 July 1997, online at www.documenta12.de/archiv/dx/lists/debate/0014.html.

Leopoldseder, H., Schöpf, C. Stocker, G. *1979 – 2004 Ars Electronica*, HatjeCantzVerlag 2004.

Lialina, O. Espenschied, D. (Eds.), *Digital Folklore*, Merz and Solitude, Stuttgart 2009.

Lieser, W. (Ed.), *Digital Art*, h.f.ullmann 2009.

Lister, M. Dovey, J. Giddings, S. Grant, I. Kelly, K. *New Media: a Critical Introduction*, Routledge, New York 2009.

Loomba, A. *Colonialism/Post colonialism*. London & New York ,Routledge. 1998.

Lovelock, J.E. *The Ages of Gaia*. Oxford: Oxford University Press, 1989.

Lovink, G. *Zero Comments, Blogging and Critical Internet Culture,* Routledge, New York 2007.

Lovink, G. "New Media Arts: In Search of the Cool Obscure. Explorations beyond the Official Discourse", in *Diagonal Thoughts*, 2007. Online at www.diagonalthoughts.com/?p=204.

Lovink, G. Niederer, S. "Eds". *Video Vortex Reader. Responses to Youtube*, Institute of Networked Cultures, Amsterdam 2008.

Ludovico, A. " Ed". *Ubermorgen.Com – Media Hacking Vs.Conceptual Art.Hans Bernhard / Lizvlx*, ChristophMerianVerlag,Basel 2009.

Lunenfeld, P. *Snap To Grid: A User's Guide To Digital Arts*, Media, And Cultures, MIT Press, Cambridge 2000.

Macey, D. Dictionary of Critical Theory. London, New York. Penguin Books. 2000.

Manovich ,Lev . The language of new media. Cambridge: MIT Press, 2001.

Mason, C. *A computer in the Art Room: the Origins of British Computer Arts 1950 – 80*, Norfolk, JJG Publishing 2008.

Macgregor, B. "Cybernetic Serendipity Revisited", undated (2008),

Manovich, L. *The Language of New Media*, The MIT Press, Cambridge 2001.

Manovich, L. "The Death of Computer Art", 1997, 1997. Online at www.manovich.net/ TEXT/death.html.

Manovich, L. "Post-Media Aesthetics", sd 2000, online at www.manovich.net/DOCS/Post_media_aesthetics1.doc

Manovich, L. "Don't Call it Art: Ars Electronica 2003", in *Nettime*, September 22, 2003. Also available at http://manovich.net/DOCS/ars_03.doc.

Manovich, L. "From Borges To HTML", In *Intelligent Agent*, 2003, Online At http://Intelligentagent.Com/CNM200/Manovich_New_Media.Doc.

Manovich ,Lev . The language of new media. Cambridge: MIT Press, 2001

Mchugh, G. *Post Internet*, Link Editions, Brescia 2012.

Mcluhan, M. *Understanding Media. The Extensions of Man*, 1964. MIT Press, Cambridge 1994.

Mc Robbie, A. *Post-modernism & Popular Culture*. London ,Routledge. 1994.

Medosch, A. *Technological Determinism in Media Art*, 2005. A dissertation submitted in partial fulfilment of the requirements of Sussex University for the degree of MA Interactive Digital Media. Online at www.thenextlayer.org/files/TechnoDeterminismAM_0.pdf. online at http://design.osu.edu/carlson/history/PDFs/cyberserendipity.pdf.

Mecaulay, T. 'Minute on Indian Education.' .The Post-Colonial Studies Reader. "Ed." Ashcroft, B. Gareth, G. and Helen, T. London and New York, Routledge. 1995.

Michaud, Y. *L'artisteet les commissaires*, Hachette Pluriel Reference 2007.

Mirapaul, M. "Museum Puts Internet Art on the Wall", in *The New York Times*, 16 September 1999, online at http://theater.nytimes.com/library/tech/99/ 09/ cyber/ artsatlarge/16artsatlarge.htm l.

Mirapaul, M. "Selling and Collecting the Intangible, at $1,000 a Share", in *The New York Times*, 29 April 2002, online at www.nytimes.com/2002/04/29/arts/arts-onlineselling-and-collecting-the-intangible-at-1000-a-share.html.

Morris, S. "Museums and new media art", New York, Rockefeller Foundation, October 2001, online at www.cs.vu.nl/~eliens/archive/refs/ Museums_and _New_Media_Art.pdf .

Miah, A. "Ed".*Human Futures – Art in an Age of Uncertainty*. Liverpool: Liverpool University Press, 2008.

Miller, B. *The Power of Art Patronage in Indian Culture*. New Delhi. Oxford University Press. 1992.

Miranda, E.R. *Mozart Reloaded*. Sargasso Publishing, 2011.

Mitter, P. *Art and Nationalism in Colonial India 1850-1922 Occidental Orientation*.New York. Cambridge University press. 1994.

Mukherjee, B. *Rasa The Indian Performing Arts in The Last Twenty Five Years, Vol-I.* Calcutta : Anamika Kala Sangam. 1995.

Nelson, C. Paula, A.T. and Lawrence, G. *Cultural studies. An Introduction.* Cultural Studies "Ed." Laurence. G. Paula. A. T. Cary.N.London and New York : Routledge. 1992.

Niranjana, T. 'The Imperative To Evaluates Notes Towards A Geneology'. Creative Arts Of India " Ed." Ratan Parimoo and Indramohan Sharma. New Delhi. Books and Books. 1995.

Nichols, J. "Documenta X", October 1997, online at www.artdes.monash.edu.au/ globe/issue7/doctxt.htm l.

Nideffer, R. F. "SHIFT-CTRL. Mediating the process of academic exhibitionism", 2000, online at www.nideffer.net/classes/135-09-W/readings/nideffer.html.

O'Riley, M.K. *Art Beyond the West.* London. Laurence King. 2001.

Olson, M. "Lost Not Found: The Circulation of Images in Digital Visual Culture", in *Words Without Pictures*, 18 September 2008, online at http://uncopy.net/wp-content/uploads/2011/01/olson-lostnotfound.pdf.

Pal, P. *American Collection of Asian Art.* Bombay. Marg Publication. 1986.

Packer, R. Jordan K. "Eds" .*Multimedia: From Wagner to Virtual Reality*, New York,W. W. Norton & Company 2001.

Palfrey, J. Gasser, U. *Born Digital. Understanding the First Generation of Digital Natives*, Basic Books, New York 2008.

Paul, C. *Digital Art*, Thames & Hudson, London 2003[2008].

Paul , Christiane and Rush ,Michael . *New Media in Late 20th-century Art*.London , Thames & Hudson,1999.

Paul, C. "Ed". *New Media in the White Cube and Beyond. Curatorial Models for Digital Art*, University of California Press, Berkeley 2008.

Perniola, M. *L'arte e la suaombra*, Giulio EinaudiEditore, Torino 2000.

Perra, D. *Impattodigitale.Dall'immagineelaborataall'immaginepartecipata: il computer nell'artecontemporanea*, Baskerville, Bologna 2007.

Piro, N. "Ed". *Etoy – Cyberterrorismo. Come siorganizzaunrapimentovirtuale*, Castelvecchi, Roma 1998.

Polveroni, A., *This is contemporary! Come cambiano i musei di arte contemporanea*, Franco Angeli, Milano 2007.

Ponzini, P. "DiVA Digital Video Art Fair", in *Digimag 33*, April 2008, online at www.digicult.it/digimag/article.asp?id=1125.

Popper, F. *Art of the Electronic Age*, Thames & Hudson, London 1997.

Popper, F. *From Technological to Virtual Art*, MIT Press, Cambridge, Massachusetts –London, England 2007.

Price, S. "Dispersion", 2002 – ongoing, online at www.distributedhistory.com/Disperzone.html.

Quaranta, D. *Net art 1994-1998. La vicenda di Äda'web*, Vita e Pensiero, Milano 2004.

Quaranta, D. "Let's Get Loud! Interview with Helen Thorington, director of turbulence.org", in *Cluster.On Innovation*, n. 5, 2005, pp. 12 – 17.

Quaranta, D. "Don't Say New Media!", in *FMR Bianca*, n° 4, Franco Maria Ricci, Bologna 2008.

Quaranta, D. "We Are All Ready for a Change. Interview with Steven Sacks", in *Rhizome*,28 June 2007, online at http://rhizome.org/discuss/view/26364#4889.

Quaranta, D. *Media, New Media, Postmedia*, Postmedia Books, Milan 2010.

Quaranta, D. "The Postmedia Perspective", in *Rhizome*, January 12, 2011, online at http://rhizome.org/editorial/2011/jan/12/the-postmedia-perspective/.

Quaranta, D. "Ed".*Gazira Babeli*, Link Editions, Brescia 2012.

Quaranta, D. *Beyond New Media Art*. Morrisville: Lulu Press, Inc,2014

Quaranta, D. *Playlist. Playing Games, Music, Art*.Exh. Cat., LABoral Centro de Arte y Creación Industrial, Gijon, Spain, December 18, 2009 – May 17,2010.Online at: http://domenicoquaranta.com/public/pdf/LABoral_Revista_playlist.pdf .

Quaranta, D. *Collect the wwworld.The Artist as Archivist in the Internet Age*.Exh.cat. Brescia, SpazioContemporanea, September 24 – October 15, 2011. LINK Editions, Brescia 2011. Online at http://editions.linkartcenter.eu/.

Quaranta, D. Bernard, Y. " Eds". *Holy Fire. Art of the Digital Age*, cat., iMAL, Bruxelles, 2008. Brescia, FPEditions 2008.

Quinn, E. "Live and Media Arts at the ICA", in *New Media Curating*, October 17, 2008.

Ray, N. *Idea and Image in Indian Art*. New Delhi. MunshiramManoharlal Publishers Pvt. Ltd. 1973.

Rastas, P. "Alien Intelligence", 2000, in *Kiasma Magazine*, 5 -99.

Reas, C. Fry, B. "Eds". *Processing: A Programming Handbook for Visual Designers and Artists*, MIT Press, 2007.

Rethinking Curating: Art after New Media . Cambridge: MIT Press 2015. Rinehart, R. "The Media Art Notation System: Documenting and Preserving Digital/Media Art", in *Leonardo*, April 2007, vol. 40, No. 2, pp. 181-187.

Rinder, L. Singer D. "Eds."*Bitstreams*, exh. cat., Whitney Museum of American Art, New York 2001.

Romano, G. *Artscape. Panorama dell'arte in Rete*, Costa & Nolan, Ancona – Milano 2000.

Rosenbaum, L. "guggenheimsoho to go high-tech", in *Artnet*, 29 March 1996, online at www.artnet.com/magazine_pre2000/news/rosenbaum/ rosenbaum3-29- 96.asp.

Rush, M.*New Media in Late 20th-Century Art*, Thames & Hudson, London 1999 [2001].

Rush, M. *New media in art*.London ,Thames & Hudson,2005

Rush, M.*New Media in Late 20th-Century Art*. London, Thames and Hudson, 2001.

Saltz, J. "My Sixth Sense", in *The Village Voice*, 2000.

Sardesai, A. "Ed." Art India. Mumbai. Issue-ii/Vol.XV/Quarter-II/. 2010.

Schneider, I. Korot, B. "Eds".*Video Art*, New York, Harcourt Brace Jovanovich, 1976.

Scholder, A. Crandall, J. "Eds". *Interaction. Artistic Practice in the Network*, Eyebeam / D.A.P., New York 2001.

Schwartz, J. "Museum Kills Live Exhibit", in *The New York Times*, May 13, 2008, on lineat www.nytimes.com/2008/05/13/science/13coat.html?_r=0.

Scudero, D. *Manuale del curator.Teoria e praticadellacuracritica*, Gangemi Editore, Roma 2004.

Selz, P. *Beyond The Main Stream*. New York. Cambridge University Press. 1997.

Sen, G. *Image and Imagination: Five Contemporary Artists*. Ahmedabad.Mapin Publishing House Pvt. Ltd. 1996.

Shanken, E. A. *Art and Electronic Media*, Phaidon Press, London 2009.

Shanken, E. A. "Art in the Information Age: Technology and Conceptual Art", 2001. Online at http://artexetra.files.wordpress.com/2009/02/shankenartinfoage.pdf.

Shanken, E. A. "Ed". "New Media, Art-Science and Contemporary Art: Towards a Hybrid Discourse?". *Artnodes*, No. 11, p. 65-116. UOC. Online at http://artnodes.uoc.edu/ojs/index.php/artnodes/article/view/artnodes-n11-shanken/artnodes-n11-new-media-art-science-and-contemporary-art-eng

Shekar, V. (2009). 'Surekha- Using the Body as a Site for Intervention and appropriation'. Art and Deal. Vol-6, No-4, Issue No-30 "Ed" Tagore, S. New Delhi. Art and Deal Pvt Ltd.

Shukla, H.L. *SemioticaIndica Encyclopaedic Dictionary of Body- Language in Indian Art & Culture.Vol- II*. New Delhi. Aryan Books International. 1994.

Sinha, I. *The Search for Ecstasy*. London. Charles Foukes Limited. 1993.

Slaton, J. "Museum Offers Webby Art Award", in *Wired*, 18 February 2000, online at www.wired.com/culture/lifestyle/news/2000/02/34414.

Slocum, P. "New Media and the Gallery", in *Artlies*, Issue 67, 2010, online at www.artlies.org/article.php?id=1993&issue=67&s=0.

Smith, A. V. *A History of Fine Arts in India and Cylone*. (3rd edition) " Ed." Karl Khandalavala. Bombay. D. B. Taraporevala sons and Co. Pvt, Ltd. 1969.

Smith, R. "A Museum's Metamorphosis: The Virtual Arcade", in *New York Times*, 18 June 1996.

Some, S.(1993). *Abanindranath Tagore and Gaganendranath Togore 'A Reappraisal'*. Lalit Kala contemporary 38. New Delhi. Lalit Kala Akademi.

Spingarn-Koff, J. "010101: Art for Our Times", in *Wired*, 28 February 2001, online at www.wired.com/culture/lifestyle/news/2001/02/41972.

Spivak, G. 'Can the Subaltern Speak' .*The Post Colonial Studies Reader* "Ed" Bill Ashcroft, Gareth Griffiths and Helen Tiffin London and New Year.Routledge. 1995.

Syman, S. "Bell Curves and Bitstreams. Stefanie Syman on the beginning of the end of digital art", in *Feed*, 27 March 2001.

Stallabrass, J. *Art Incorporated. The Story of Contemporary Art,* Oxford University Press 2004.

Steyerl, H. "In Defense of the Poor Image", in *eflux journal*, Issue 10, November 2009, online at www.e-flux.com/journal/in-defense-of-the-poorimage/.

Stocker, G. "The Art of Tomorrow", in *a minima*, n° 15, 2006, pp. 6 – 19.

Subramanyam, K.G. (1978).*Moving Focus, Essays on Indian Art*. New Delhi. Lalit Kala Akademi.

Sudhi, P. *Aesthetic Theories of India, Vol-III*. New Delhi. Intellectual Publishing House. 1990.

Tapscott, D. *Grown Up Digital*, McGraw-Hill eBooks 2009.

Terraroli , V. "Ed". *Art of the Twentieth Century*, 5 vv, Milano, Skira 2006 – 2010.

Thornton, S. *Seven Days in the Art World*, W. W. Norton & Company 2009.

Tiwari, M.N. (2003). *Kala.The Journal of Indian Art History Congress Vol VIII*. New Delhi. Sundeep Prakashan.

Tuli, N. *The Flamed Mosaic, Indian Contemporary Painting*. New Delhi.Heart in association with Mapin Publication Pvt. Ltd. 1997.

Tribe, M. Jana, R., *New Media Art*, Taschen, Köln 2006.

Tribe, M. New Media art (Taschen Basic Art Series). Cologne: Taschen, 2006.

Troemel, B. "What Relational Aesthetics Can Learn From 4Chan", in *Artfagcity*, September 9, 2010. Online at http://www.artfagcity.com/2010/09/09/ img- mgmt-what-relational-aesthetics-can-learn-from-4chan/ .

Tribe, M. "Why Your .JPEGs Aren't Making You A Millionaire", in *The Creators Project*, May 14, 2012, online at http://thecreatorsproject.com/blog/digart-why-yourjpegs-arent-making-you-a-millionaire.

Tribe, M. *Peer Pressure*, Link Editions, Brescia 2012.

Vanderbilt, T. "The King of Digital Art", in *Wired*, issue 13.9, September 2005, online at www.wired.com/wired/archive/13.09/sacks.html.

Varadhande, M.L. (1978). *Traditions of Indian Theatre*. New Delhi. Abhinav Publications.

Virilio, P. *The Lost Dimension*. New York, Semiotext(e), 1991.

Walsh, J. "Ed".*Bill Viola – The Passions,* exh.Cat., Los Angeles: The J. Paul Getty Museum, 2003.

VVAA, *Deep Screen. Art in Digital Culture*, exh. cat., Amsterdam :Stedelijk Museum, 2008.

VVAA, *Eva & Franco Mattes: 0100101110101101.ORG*, Charta, Milano – New York 2009.

VVAA, *Mediascape,* exh. cat., New York : Guggenheim Museum Publications, 1996.

VVAA, *Postmedia Condition*, exh. cat., Madrid : Centro Cultural Conde Duque, 2006.

VVAA, *Olafur Eliasson. Colour memory and other informal shadows*, Oslo: Astrup Fearnley Museet for Moderne Kunst, 2004.

VVAA, *XLII Esposizione Internazionaled'Arte La Biennale di Venezia.Arte e scienza.Biologia / Tecnologia e informatica*, exh.cat., Electa, Venezia 1986.

VVAA, *010101: Art in Technological Times*, exh. cat., Sfmoma, San Francisco 2001.

VVAA, "Media Art Undone", conference panel at transmediale 07, Berlin, February 3, 2007. Full transcript of the presentations is available here: www.mikro.in- berlin.de/wiki/tiki-index.php?page=MAU

Verschooren, K. A., .*art. Situating Internet Art in the Traditional Institution for Contemporary Art*, 2007. Master of Science in Comparative Media Studies,Massachusetts Institute of Technology, online at http://cms.mit.edu/research/theses/KarenVerschooren2007.pdf.

Vicente, J. L. "Unahistoria del arte y la tecnología en ARCO", in *El Cultural*, February 2008. Available online in *Elastico*, at http://elastico.net/archives/ 2008/02/post_59.html.

Vierkant, A. "The Image Object Post-Internet", in *jstchillin*, 2010, online at http://jstchillin.org/artie/vierkant.html.

Voropai, L. "Institutionalisation of Media Art in the Post-Soviet Space: The Role of Cultural Policy and Socioeconomic Factors", in *Re:place*, November 2007, online at http://pl02.donau-uni.ac.at/jspui/handle/10002/449.

Wands, B. *Art of the Digital Age, Thames & Hudson*, London – New York, 2006.

Wands ,Bruce . *Art of the digital age*.London, Thames & Hudson, 2007.

Wardrip- Fruin N. Montfort, N. "Eds". *The New Media Reader*, The MIT Press, Cambridge – London 2003.

Weibel, P. Druckrey, T. "Eds".*net_condition: art and global media*, The MIT Press, Cambridge (Massachussets), 2001.

Welch, S. (1985). *India Art & Culture 1300-1900*. Chidambaram. Prestel Mapin Publishing Pvt. Ltd.

Wishart, A. Bochsler, R. *Leaving Reality Behind. The Battle for the Soul of the Internet*, 4th Estate, 2002 (Ecco – Harper Collins 2003).

Wolfe, T. *The Painted World*, New York 1975. Trad.it. *Come ottenereilsuccesso in arte*, Torino, Allemandi 1987 (2004).

Journal

Tagore, S "Ed."Art & Deal. New Delhi. Issue 32/Vol.7.No.2/. 2010.

Tagore, S. "Ed." Art & Deal. New Delhi. Issue 36/Vol.7.No.6/. 2011.

Tagore, S. "Ed." Art & Deal. New Delhi. Issue 37/Vol.7.No.7/. 2011.

Tagore, S. "Ed." Art & Deal. New Delhi. Issue 46/Vol.8.No.15/.2012.

Tagore, S. "Ed." Art & Deal. New Delhi. Issue 49/Vol.8.No.19/. 2012.

Sardesai, A. "Ed." Art India. Mumbai.Issue-ii/Vol.X. 2005.

Sardesai, A. "Ed." Art India. Mumbai. Issue-iii/Vol.X/. 2005.

Online Resources and Magazines

http://resourceguide.eai.org/The EAI Online Resource Guide for Exhibiting, Collecting & Preserving Media Art, produced by the Electronic Art Intermix, New York.

http://www.nettime.org/Mailing lists for networked cultures, politics, and tactics. In its archives you can find hundreds of texts, interviews and discussions about New Media Art.

http://rhizome.org/Rhizome, mailing list and no-profit organization "dedicated to the creation, presentation, preservation, and critique of emerging artistic practices that engage technology."

http://www.yproductions.com/Steve Dietz's website.

http://www.fondationlanglois.org/Daniel Langlois Foundation for Art, Science, and Technology, Montreal (Canada).

http://www.mediaarthistory.org/Conference series on the Histories of Media Art, Science and Technology.

http://www.nytimes.com/library/tech/reference/indexartsatlarge.html/Arts At Large, Matthew Mirapaul's column on art and technology in the *New York Times*.

http://crumbweb.org/CRUMB, Curatorial Resource for Upstart Media Bliss. It hosts the mailing list *New Media Curating.*

http://www.we-make-money-not-art.com/RegineDébatty's blog.

http://gallery9.walkerart.org/Gallery 9, the online gallery of the Walker Art Center, Minneapolis.

http://www.tate.org.uk/intermediaart/The "Intermedia Art" section of the Tate Gallery, London.

http://variablemedia.net/The Variable Media Initiative.

http://www.aec.at/Ars Electronica Center, Linz.

http://www.mediaartnet.org/An "online encyclopedia" on New Media Art, edited by Rudolf Frieling and Dieter Daniels.

http://www.archimuse.com/The international conference *Museums and the Web*.

http://switch.sjsu.edu/Switch, "Online Journal of New Media".

http://vagueterrain.net/Vague Terrain, an online magazine on digital culture, art and technology.

http://www.laudanum.net/cream/Cream, a newsletter on digital culture .

http://www.kurator.org/The online curatorial platform Kurator, developed by Joasia Krysa.

http://www.intelligentagent.com/Intelligent Agent, an online magazine edited by Christiane Paul and Patrick Lichty.

http://pooool.info/Pool Magazine, "an online platform and publication dedicated to expanding and improving the discourse between online and offline realities and their cultural, societal and political impact on each other", edited by Louis Doulas.

http://www.artfagcity.com/Art Fag City, an independent New York-based art blog dedicated to providing exposure to emerging contemporary art and under- known artists, edited by Paddy Johnson.

http://www.e-flux.com/journals/The magazine developed by the international network e-flux.

http://dismagazine.com/DIS Magazine, "a post-Internet lifestyle magazine about art, fashion and commerce."

www.ingramcontent.com/pod-product-compliance
Lightning Source LLC
LaVergne TN
LVHW061607070526
838199LV00078B/7203